Planning Library Interiors

Planning Library Interiors
The Selection of Furnishings for the 21st Century

by Carol R. Brown

First edition titled *Selecting Library Furniture: A Guide for Librarians,
Designers, and Architects*

Oryx Press
1995

© 1995 by Carol R. Brown
4041 North Central at Indian School Road
Phoenix, Arizona 85012-3397

Published simultaneously in Canada
Printed and Bound in the United States of America

∞ The paper used in this publication meets the minimum requirements of
American National Standard for Information Science—Permanence of Paper
for Printed Library Materials, ANSI Z39.48, 1984.

Library of Congress Cataloging-in-Publication Data
Brown, Carol R.
  Planning library interiors : the selection of furnishings for the 21st century / by Carol
R. Brown
    p. cm.
  Rev. ed. of: Selecting library furniture. 1989.
  Includes bibliographical references and index.
  ISBN 0-89774-850-6
  1. Library fittings and supplies—United States—Purchasing. 2. Library architec-
ture—United States. I. Brown, Carol R. Selecting library furniture. II. Title.
Z684.B86 1995   94–30430
022'.9—dc20   CIP

For my two best friends,
my sons,
Ian Robertson Brown
and
Kevin William Brown

CONTENTS

PREFACE

Several factors contributed to the decision to publish a second edition of *Selecting Library Furniture*, now titled *Planning Library Interiors: The Selection of Furnishings for the 21st Century*. In 1993 Oryx Press inquired about the possibility of revising the book to provide new information about changes that had occurred or were occurring in libraries. Included in these changes were such issues such as compliance with the Americans with Disabilities Act and new technologies that required special equipment. My knowledge of furnishings for libraries had broadened as the result of more than five years of consulting work since the first edition of this book was written. As I reviewed the first edition in detail, I realized that a second edition needed to be published.

I approached the task of revising the book with the belief that the second edition had to have a substantial amount of new information to justify its purchase by people who already owned the first edition. To this end, the book has been completely reorganized and rewritten. The only discussion that remains essentially the same in the second edition is the basic information about wood construction.

In gathering updated information, I interviewed many of the furniture specialists who assisted me with the first edition. I also studied recent periodical literature on general contract office furnishings and the planning of office areas. Several new experts, noted in the acknowledgments, came to my attention and provided assistance with spe-

cialized topics. My clients in the consulting business were all aware that I was revising the book, and many of them provided me with suggestions and information; for example, I was given an opportunity in San Francisco to interview several individuals who were involved in planning barrier-free access to the new Main Library.

The scope of the book has been broadened in the second edition. Because of my belief that library interiors and library buildings must be designed concurrently, more information has been added about the planning of library facilities and spaces, generally. An example of library goals and objectives written specifically to tie building needs to library collections and services has been included in the appendix to this book. The discussion of children's furnishings and areas has been expanded into a separate chapter in order to cover the topic more thoroughly. The information about furnishings for electronic equipment has been expanded with a detailed discussion of how to coordinate plans and furnishings for computers with plans for power and data distribution in the building. The second edition has more information about performance testing and existing and future standards that are relevant to selecting furnishings for libraries. The information about planning work areas has been expanded.

Many of the illustrations included in the first edition have been replaced by new photographs. Most references to particular products have been removed from the text. Information about specific items is, for the most part, provided with the photographs. The bibliography and list of furniture manufacturers have been updated and expanded.

In addition to expanded coverage of existing material, the second edition covers topics that have become vital concerns in furniture selection in the past five years. Since the passage of the Americans with Disabilities Act of 1990, Public Law 101-336 (ADA), most librarians and design professionals have participated in assessing existing buildings and/or planning new facilities that comply with the spirit, as well as the letter, of that law. In order to update the criteria for furniture selection, information about compliance with ADA and barrier-free access to libraries, as these topics relate to library furnishings, has been included in the second edition. Also, a discussion of indoor air quality has been added in response to growing general concern over environmental issues and in anticipation of new regulations and standards that will seek to control indoor air quality as it relates to the construction of buildings and the manufacture of furnishings.

Because of my familiarity with the project, information about the new Main Library of San Francisco Public Library has been included in several discussions. I believe that the San Francisco planning process is exemplary and that the concerns addressed in that building project should be addressed in designing any state-of-the-art library today.

Since the first edition was published, I have had opportunities to work on much larger building projects than I had prior to 1989. My consulting experience has, therefore, resulted in broadening my perspective in writing the second edition. In revising the book, I attempted to present the information in such a manner that it will be useful to librarians working with design professionals, to librarians selecting furnishings themselves, and to designers and architects working with librarians. Once again, my goal has been to present information about selecting furnishings that can be applied to products that will become available in the future, as well as to those existing currently.

Many specific items of furniture discussed in this edition are made by companies whose primary business is libraries; however, libraries are frequently furnished satisfactorily with items sold by companies that are considered general contract furniture manufacturers. The planning process and the selection criteria presented are intended for application to any furnishings used in a library, regardless of whether the items are manufactured by a general contract furniture manufacturer, a library furniture manufacturer, or a local millwork house.

For additional questions you may have about library planning and the selection of furnishings, please contact me at Carol Brown Associates, 11706 S. Kirkwood, Stafford, TX 77477, (713) 530-6221.

ACKNOWLEDGMENTS

Many individuals and organizations contributed to the preparation of *Planning Library Interiors*. I am grateful to everyone who provided assistance. I want to thank every company that supplied photographs for this book and the individuals working for these companies who made the arrangements for the pictures.

Special thanks are expressed to Bill Hendrick, Bob Boardman, and Fred Schutmaat of the Worden Company for their valuable support and assistance in providing information and photographs for this book. I would also like to thank the following for their assistance and information: John Buckstaff, Frank Yench, Richard Pata, and the Buckstaff Company; Jean Gayle and Steelcase, Inc.; Lynne Nibbelink, Linda Folland, and Herman Miller, Inc.; Geoff Allen and Haworth, Inc.; Richard Silberman and Healthy Buildings International; Gary Chappell and Spacesaver Corporation; Paula Wenstrom; Earl Siems; Judy Kugle; and Patty White.

Several libraries and many of my friends working in libraries provided assistance in revising this book. Special thanks are expressed to my friend, Roxanne Dolen, at Looscan Branch, Houston Public Library, who served as my "local public librarian" during this project. Roxanne answered numerous reference questions on a variety of topics and located a number of books for me.

I am grateful to all of the libraries who hired me for consultations over the past few years. Every project provided new challenges and new learning experiences that eventually contributed to this book. I would like to acknowledge three libraries in particular whose staff have provided assistance throughout the preparation of the second edition. First, I would like to thank City Manager Dan Johnson, the members of the City Council, Director of Library Services Beth Little Bormann, and the staff of Carrollton Public Library, Carrollton, Texas, for their support of my work. Beth and her staff supplied me with a wealth of information relevant to the book and have answered numerous reference questions. Second, I would like to express my appreciation to the staff of Fort Bend County Libraries, Richmond, Texas. I would like to thank Library Director Roman Bohachevsky and Assistant Director Jane Powell for their support. I would also like to thank Linda Lupro for assisting with research and Molly Krukewitt for providing information about children's services and for reviewing part of the book.

Finally, special thanks must go to Library Director Ken Dowlin and Facilities Development Coordinator Kathryn Page of the San Francisco Public Library. Kathy provided information about many topics covered in the book, arranged several important interviews for me, and reviewed the information in the manuscript pertaining to the San

Francisco Public Library. I would like to thank Jerry Kuns, Stanley Pauer, and Marti Goddard, who provided information during interviews about planning barrier-free access to the new San Francisco Main Library. I would also like to acknowledge the assistance of Pei, Cobb, Freed and Partners and Simon, Martin-Vegue, Winkelstein, Moris (SMWM), associated architects, in providing information about the San Francisco Public Library project. I am particularly grateful to Bev Moris and Anthony Bernheim of SMWM, who supplied valuable information for the book.

Finally, I would like to thank several people who helped me complete the second edition: Linda Bennett, who edited the manuscript; Paul Colburn, who traveled from Denver, Colorado, to photograph furnishings in Carrollton; and Mary Beth La Vergne, who helped me with numerous details in finishing the second edition. Thanks also to Julie, Sondra, and Connie and all my other friends who provided me with support and listened to my stories.

INTRODUCTION

For many librarians, the selection of furniture for a new building or the major refurbishing of an existing facility is a once-in-a-lifetime task. A project usually involves a number of people in addition to the librarian: architects, facilities planners, interior designers, consultants, purchasing agents, library board members, Friends of the Library, and representatives of governing bodies. Several of these individuals or groups may be involved in making decisions about furniture selections. The library manager, the staff members, and the users are, however, the ones who remain on the site, long after the others are gone, to test whether the design of the building and the furnishings selected are satisfactory.

In most building projects, interior designers or consultants complete the space planning and the selection of furnishings. Sometimes the architectural firm planning the building has designers on staff to perform the interiors work, or sometimes a separate interior design or consulting firm is hired by the library or the architect to complete the interior design. In building and refurbishing projects for small and medium-sized facilities, the job of furniture selection may be the responsibility of a library manager or a purchasing agent who may or may not have previous experience obtaining furnishings for libraries.

Regardless of who has primary responsibility for furniture selection, active involvement of librarians in the process is necessary to ensure that the completed library interior is functional. After all, a library is not just a general office area. Library space has a very specific function that must be addressed in furnishing the interior, and no one is as attuned to the specialized needs of the staff and users as the library manager.

Librarians are the most important professionals in the library planning process. With adequate knowledge of library furnishings, they will have the confidence needed to ask reasonable questions of vendors and designers. The information included here should provide librarians with the foundation needed to assess products, to make informed decisions regarding furniture selections, to work confidently and knowledgeably with design professionals, and to ensure that the library is obtaining the best furnishings for the funds available.

Furnishings for general offices are often selected to be used only by the staff, perhaps for a period of five to ten years. Library furnishings, however, are selected to be used by the public or a groups of users, as well as the staff. In some instances, larger items and shelving are expected to be serviceable for the lifetime of the library—30, 40, even 50 years.

In the past, libraries were seen as specialized institutions with stereotypical needs in furnishings. The process of furniture selection involved considering what standard products were available. Most library chairs and tables looked about the same—sturdy and nondescript. Library interiors were generally pleasant but serviceable, institutional-looking places.

Library interiors and the furniture selection process have changed, however. Architects design the interiors of libraries with distinction and style. A wider variety of products is now available for furnishing the library. Furniture manufacturers are more customer-responsive and are offering more products that address current trends in libraries, such as automation, the marketing and merchandising of library materials and services, and barrier-free design.

As will be explained in chapter 1, the furniture selection process now involves much more than considering what products are available. The acquisition of furniture and shelving includes the following steps: (1) "look around" the existing library space to determine which furnishings work effectively and which ones are a problem; (2) study specific service and collection plans for the library (as stated in the goals and objectives) and consider how these plans relate to the library interior; (3) determine what the new furnishings should accomplish for the particular library involved; (4) consider what is available on the market, or what can be obtained to fulfill the requirements determined in steps 1, 2, and 3; and (5) make responsible selections and purchase the furnishings.

The following chapters provide useful information for architects, designers, and vendors, as well as librarians. The information can be shared with any group or individual who will be involved in making or approving furniture selections. Furniture manufacturers and salespeople may want to read this book in order to improve their knowledge of the market from the viewpoint of the librarian.

Chapter 1 discusses a process for determining furniture requirements and provides examples of applying the selection process to particular items. Chapters 2 through 9 provide background information about the construction of furniture and shelving and discuss particular kinds of furnishings and shelving that are available. The last two chapters discuss bid procedures and the library furniture market.

Although products of specific manufacturers are mentioned, the reader should note that these items are mentioned only as examples. The emphasis is on criteria for evaluating products—those now available and those to be manufactured in the future. Specific products are discussed to answer questions concerning what particular qualities and materials make some of them more reliable, more serviceable, etc., than others. The resulting criteria or considerations for evaluating a product can also be applied to brands not mentioned here or not yet manufactured. The reader is cautioned neither to assume that because a product is *not* discussed here, it is not worthy of consideration, nor that inclusion of a particular brand constitutes an endorsement of that product.

Library Planning and the Furniture Selection Process

The most important lesson librarians have learned about library buildings over the past few years is that the interiors must be constructed with built-in flexibility. Who hasn't experienced the challenge of automating a building designed for manual operations? Or the challenge of adding a growing audiovisual collection to a library designed primarily for books? It is apparent that library services and collections change frequently. In order to remain functional, therefore, libraries must be built to accommodate future changes in services, collections, equipment, staff, and users.

As with library management generally, planning is the key both to designing workable buildings and to using project resources effectively. Thorough planning prior to beginning a project will help to ensure that the completed library will be satisfactory, not only when the project is finished, but also for a long time thereafter.

Extensive use of electronic equipment throughout a library makes it imperative that furniture layouts, actual furniture selections, and equipment placement be determined in conjunction with the architectural design of a building. Because of the need to coordinate electrical and data distribution in a building with electrical and data transmission systems in the furniture, furnishings cannot be determined after the final blueprints for building construction are completed. Every phase of architectural planning should include corresponding planning of the building interior in order to ensure that the completed building is safe, tidy, and functional. Without coordinated planning, the location and use of particular pieces of furniture and equipment may be dictated by building constraints that prevent satisfactory furniture layout and preclude selecting furnishings that are the most desirable from a functional standpoint. (See p. 30 for additional discussion of coordinating electrical and data systems in buildings and furnishings.)

GATHERING INFORMATION

In most situations, new buildings replace other facilities and renovations and refurbishing projects involve making improvements on existing spaces. Like the Public Library Association (PLA) Planning Process, therefore, one of the first steps in a building project is "looking around," that is, determining what works and what doesn't work in an existing library. Many times staff and users have griped about problems with a facility and furnishings for years prior to actually working on a library improvement program. "Looking around," in this event, involves converting complaints into statements of constructive criticism and determining what can be done in new or renovated space to eliminate problems. Both staff and users should be involved in assessing the existing space and in providing input regarding their expectations for a new facility. (McClure et al. 1987)

Staff assessment of a building may involve an informal walk-through that begins and ends with the parking lot. While studying the existing library space, staff members can ask themselves questions about their particular library. For example, what works well currently for the staff and the users in the library? What doesn't function well? Are there elements of the building that aren't used by the public or about which the public complain? What looks attractive and tidy in the old library? What is usually a mess? What kinds of materials or services are not handled effectively in the existing building?

In designing a building, most of the effort and concern are concentrated on planning the large public areas of the library. The planning team naturally studies the adjacency of the various interior spaces, the layout of the bookstacks, and the number and arrangement of readers' seats. Unfortunately, however, some of the small details that make a library attractive to the public and workable for the staff are ignored, or are just an afterthought, in the planning process. The staff can be particularly helpful in taking note of the detailed aspects of the library that should be improved during a building project.

If a more formal building assessment is desired, a library staff can use the American Library Association/ Library Administration and Management Association (ALA/LAMA) publication *Checklist of Library Building Design Considerations* (Sannwald 1990) as an instrument for assessing the existing library building. (The *Checklist* can also be used as a guide in writing the building program for a new facility and as a tool for assessing the design of a new building.)

In a small library, gathering information from the public may be as simple as talking to patrons using the building. Often, staff members on the front lines receive input from patrons on a regular basis, without even asking questions. Information can also be collected by means of a formal survey. At the Baltimore County Public Library, for example, a committee headed by Jane Eickhoff developed an instrument that was used to assess patron reaction to library buildings in the system. The "Visitor Impact Survey" asks questions about the convenience, comfort, appearance, and maintenance of the libraries. The survey covers items such as building access, parking, signage, lighting, rest rooms, arrangement of furnishings, and the overall appearance of the building. A survey similar to

the one developed by Baltimore County can be useful in gathering information from users prior to beginning a building project.

The process used by library director Ken Dowlin and his staff in designing the new Main Library for San Francisco serves as a model procedure for gathering input from staff and users in planning new facilities. During the initial planning stage of the project about 20–25 focus group discussions took place. The information gathered during the focus group discussions was used in writing the building program for the new building.

According to Kathryn Page, facilities development coordinator for the San Francisco Public Library (SFPL), focus group discussions were initially conducted with 18 different client groups. Individuals representing groups, such as day care providers, government officials, local authors, and publishers, were invited by mail to attend meetings to discuss the new library. When all of the information from the focus groups was recorded and compiled, particular patterns emerged; for example, accessibility and safety were issues of concern in all of the groups. As the planning process continued, follow-up meetings to collect more information were held with representatives of the business community, with child care providers, and with users living in the immediate neighborhood of the Main Library.

In order to receive input from various segments of San Francisco's multilingual and culturally diverse population, focus group meetings were held with library staff members, including those working in SFPL's two flagship branches in Chinatown and the Mission District, as well as representatives of the city's major cultural groups. Information to ensure library accessibility to everyone was gathered during three additional meetings: one with hearing-impaired users, one with visually impaired users, and one with physically disabled users.

In Denver, five focus group discussions were conducted to gather information to be used in designing the Children's Library at the Denver Central Library. Reporting in *Public Library Quarterly*, Pam Sandlian, manager of the Children's Library, stated that the focus groups included a cross-section of children and parents throughout the city. "Children of varying age groups, ethnic backgrounds, and geographic locations within the city were represented. The objective of this research was to understand how children currently use the library and to explore their preferences for new technologies and innovative services." (Sandlian 1993, p.18)

At the San Francisco Public Library, everyone on the library staff was given an opportunity to provide input during the planning process. Thirty-five staff committees representing each library service unit or department were involved in space planning the interior of the library and, later in the process, in providing feedback on specific questions regarding the furniture selections. The members of each committee were charged with gathering input from all of the individuals working in their department and bringing that information into the planning process. Each of the committees met at least three times with representatives from the architectural firms developing the space plans: once to provide input regarding what was desired in their space, once to review the initial space plans developed, and once to review the space plans after modifications had been made.

In addition to the work of the initial space planning committees, staff were kept informed of the development of the building plans and given an opportunity to voice opinions during several general staff meetings, which all employees were invited to attend. A Staff Furniture Committee and a Public Furniture Committee also provided information in the early planning stages of the project.

During the "looking around" phase of a library building project, information should be obtained about other libraries. Many librarians tour a variety of buildings with board members, architects, and officials to gather information, to get new ideas, and to develop opinions prior to designing a building and selecting furnishings. Tours with architects give library directors an opportunity to point out specific features of buildings or furnishings that the director finds desirable or undesirable in a facility.

During site visits, information can be obtained about which furniture items do or do not function well, what users do or do not like, which furnishings look attractive or unattractive after heavy public use, and which furnishings are easy or difficult to maintain. It is also useful to sit down in the chairs to see if they are comfortable, observe how well the circulation desk functions for the staff, shake the shelves to check their stability, and notice which furniture is getting the most use by patrons. Nothing, however, should be planned for a specific library just because it looks good in another building. Before borrowing an idea from another library, the planning team should consider whether a supposedly desirable element really fits the needs of their particular library.

Information for planning a new building or space can also be obtained by telephone interviews with other libraries. At the San Francisco Public Library, for example,

plans for the new library included an area for a telephone reference service, a "new" space for that library. The facilities development staff prepared a list of questions regarding telephone reference areas, then used it to conduct telephone interviews with staff at several other large libraries that already have spaces designated for telephone reference services.

RELATING BUILDINGS AND SPACES TO THE LIBRARY'S MISSION

Library buildings and interiors should be planned to support a particular library's mission. In addition to gathering information and assessing the existing library space, the design process for a new or renovated library begins with general plans for a library's services and collections as expressed in the library's mission statement and long-range goals and objectives. The completed building should (1) allow the staff to carry out the library's mission and stated goals and objectives efficiently and (2) have the built-in flexibility to accommodate changes in the services and collections in the future.

Some libraries have formal written documents stating the library's mission and short- and long-term goals and objectives; other libraries have only informal plans of service. Many public libraries have plans based on PLA's process as outlined in *Planning and Role Setting for Public Libraries*. Regardless of the format of the service and collection plans, however, staff that are launching a building project or refurbishing a library should establish what they expect to accomplish in the space.

A library's strategic plans as expressed in its goals and objectives may be written specifically to provide guidance to architects, designers, and consultants in planning new buildings or renovated spaces. Specific objectives may note the number of square feet needed in a building for a particular service or function. Other objectives may outline the space and furnishings needed to support a new service that the library will be able to offer as a result of building improvements. For example, a library without a meeting room may develop an objective to provide adult programming, literacy tutoring, and adult education classes in the future. In order to accomplish the objective, the library building will have to be expanded to include a meeting room. In developing goals and objectives directly related to building improvements, a useful question to ask is: What do we want to be able to do in the new building that we can't do in the old one?

Library goals and objectives that are directly tied to the parameters of a building program provide guidance during both the building design and furniture selection processes. For example, here is a goal and related objectives developed in conjunction with writing a building program for the expansion of Watsonville Public Library in Watsonville, California.

Goal: As the community's major information center, the library serves to improve and enhance the quality of life of Watsonville's diverse, multicultural population by providing well-balanced collections of books in both English and Spanish for residents of all ages.

Objectives:
1. To expand the adult area in order to shelve a maximum of 75,600 books (73,600 adult and 2,000 young adult) and provide seating for 82 adults, and to expand the children's area to shelve a maximum of 38,400 books and provide seating for 30 children.
2. To expand the adult Spanish-language collection by approximately 2,000 books and to improve the depth of the Spanish-language collection in order to serve a variety of reading levels and interests on the same subject.
3. To add four double-faced sections of 84-inch-high shelving in the workroom for storing multiple copies of books in Spanish that go out of print quickly.
4. To establish a browsing area near the entrance to the building for the merchandising of new books, high-demand titles, and audio-visual materials on attractive, lighted display shelving or racks.

In the example above, the goal provides several items of information that have an impact on plans for the renovated building: (1) Because the library is the city's major information center, staff and user space for reference functions will be important considerations in designing the library. The information function may have an impact on the design of the reference desk(s); (2) because Watsonville has a diverse, multicultural population, the building and interior design should reflect the particular library needs and expectations of the various user groups; (3) space and convenient access will be required for extensive collections in both English and Spanish; and (4) space will be needed for collections in both languages for young people as well as adults.

The objectives in the Watsonville example provide even more specific information about building needs. By stating the quantity of books in the collections, it is possible to calculate how much building space will be needed for adult, juvenile, and Spanish-language books, and therefore, how many bookstacks will be required for the various collections. The objectives also indicate the kind of

furnishings needed to house the browsing collection effectively. (See Appendix p. 139 for an example of one library's long-range goals and objectives, written specifically to guide a library in planning a new building.)

CONSIDERATIONS IN SELECTING FURNISHINGS

Once long-range plans for services and collections have been established, the next step in planning a new library is the preparation of a building program that serves as a guide to the architect or other professionals designing the facility. The program defines the environment in which the facility will be built, outlines the general requirements of the building from the standpoint of the owner, and describes the functions and relative size of various spaces. The architect interprets the program guidelines set down by the owner and translates the information into a set of drawings that can be used to construct the building.

Similarly, the process of selecting library furnishings begins with the development of a set of guidelines to be used in determining the specific products to be purchased. This "furniture program" may be a written document or just informal notes. In either case, the information will be used by the librarian when making specific furniture selections or in guiding others involved in decision making: the interior designer or consultant hired to write specifications; the architectural firm assisting with the selection of furnishings; or the purchasing agent responsible for the acquisition of the interior items.

Whether a project involves a public, school, academic, or special library, the initial task in the furniture selection process is to establish just what the owner of the facility wants or needs to accomplish with the various items purchased. As a rule, this task will depend on many of the general functions and requirements as spelled out in the building program; for example, the primary building use; the age of the users; the amount of use expected; the kinds of materials to be stored, organized, and displayed; the number of staff members; and future changes anticipated. More specifically, three major factors should be considered when making furniture selections: the function of the item, its maintenance, and its appearance.

The function consideration will include determining not only *what* use will be made of the item, but also *who* will use it and *how* it will be used. In some cases, function may further involve deciding how long the item will be used at any one time, how often it will be used, and whether built-in flexibility is needed for future changes in use. Maintenance considerations will include the ability to withstand heavy use over a long period of time, ease of day-to-day cleaning and upkeep, ease with which repairs can be made or parts replaced, and flexibility of the item in regard to changing its location or use in the future. The appearance of the item will, of course, involve considering how it adds to the attractiveness of the building, whether it is compatible with the other furnishings and the design of the building, and whether it contributes to the general atmosphere desired for the facility.

Other examples of function, maintenance, and appearance will be given later as the furniture selection process is applied in individual situations. Although all three factors should be considered, those bearing the most weight in making any given selection will, of course, depend on the particular circumstances. For example, in selecting task chairs, function and maintenance may be more important than appearance. When choosing chairs for the boardroom, on the other hand, appearance may be a more important factor than maintenance.

In addition to the three considerations suggested here, the furniture selection process also includes planning for compliance with the Americans with Disabilities Act (ADA) of 1990, Public Law 101-336. The implications of the law on the library furniture and shelving are discussed on p. 25.

On the basis of input from staff and users, the building program, and other information gathered, the qualities desired in the various items to be purchased can be determined. These ideas, regardless of whether they become a formal document or remain as notes for future reference, become the furniture program. The furniture and shelving layout and the quantities of items to be purchased vary in academic, public, special, and school libraries. The furniture and shelving used are the same, however, regardless of the kind of library: reading tables and chairs, bookstacks, computer workstations, index tables, and carrels.

The following examples are notes written for reading chairs for a fictitious public library; the same kind of notes can describe any furnishings to be used in any kind of library situation. In deciding which reading chair to purchase for adults, the staff might outline their ideas in the following manner:

Function. For the new library, we want a chair that is comfortable for reading or studying for long periods of time (as long as two or three hours). We want a chair that has plenty of padding on the seat and back, so we want one that has a wooden frame and an upholstered seat and back.

We want one with good back support and a seat large enough to be comfortable for both large- and average-sized users. We have decided that a chair with arms and a sled base is desirable for our users.

(Or the choice might be for a chair with a metal frame with a chrome or epoxy finish, or for an all-wooden chair, or for one with vinyl upholstery. The library may opt for a chair with no arms, and a leg base rather than a sled base.)

Maintenance. The reading chair should be one that has been performance-tested and has proven to be sturdy enough to withstand heavy use for at least 15 years. The legs should not break if someone rocks back and forth in the chair. The arms should be at the correct height to fit under the edge of the table without doing damage to either the arms or the table edge. The chair should have fabric that can be easily maintained and cleaned and should have a design that makes it easy to reupholster. The chair should not have a crevice between the seat and back where dirt can collect. The chair should be constructed so that it will not come apart where the various parts are joined. The back of the chair should be attached to the seat in such a manner that the back will not break away from the seat.

(Maintenance considerations might include choosing specific materials because of ease of upkeep; e.g., vinyl rather than fabric upholstery or a wood seat and back.)

Appearance. Because the building is fairly traditional, we want a reading chair that is attractive but compatible with the design of the library, including the wooden staircase. If possible, we want a chair with a slight arch across the back, or some other element to give it a little distinction. Because the library board has indicated a strong interest in a dark oak finish on the staircase, we want to choose a wooden frame that will work well with the wood used in the building itself.

Other seating for adults in the public area could include stools or benches for use at index tables or tables holding various kinds of computer equipment. In this case, considering the function of the item, seating without a back may be desired in order to discourage users from tying up the equipment by using the seat for reading or studying. Here again, other options to be considered might be a sled or leg base and an upholstered, wood, or metal seat. With stools, maintenance and appearance considerations may be similar to those for the chairs. On the other hand, if there are other kinds of materials in the building or other design elements that are significant, the appearance of the stool could be tied in more with those other elements rather than with the chairs.

In a children's area, the function consideration of chairs should include the fact that the chairs will inevitably be used for activities other than sitting, including climbing, jumping, piling, building, etc. Also, chairs of more than one height should be provided to accommodate children of different ages. Even the smallest chairs will also be used by parents and should be strong enough to hold adults. In the children's area, maintenance is a very important consideration for any seating provided. Just as it does for adults, the library may wish to use several kinds of seating—chairs at reading tables, stools at tables where audiovisual and computer equipment are used, step stools scattered around the picture book area, or cushions.

Although the function of a lounge chair is easily distinguished from the use of a reading chair at a table in the library environment, the library function of a lounge chair differs clearly from the corresponding use of this type of furniture in other waiting areas, such as in the airport or a doctor's reception room. In the airport, for example, rows of ganged (connected) seats are used by waiting passengers who are willing to sit elbow-to-elbow for short periods of time, out of necessity. As research on personal space has indicated, however, many of us are uncomfortable sitting this close to a stranger. Users in library situations, then, with a choice of seats, will not take the chair that puts them right next to another person. Lounge furniture in the library may be used for long periods of time by someone reading, or for a short time by someone taking a break from studying. In either case, long sofas, or the type of ganged seating used in waiting areas, will not be particularly functional because of our feelings about personal space.

Maintenance considerations for lounge furniture will certainly be important in public areas with heavy use. The amount and kind of upholstery, the choice of material used for the frame, and the design of the chair will all affect maintenance. For example, the library may want a chair upholstered with fabric because it is comfortable and attractive. On the other hand, the choice may be one that has an upholstered seat and back, but with wooden or metal arms, because they are the parts of the lounge chair that get dirty most quickly with heavy use.

Lounge furniture is used not only to provide an alternate form of seating but to break up the monotony of having rows and rows of reading tables or ranges of shelving. In other words, such furniture plays a definite role in the appearance of the library. Large, comfortable-looking chairs make the interior more inviting, and suggest that the library is a pleasant place to spend some time, perhaps doing some leisure reading. The style of chair used can also be significant in relating the furnishings to the

design of the building and in contributing to the particular atmosphere desired. For example, a large, fully upholstered lounge chair may be appropriate in some libraries, while a chair with an epoxy-coated metal frame and an upholstered seat and back may be a better choice in another building.

Function will be the highest priority to consider when choosing chairs to be used by the staff. Several different kinds of chairs may eventually be selected because of the variety of tasks carried out by the staff. Some staff members will need to have a chair that allows them to work comfortably when seated in front of a terminal for long periods of time. The reference staff will probably need chairs that will allow them to sit comfortably but get up and down easily and frequently. Because many chairs in the library have to be shared by several staff members, ease of adjustability for different-sized individuals is important. Some chairs will need to be the right height for a 29 inch worksurface and some may be needed for worksurfaces that are 38–42 inches high.

A chair that can be cleaned easily is, of course, desirable. The kind of upholstery selected, the availability of replacement parts, and the ease with which the chair can be reupholstered or repaired are also important maintenance considerations.

The appearance of the work chair plays an interesting role in the library, as in other office settings, in identifying the chain of command. In many organizations the higher in the hierarchy the staff member is, the larger and more expensive the chair will be. The clerk in the workroom at the terminal sits in a secretarial posture chair with no arms and a low, or intermediate, back height. Reference librarians are more likely to have a full back and arms on their chairs, while the manager will have an executive chair with a high back and fully upholstered arms. In many cases, the chairs may be equally functional for the situation in which they are used, but they do play a role in office politics: the boss wants a larger, more elaborate chair that represents her/his status in the chain of command. Other appearance considerations are the upholstery, style, and base finish.

In determining the library's needs in reading tables, functional considerations will be fairly simple. The table's height depends on its use and the age of its users: 31–32 inches high for wheelchair use; 29 inches high for adults reading and studying; 27 inches high for young adults; 26–29 inches high for typing and computer use; and 20–25 inches high for children. The size and shape of tables needed will depend on whether users will be working singly or in groups, how much material they will need to spread out on the table, and whether they will use equipment on the worksurface. Some tables may include electrical raceways and a wire management system or task lighting, depending on their function.

The description of reading tables could very simply be as follows:

Function. We want reading tables for adults that are 29 inches high, which can be used for reading and studying for long periods of time. Most of our users will work alone or with one or two other people, so we want several tables to seat no more than four people. We want some rectangular tables, 48 inches by 72 inches , and some 48-inch round tables. Some of the tables should be designed so that they can be retrofitted with electrical systems later, if we need more space for computers in the future. In the children's area, we want some tables small enough for preschoolers and some for children in grades K–3. We also want two or three tables 27 inches high, if there is enough room.

The construction and finish of the tabletop are major elements in maintenance considerations for tables. The library might choose a tabletop constructed of butcher block, three-ply flakeboard, or five-ply lumber core. In some situations, a veneer or other wood surface can be maintained on a day-to-day basis and, if necessary, refinished. In libraries that are used heavily by the public, a high-pressure laminate may be maintained more easily and for a longer period of time. The strength of a table depends on the materials used in the base and the joinery between the base and top. Because these elements affect how sturdy the table will be, they are important maintenance considerations. Tables are discussed further in chapter 6.

Appearance considerations for a table include the materials used, the design or style, and the finish. A leg-base, panel end, or pedestal table could be chosen, with either a wood or metal base, in any number of different styles and finishes.

Decisions regarding computer and microform workstations, index and stand-up reference tables, staff worktables, folding tables for meeting rooms, and carrels will include considerations similar to those noted for reading tables. In the same building, the staff might decide to have some leg-base tables for reading, and tables or workstations with panel ends for computer equipment. Rectangular tables that have wooden legs might be desired in some areas, while round tables with a metal base might be used in other areas. In order to have the design of all of the furnishings coordinate, decisions regarding tables will prob-

ably determine the style of technical pieces, such as the index tables and atlas and dictionary stands.

Circulation and reference desks are the major workstations for interacting with the library's public, so the staff should consider the function, maintenance, and appearance of these items very carefully and thoroughly. The description of the function of the circulation desk, for example, should include how many people will be working there, what they will be doing, how they will do it, and what equipment will be used. For example:

Function. The circulation desk should be large enough to accommodate five people working there at any one time. We want one 36-inch-wide workstation with a 32-inch-high worksurface to comply with the ADA, at least four stations at stand-up height (39 inches), and one station at sit-down height (29 inches). The workstations should be open under the desk for knee space. Because we don't know what kind of equipment we will be using in the future, we want the stations at stand-up height to have one continuous flat surface. We want the top to be 30–36 inches wide so it will be wide enough for equipment, but not too wide to reach across to hand books to patrons. If possible, the desk top should be built in such a manner that electrical cords from equipment can go down through the top at 12-inch intervals, so that equipment can be moved along the surface as library needs change. Under the desk, there should be a wire management system to handle the cords and cables from telephones, data lines, terminals, etc. At each check-out station, we will need slots or drawers to hold the forms and other supplies that we use frequently. We will need at least 36 linear feet of shelf space to store books we are holding for users.

The staff might also want other kinds of units in the circulation desk, such as vertical-file drawers, cabinets with doors, or storage units for a particular kind of library material. The shape of the desk can be a functional consideration if the staff plans to have other tasks or activities take place in the same area.

The most important maintenance considerations involve the worksurface of the desk. The top should be covered with a material that does not get marred when heavy materials and equipment are dragged across or dropped on it. The surface should be one that can be cleaned easily on a daily basis. Ideally, the desk top will be constructed in such a manner that the top only can be replaced. The staff might want to note that neither the cabinet nor the top of the desk should have sharp edges that can be easily damaged.

As with the other items in the building, the style, finish, and design of the desk should also be considered in regard to appearance. Because the circulation desk is often the first thing that is seen by patrons entering the library, the desk's appearance plays an important role in creating a first impression. The design should, therefore, be inviting, and the function of the desk should be immediately apparent.

All of the considerations in regard to the circulation desk are applicable to the reference desk as well. Although the functions are different, the staff will consider similar factors in describing reference area needs. They might want to have a worksurface 29 inches high and a transaction top across the front of the desk 36–39 inches high. Different libraries will require different types of storage behind the reference desk. Some libraries will require special accommodations for ready-reference material of various types. An electrical and wire management system will probably be needed. Some tasks carried out at the circulation desk in one library may be carried out at the reference desk in another. Also, in small libraries, one desk may be used for both circulation and reference for some—or all—of the time.

Early discussions about the function of the shelving to be selected should center around anticipated amounts and kinds of materials to be stored. In an academic library, book storage will probably involve storing large numbers of books as efficiently as possible. In a school or public library, bookstacks will be needed for picture books, for children's fiction and nonfiction, and for adult books. There may also be a need for book and audiovisual display shelving. A special library may require heavy-duty shelving for large volumes and specialized storage for other kinds of materials. Many libraries will require shelving for periodicals as well as books.

Maintenance considerations for shelving for a public library might involve the following:

Maintenance. We want bookstacks that have shelves that can be moved easily from section to section as the library changes. The shelving should be easy to assemble and disassemble, if we want to move the ranges some day. Specialized hardware should not be required in order to keep the shelving stable. The shelving should be so well-made that it remains stable even though it is moved several times. The parts of the shelving should be interchangeable, so we can adapt it to changing conditions. There should be some way of leveling the shelving easily. The finish on the shelving should not nick or scratch easily.

In many libraries, appearance is not going to be the primary factor to consider when selecting shelving. Although the staff of a small public or school library might prefer the look of wooden shelving, budget constraints may force it to consider steel shelving, or steel shelving with wooden end panels. In the closed-stack areas of most libraries, function and maintenance will be the important factors to consider; appearance will have very little to do with the selection of the shelving.

Similarly, with lateral or vertical files, microform storage, etc., function and maintenance will be more important factors than appearance. For example, there are many attractive lateral or vertical files. Therefore, the staff should describe the files needed in terms of function and maintenance: They should store the materials efficiently, be safe to use when fully loaded, have drawers that open and close satisfactorily with heavy use, have parts that can be replaced or repaired, withstand moving from place to place, and have a finish that is not easily marred.

The information compiled at the beginning of the furniture selection process becomes, in effect, the furniture program to be used when selecting specific products. As noted earlier, in small library projects, the parties involved may be so familiar with the needs of the library that no formal written document will be necessary. Whether or not the information-gathering process results in a written report, the thought process is necessary in order to ensure that the librarian, or others involved in the selection, can speak confidently and intelligibly to the design team and to potential suppliers.

The furniture program establishes the level of quality to be expected in the building interior when it is completed. Decisions made early in the project may ensure that the furnishings purchased will continue to be useful and attractive for many years to come.

MAKING FURNITURE SELECTIONS

In many cases, more than one furniture or shelving product will fulfill the needs and wants of a particular library. Prior to making furniture selections those involved in the process should study catalogs or literature for several products and visit the showrooms or conference exhibits of suppliers of similar products. No single manufacturer or supplier can do everything. Be wary of a salesperson who claims to be able to supply anything needed or wanted, regardless of materials used, construction, or amount of funds available. The name of the dealer or manufacturer's representative for a specific area can be obtained by calling the company headquarters. (The addresses and phone numbers of many of the manufacturers discussed in the following chapters can be found beginning on p.149.)

In addition to gathering information about specific products, these questions can be asked of the supplier:

1. How long has the vendor been in business?
2. How long has the vendor been selling the product being considered?
3. Who manufactures the product?
4. How long has the manufacturer been in business and is the company financially stable?
5. Who will install the product?
6. Is the installer familiar with the product?
7. What is the anticipated delivery time on the product?
8. Has the vendor/manufacturer/installer done other projects similar in scope to the one now planned?
9. Who will be responsible for following up on the project once the installation is complete; that is, who will handle problems that might arise later?
10. What are the warranties and guarantees offered on the products and labor supplied?

Although the length of time vendors have been in business does not provide any insurance for the future, a company that has been in existence for several years can provide a list of references of successfully completed projects that have stood up over time. Obviously, the longer vendors have sold the product, or a similar one, the more they should know about it. References should be carefully checked to see if the earlier projects were similar in scope to the current one, and to determine whether or not the products, installation, and service provided were satisfactory.

Do not assume that the name on a product reveals who actually manufactures the item. For example, although most library supply houses include steel shelving products in their catalogs, not all of them own a manufacturing plant. Several companies purchase a product from another manufacturer and sell it under their brand name. It might be cheaper to buy directly from the manufacturer rather than from the supplier. Also, knowing the product's manufacturer may tell you more about it, if the manufacturer has an established reputation.

In some cases, it is not only important to know how long a manufacturer has been in business, but how long the current owner has held the company. Product quality sometimes changes as owners change, even though the name of the company stays the same. For that reason, it is best not to assume that because Brand A was an unreliable product 10 years ago, it should not be considered

reliable now, or vice versa. Furniture or shelving made by a company that has changed ownership should be evaluated like any new product, on the basis of the criteria discussed in later chapters.

Some products require installation by someone who is factory-trained. In any case, the installer should be familiar with the product or the kind of product. In large projects, it is obviously very important to ascertain whether the manufacturer, the supplier, and the installer have successfully handled jobs of the size planned. Occasionally a company will bid on a job that is outside the scope of its capabilities in terms of quantities needed, delivery time expected, type of construction desired, etc. In that event, furnishings may not be delivered on schedule, and the level of quality of the items received may not meet specifications.

During the process of making furniture selections, the question arises: Does the library have adequate funds to purchase furnishings with the level of quality desired? The question will be answered during the selection process as available products are researched and as prices for specific items are obtained.

The price of a product is based upon many factors, including the quality and cost of the materials used, the quality of workmanship that goes into making it, volume of sales, competition in the marketplace, and whether or not the item is a standard or customized product for that manufacturer. Here is one possible scenario that might take place in the course of obtaining product prices: The representative of Company A may say the company can provide just what is wanted, but the representative knows the requested item will have to be custom-made by the manufacturer. Company B, on the other hand, may be able to supply the item as a standard product. In that case, Company B may offer a better price because the product can be manufactured for less.

It is important to remember that an initial expenditure should be viewed in terms of the cost to the library over the number of years a piece will be used (life-cycle costing). In the long run, a less expensive item may cost the library more, in terms of total dollars, if it has a fairly short life span and has to be replaced or repaired more quickly.

After completing the process of deciding what furnishings and shelving the library would ideally like to have, a preliminary list of furnishings and shelving items should be prepared. The list should include the quantity and a brief description of each item needed. The description may refer to a particular product or may provide information that will establish the level of quality, function, and appearance of the product desired (for example, oak reading table, 48" x 72" x 29", full panel ends faced with veneer, laminate top with wood edge bands, particleboard core).

Vendors will provide ballpark estimates of the price of the products on the initial list. If it is immediately evident that the first-choice product is too expensive, salespeople will be willing to offer alternatives that will provide a similar level of quality without the refinements or extras that a luxury item has. Compromise is often necessary on matters that deal strictly with appearance. A library may choose to give up some stylistic elements in particular pieces in order to get a higher level of quality in other items. For example, because of the electrical requirements of the circulation and computer catalog stations, a library may choose to buy standard leg-base tables and less expensive reading chairs, so that more funds will be available to purchase a circulation desk and computer workstations that contain a top-of-the-line electrical system.

Although vendors cannot be expected to spend a lot of time figuring exact prices at this point, they should be able to provide enough information to determine whether or not a desired product falls within the budget. (A more in-depth discussion of the vendor's responsibilities will be found in chapter 11.)

There are several ways to purchase library furnishings. In many cases, the purchase is handled on a bid basis, so that suppliers are competing against each other. In a bid situation, the purchaser is dependent upon the vendor to provide a price determined by the conditions of the particular job. Furnishings can also be purchased from a catalog at a list price. Although ordering through a catalog may be viewed as an easy way to handle a small purchase, it is not the best way to obtain a competitive price, nor does it necessarily allow the buyer to ask questions about the product and specify exactly what quality is demanded. In some situations, a library may put out a request for proposals (RFP) and, in effect, negotiate the job with vendors. Regardless of the purchase method used, however, decision makers should talk with suppliers, ask questions about the construction of products, obtain written specifications, and ask for the names of libraries using the product for more than a year.

In summary, everyone involved in making decisions about furniture selections should ask lots of questions. In order to be able to ask the right questions and make informed decisions, knowledge of what ensures quality in a product is needed. The following chapters provide information to help in evaluating product quality.

CHAPTER 2

Quality Construction and Issues in Furniture Selection

Level of quality in library furnishings and shelving is indicative of the length of time a product will remain in good repair and maintain a satisfactory appearance. High quality furnishings that were purchased 20, 30, or more years ago are still in use in many libraries; sometimes staff and users want new furniture in order to update the look of the library long before the furnishings wear out.

Library furnishings with an undesirable level of quality, on the other hand, have a limited life and must be replaced within a few years. A low level of quality is indicated, for example, by tables that become unstable and rack with use, by chairs or parts of chairs that break, by laminate or veneer finishes that chip or fall off, and by drawers that fail to operate easily.

High quality in furnishings is determined by a number of factors that work together to ensure that a product will be usable for many years. Developing furniture with a high level of quality involves taking a "systems" approach to furniture design. (The approach might also be termed "holistic.") According to Richard Pata, engineering director of Buckstaff, a high level of quality is ensured, not by any one feature of a product, but rather by sound engineering and construction of each element into one well-crafted piece of furniture. Engineering for a high level of quality involves taking into consideration, for example, the physical dimensions of a piece of furniture, the physi-

cal and mechanical properties of the materials used to make it, and the joints and connections that hold the piece together.

DETERMINING HIGH QUALITY IN FURNISHINGS

Most people selecting furniture do not have the knowledge and expertise needed to evaluate the engineering and design of a particular piece of library furniture. How, then, can specific products be assessed to ensure the highest level of quality for the money? Sound evaluation of a product involves reading product literature, looking at an item, and, more important, studying evidence of the product's long-term performance.

Information that provides evidence of satisfactory furniture design and performance is collected by field testing and by product testing in a laboratory. Older products have, in effect, been field tested in other libraries. A vendor will supply the names of libraries that are similar in size, that have a similar amount of business, and that currently use the product in question.

When checking furniture references, detailed questions about how well an item has held up over time should be asked. Posing a general question, such as "Do you like the chair?," doesn't provide enough information. Specific questions should be asked that can reveal any detail of construction or materials, in even one piece of furniture, that has failed. If the answer to an inquiry is, for example, "Yes, we really like the chairs. We have figured out how to fix the stretchers on them when they break," find another product!

Information about performance is also obtained by testing products in a laboratory. Performance tests are conducted by manufacturers or industry groups in in-house laboratories and in independent testing facilities. Performance tests in laboratories use machines and methods that simulate the forces exerted on a product in actual use. The simulated action is repeated a number of times with force applied in increasingly larger amounts through a specified number of cycles (often more than 100,000) until the product, or a particular part of a product, fails or proves to withstand the test at a specific level.

Performance tests can become the basis for standards that are used to evaluate products. For example, the tests of steel shelving that have been conducted by *Library Technology Reports* (*LTR*) and adopted as an American National Standards Institute (ANSI) standard (see discussion in chapter 3, p. 37) provide consumers with the means for evaluating and comparing steel shelving products.

The purchase of furniture and shelving that has been performance-tested for safe, long-term use helps to ensure that the library is obtaining the highest quality products for the funds available. During the furniture selection process, vendors should be asked to supply performance testing data for specific products that can be compared with similar information from other companies.

One word of caution: Many companies make products that are similar; however, not all manufacturers routinely do performance tests. Sometimes a salesperson will tell a consumer that testing results for a specific product apply to a similar product made by another manufacturer. As a sales technique, this only works if the consumer does not understand the rationale behind the need for the standard and is willing to take the word of the salesperson for the technical details involved in compliance with the standard.

One of the motivating factors that leads manufacturers to implement a performance testing program is the threat of possible product liability lawsuits that can result from selling below-standard furnishings. An excellent discussion of the subject of product liability is presented in *Specifications for Commercial Interiors* by S. C. Reznikoff (1989). Reznikoff defines product liability as follows:

> Product liability is primarily concerned with negligence. It is considered the "duty" of the manufacturer to provide products that will not expose the consumer to undue risk, bodily injury, death or property damage as a result of the construction, design, installation, and assembly of the product. Also included in product liability actions is the manufacturer's failure to ward against a danger or hazard in the use or misuse of the product and failure to provide adequate instructions for the use of the product. Violation of *express warranty* may also be involved. An express warranty is a guaranty of performance and includes all advertising claims made by the manufacturer.(p.17)

Product liability should be a concern to consumers, as well as to manufacturers, who want to avoid liability suits involving furnishings. Decisions regarding the selection of particular furniture items that have been made by the owner (the library) and that are reflected in bid specifications may make the owner liable. The outcomes of prior liability cases indicate that the judicial system transfers much of the responsibility in lawsuits from the manufacturer to the owner after a product has been used approximately 10 years. Furniture and shelving selections should, therefore, be based on performance testing data and the most stringent industry standards whenever possible. Also, products and finishes selected should be in compliance with any relevant local, state, and national regulations that affect furnishings.

Quality and performance testing methods, standards, and regulations are established by a number of agencies and organizations. Some guidelines are established by organizations that support a particular industry or user group, such as the Business and Institutional Furniture Manufacturers Association (BIFMA). Other standards are established by governmental or quasi-governmental agencies, such as the General Services Administration (GSA) and the American National Standards Institute (ANSI).

Standards that relate to particular kinds of furnishings are discussed in the chapters that follow. Here are some of the organizations that develop standards or guidelines that affect the furniture and shelving industries.

American Association of Textile Chemists and Colorists (AATCC)
Recognized as an authority for test methods of textiles. "Develops standard test methods; conducts textile test method research; disseminates scientific information."

American National Standards Institute (ANSI)
"Serves as a clearinghouse for nationally coordinated voluntary standards for fields ranging from information technology to building construction. Gives status as American National Standards to standards developed by agreement from all groups concerned, in such areas as: definitions,

terminology, symbols, and abbreviations; materials, performance characteristics, procedure, and methods of rating, methods of testing and analysis; size, weight, volume, and rating; practice, safety, health, and building construction. Provides information on foreign standards and represents United States interests in international standardization of work."

American Society for Testing and Materials (ASTM)

"Establishes standards for materials, products, systems, and services. Has 133 technical committees. Has developed more than 9,000 standard test methods, specifications classifications, definitions, and recommended practices now in use."

Architectural Woodwork Institute (AWI)

Members are manufacturers of architectural woodwork products (casework, fixtures, and paneling) and associated suppliers. The association works to raise industry standards, researches new and improved materials and methods, and publishes technical data helpful in the design and use of architectural woodwork.

Business and Institutional Furniture Manufacturers Association (BIFMA)

Members are "firms engaged in the manufacture of furniture intended for use in offices, public spaces, and non-live-in institutional spaces (seating and space divider manufacturers included). Activities are in areas of: engineering standards development for all primary products; industry relations; government relations; executive development; industry information and statistics. Research programs include: industry statistical analysis; upholstery flammability research; product safety research."

General Services Administration (GSA)

Develops and implements federal government acquisition policies and procedures and administers federal acquisition regulations for civilian agencies.

International Organization for Standardization (ISO)

A multinational association of national standards bodies that develops and publishes international standards.

National Fire Protection Association (NFPA)

"Develops, publishes, and disseminates standards, prepared by approximately 250 technical committees, intended to minimize the possibility and effects of fire and explosion; conducts fire safety programs for the general public." Publishes *National Fire Codes*, an annual compilation of more than 270 fire codes, standards, recommended practices, manuals, and guides on fire protection. With ANSI,

adopts, publishes, and distributes the *National Electrical Code* (NEC).

Occupational Safety and Health Administration (OSHA)

An agency within the U.S. Labor Department that develops and enforces mandatory safety and health standards to protect workers in four major categories: general industry, maritime, construction, and agriculture.

Underwriters Laboratory (UL)

A product safety certification laboratory that "establishes and operates product safety certification programs to ascertain that items produced under the service are safeguarded against reasonably foreseeable risks."

(Above information from the *Encyclopedia of Associations*, 1994)

Consumers (as well as manufacturers who compete in the global market) may need to be familiar with ISO 9000, a series of general standards, published by the International Organization for Standardization since 1987, that address various aspects of quality assurance and consist of numerous sets of technical standards overseen by a variety of institutions. ISO 9000 standards have been adopted by more than 50 countries, including the United States. Companies wishing to sell products in countries that have adopted ISO 9000 may be required to have ISO 9000 registration. Registration provides evidence that a company has set up a consistent system for manufacturing a product. Each country that has adopted the standards interprets the guidelines differently, and each country has its own system of accreditation for registering companies. (Material for this brief discussion was obtained from "ISO's Implications," *Interiors*, May 1993, p. 52. Additional information about ISO 9000 can be obtained from major furniture manufacturers and from other associations listed on p. 153.)

Individual libraries can have an effect on the library furniture and shelving industries by demanding a high level of quality in products and services. Librarians as a group are, of course, a major market for several companies. The leading manufacturers in the library and contract furniture markets performance test their products to meet or exceed industry and market standards and to comply with local, state, and national regulations. Librarians and design professionals who specify products that meet the most stringent standards and who stand behind their specifications in a bid process give a message to all manufacturers about the high level of quality expected in the library marketplace.

WOOD FURNITURE CONSTRUCTION

Most fine quality library furniture is constructed of wood. It is essential when selecting furnishings, therefore, to have some background knowledge of wood and wood products, joinery, construction, and wood finishes. The actual construction of a piece of wood furniture cannot necessarily be determined by looking at the finished product. What may look like a solid piece of wood may actually be a veneer, or a thin slice of wood, used to face a core of another kind of material. This is one reason it may be risky to purchase inexpensive furniture from an office supply catalog: The information given may be incomplete or misleading. A $200 desk may look fine when it's purchased, but it can't be expected to provide a library with the same reliable use over a period of years as an $800 desk.

Most people don't have, and don't care to have, any more than a rudimentary knowledge of wood and wood construction. For that reason, it is advisable to work with companies that have engineers on staff with expert knowledge of and experience with wood and the use of wood in furnishings. Representatives of reliable wood manufacturing companies should be able to discuss the elements of wood and wood construction that affect the quality of their end products.

Information about wood can be found in *Architectural Woodwork Quality Standards*, published by AWI (1993) and the *Wood Handbook*, published by the U.S. Department of Agriculture (1987). The AWI publication includes a special advisory (p. 49) regarding dimensional change problems in wood that should be considered in planning a new library facility that will house wood furnishings. Wood is a hygroscopic material that absorbs moisture and swells in high humidity and releases moisture and shrinks in low humidity. AWI states that "together with proper design, fabrication and installation, humidity control is obviously the important factor in preventing dimensional change problems." Every wood furniture manufacturer has had the unfortunate experience of receiving complaints about originally well-made wood furniture that develops cracks because of low humidity or swells because of high humidity in the environment in which the furniture is placed. AWI recommends that relative humidity be maintained within the range of 25 percent to 55 percent, and states that uncontrolled extremes below 25 percent and above 55 percent relative humidity can cause problems. Failure to provide adequate humidity control in a facility and resulting problems with wood furniture are the responsibility of the owner, not the furniture manufacturer. (Concern about the maintenance of wood furniture is consistent with concern about preserving books in the library. Most paper is manufactured using wood fibers. According to Richard Silberman with Healthy Buildings International, libraries should maintain relative humidities between 40 percent and 50 percent in order to optimize the balance between occupant comfort and paper preservation. [Silberman, 1993])

Wood furniture selection involves considering which of the primary types of wood construction will be acceptable in the furnishings selected. Wood library furniture is currently constructed of three-ply flakeboard or particleboard, five-ply lumber core, medium-density fiberboard, plywood or veneer core, solid butcher block and, occasionally, of solid wood plank. (The major types of construction are defined below, but this list will undoubtedly grow as new products are continually being developed.) (See Figures 1A–D.)

According to AWI's *Architectural Woodwork Quality Standards*, flakeboard or particleboard is manufactured from "wood particles of various sizes that are bonded together with a synthetic resin or binder under heat and pressure" (p. 52). Most high-quality flakeboard used in furniture is medium density, that is, 45 pounds per cubic foot. The term "three-ply" refers to the particleboard core and the face and back veneers (or the plastic laminate and backing) that are applied over the core.

Some particleboards (those manufactured using urea-formaldehyde resins as an adhesive) are now under scrutiny for emitting noxious levels of formaldehyde (See the discussion on indoor air quality, p. 23.) Other particleboards, those bonded with phenolic-resins, are more resistant to swelling when exposed to moisture and do not emit significant quantities of formaldehyde.

Lumber core consists of strips of kiln-dried wood, often common poplar, basswood, or aspen, of random widths (usually from 2½ to 4 inches wide) and lengths that are edge-glued into panels. Crossbands of wood running perpendicular to the grain of the lumber core are then placed on either side of the core. Finally, face and back veneers (with the grain running parallel to the core and the opposite direction of the crossbands) are applied to make up the five plies.

Medium-density fiberboard (MDF) is becoming increasingly popular as a core material. MDF is defined as "wood particles reduced to fibers in a moderate pressure steam vessel, combined with a resin, and bonded together

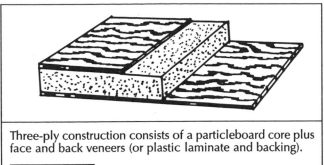

Three-ply construction consists of a particleboard core plus face and back veneers (or plastic laminate and backing).

FIGURE 1A

Five-ply construction includes a lumber core, two crossbands running in the opposite direction of the grain of the core, and face and back veneers with the grain running parallel to the core.

FIGURE 1B

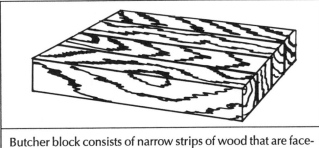

Butcher block consists of narrow strips of wood that are face-glued.

FIGURE 1C

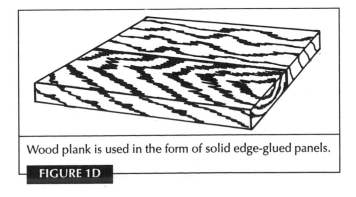

Wood plank is used in the form of solid edge-glued panels.

FIGURE 1D

under heat and pressure. . . . The surface of [MDF] is flat, smooth, uniform, dense and free of knots or grain pattern." (AWI, 1993, p. 52)

Veneer core consists of "three or more layers (plys) of wood veneers pressed and glued into a single sheet." (AWI, 1993 p. 53) Butcher block construction involves the use of solid staves or narrow strips of wood which are face-glued. Wood plank is also occasionally used in the form of solid edge-glued panels.

The use of wood materials with several plies minimizes the effect of moisture absorption by the wood. Robert Boardman of the Worden Company notes that one of the major disadvantages of working with wood in any form is the ability of this natural material to absorb moisture from the atmosphere. "The most important development with regard to the control of hygroscopic expansion and shrinkage of furniture panels is the cross-lamination of wood," that is, applying the layers of wood so that the grain of a layer is at a right angle to the grain of the ply below it. Cross-lamination is only advantageous if the plies are perfectly balanced. The plies on opposite sides of the core must be of the same thickness, moisture content, and species, in order to avoid warping of lumber core panels.

Manufacturers and vendors offer consumers differing opinions on the quality of construction that is possible using particleboard, lumber core, or butcher block. Usually, a company preference is based to a some extent on the material selected for use in their standard product. For example, some companies use solid lumber core tops on all of their tables as a standard; other manufacturers use flakeboard or particleboard core as standard construction material. Most of the major library manufacturers will, however, build furniture with either three-ply flakeboard or five-ply lumber core, depending on what the purchaser specifies.

Several factors should be considered in deciding whether to specify particleboard or five-ply lumber core construction for furniture. Boardman notes two major advantages to five-ply lumber core construction: (1) form stability, or the structural strength to withstand long-term loading and (2) a solid edge that can be shaped and finished, and that provides good holding power for mechanical fasteners on the edge grain. Particleboard, however, is less expensive and has some other advantages over lumber core or butcher block. For example, particleboard has more dimensional stability; it has greater "resistance to linear and thickness expansion or shrinkage of a panel as a result of changes of the wood moisture content." If the materials on either side of the core are balanced correctly, there is less likelihood of a particleboard warping than a lumber core panel.

The most frequently mentioned disadvantage to particleboard is its screw-holding power. According to Boardman: "Screws driven into the edges of particleboard have a screw-holding power considerably less than that of solid wood, while the screw-holding power on the face of the board is entirely satisfactory. Usually, in order to increase the edge screw-holding power, the particleboard edges must be reinforced with solid wood members." (Boardman, 1981) Other factors that affect the satisfactory use of particleboard construction are the density of the particleboard, the sizes of the screws used in the construction, backer sheets used, and any other components that go into making the panel.

In the future, consumers may have another factor to consider in selecting core material. In some localities, regulations regarding flammability may dictate the use of core materials treated for fire retardancy. Such regulations may affect the choice of core material; not all particleboards nor all lumber core materials are fire retardant. In areas covered by these regulations, furniture contractors will be required to provide information about the fire rating of the materials used in their furniture construction.

It is unlikely that in a building project all wood construction in the furniture will have the same core material: Some items will be made using five-ply lumber core, while other items will be made using three-ply flakeboard. Parts of tables, shelving, or chairs that are important to the structural strength or stability of the item should ideally be constructed of lumber core. Items like end panels for steel shelving, which are added mainly for the sake of appearance, can be constructed of the less expensive particleboard. Several types of construction may even be used in different parts of the same piece of furniture, if function demands it. In summary, particleboard, lumber core, fiberboard, and solid wood are all acceptable types of material for wood furniture construction, if the finished items are engineered correctly and made by a reliable manufacturer.

Most library furniture manufacturers use northern-grown red oak or hard maple for face veneers and for parts of their standard products where solid wood is specified, such as edge bands of tables, shelves, and stabilizing keels. The wood is kiln-dried to an acceptable moisture content of between five percent and seven percent. It is the responsibility of a manufacturer to control environmen-tal conditions throughout the furniture manufacturing process and shipping, so that wood products arrive at an installation site with an acceptable moisture content.

When a finish other than natural oak or maple is desired for furnishings, wood is often stained to simulate the color of other woods, such as mahogany or cherry. If a consumer is willing to pay the price, most manufacturers will also work with solid woods other than oak and maple on special projects.

The finished look of a piece of high-quality furniture is often determined by the face veneer used. Face veneers used by domestic manufacturers are usually no less than 1/36th of an inch thick. The appearance of the grain in different types of veneer is the result of the way in which a log segment is cut with relation to the annual rings. (See Figure 2.) Veneer cuts include the following:

> *Half-round slicing:* Logs are mounted off-center in the lathe, so that the result has some of the characteristics of both rotary- and plain-sliced veneers.
>
> *Plain or flat slicing:* The half-log is sliced parallel to a line through the center of the log. The grain figure is similar to that of plain sawn lumber.
>
> *Quarter slicing:* The quarter-log is sliced so that the growth rings of the log strike the blade at approximately right angles, making the grain show as a series of stripes.
>
> *Rift-cut:* Produced from "various species of oak. Oak has medullary ray cells which radiate from the center of the log like the spokes of a wheel. The rift is obtained by slicing slightly across these medullary rays. This accentuates the vertical grain."
>
> *Rotary:* As the name implies, the log is mounted in a lathe and cut against a blade, like unwinding a roll of paper. A bold grain figure is produced.

Other visual aspects of veneer are the result of the way in which the individual pieces of veneer, called "leaves," are arranged or matched. Most matching is done with sliced, rather than rotary cut, veneers. (See Figure 3.) Matching between adjacent veneer leaves includes the following:

> *Book matching:* "Every other piece of veneer is turned over, so that adjacent leaves are 'opened' as two pages in a book." The visual effect is that

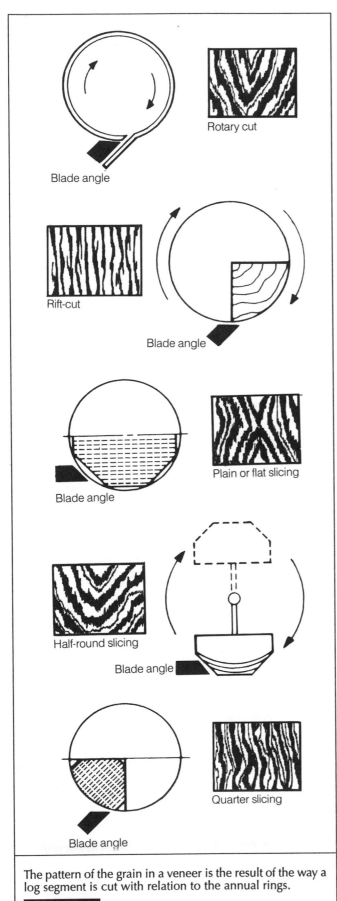

The pattern of the grain in a veneer is the result of the way a log segment is cut with relation to the annual rings.

FIGURE 2

A veneer match is the result of the specific way the individual pieces of veneer, called leaves, are arranged.

FIGURE 3

"veneer joints match, creating a symmetrical pattern." Book matching within a panel may be a running match in which "each panel face is assembled from as many veneer leaves as necessary"; a balance match in which "each panel face is assembled from leaves of uniform width"; or a center match in which "each panel has an even number of veneer leaves of uniform width. Thus, there is a veneer joint in the center of the panel, producing horizontal symmetry."

End matching: "leaves are book matched end to end as well as side to side."

Random matching: The arrangement of the leaves from one or more logs resulting in a casual, board-like effect.

Slip matching: "adjoining leaves are slipped out in sequence [as they were cut from the log], with all the same face sides being exposed."

(*Architectural Woodwork Institute*, 1993, pp. 59-62)

Library furniture manufacturers use different cuts of veneer or matches as their standard. Buckstaff, for example, uses slip-matched veneers as standard, while Worden uses book-matched veneers with some woods and slip-matched veneers with others. Both slip- and book-matched veneers cost the same. It is important to understand that different matches produce different visual effects. The visual effects also vary according to the type of wood and the finishing method used. In purchasing products with veneers from several different vendors for one library, make sure that the specifications are consistent so that the wood throughout the building will match. Ask the furniture vendor to provide a sample of the veneer to be specified (or a photograph of typical veneer matches) in order to see the visual effects that can be expected in the finished furniture.

Although the type of veneer used has an effect on the appearance of furniture, a more important maintenance consideration is the finish that is placed on the wood. Almost any finish will look good on a new piece of furniture, but it is important to consider what happens to a finish after heavy use. *Architectural Woodwork Quality Standards* includes a detailed table (p. 263) that compares performance data on a number of wood-finishing systems. Wear and chemical resistance and ease of repair are some of the characteristics that are compared.

Some wood furniture is finished with only a natural penetrating oil. An oil finish scratches relatively easily and has poor abrasion resistance; however, a natural oil finish can be repaired easily and acquires an attractive patina over time. An oil finish requires more maintenance than a film finish, such as catalyzed lacquer, because a reapplication of oil or wax is required from time to time, usually a minimum of every six months. Also, if an oil finish is used on a porous wood such as oak, the oil may leach out onto the surface as the wood contracts.

The most commonly used finishes for wood furniture are *catalyzed* (not standard nitrocellulose) lacquer and alkyd-urea conversion varnish. Catalyzed lacquer is a nitrocellulose-based finish with a catalyst added to improve its performance. Conversion varnish is a catalyzed alkyd-based finish. Both catalyzed lacquer and conversion varnish are considered to be tough and resistant to household chemicals. Both of these finishes are selected because of their wear resistance and because they can be repaired or refinished relatively easily.

The most impact-resistant finishes are catalyzed vinyl, catalyzed polyurethane, polyester, and polyester/polyurethane. Catalyzed vinyl is a catalyzed finish with a vinyl resin base. It is extremely durable and resistant to most chemicals. Polyester is a high-solids content plastic finish that leaves a deep wet-look finish. The finish can be clear or colored. Both polyester and polyurethane finishes are very durable but difficult to repair. (AWI, 1993, p. 261)

The choices available for finishing wood furniture may change in the next few years as expected new environmental regulations are enacted and enforced. Concern over indoor air quality, especially during the manufacturing process, may result in restricted use of solvent-based finishes, such as catalyzed lacquers, and an increase in the use of water-based finishes, such as polyurethane.

Several kinds of materials other than veneers are used to face wood furniture. High-pressure laminates, for example, are frequently preferred over wood veneers as facing materials. Standard laminates used on furnishings are .050 inches thick for horizontal surfaces and .028 inches thick for vertical surfaces; a backing that is .020 inches thick is used to balance the construction. Although a manufacturer may maintain a supply of certain laminates as part of its standard product line, a purchaser can specify a laminate from the lines of any of the major suppliers, such as Formica, Nevamar®, and Wilsonart.

Some manufacturers now offer laminates that are treated to provide superior abrasion and scuff resistance.

For example, Nevamar's "ARP®" surface consists of a very thin layer of microscopic particles of aluminum oxide deposited on the conventional laminate surface. The special coating protects the surface from scuffing, abrasion, and gloss change and, according to the manufacturer, keeps surfaces "looking new longer."

Library service desks are, of course, sometimes constructed of marble or granite, rather than wood. Sometimes the cabinet of the desk is constructed of wood, and either granite or marble is used to provide a durable worksurface. Synthetic "solid surface" materials are also used on library furniture, primarily for the tops of service desks. These materials were first used as countertops in residential kitchens and bathrooms. The plastic materials are frequently referred to by brand names, such as DuPont's Corian®, Nevamar's Fountainhead®, Formica's Surell™, and Avonite®. The solid surfacing materials are all fabricated differently. Corian, for example, is a mineral-filled acrylic; Fountainhead is a mineral-filled acrylic-polyester alloy; Surell is a mineral-filled polyester; and Avonite is an unfilled polyester. The materials are available in solid colors, stone-look, and other patterns. The solid surfacing materials offer several advantages over plastic laminates. When used on a worksurface (for example the top of a circulation desk), the material can be molded to form an edge or bumper rail that is more durable than a plastic laminate or wood edge band. Also, surface scratches on the material can be repaired by sanding lightly. Solid surfacing materials do, however, expand and contract; therefore, it is important to discuss the specific properties of a material with the supplier prior to using it on a worksurface.

As mentioned earlier, in taking the "systems" approach to furniture construction, the manner in which an item is put together, as well as the materials and finishes used, contribute to the quality of a product. The use of appropriate joints, or joinery, between the various parts of a piece of furniture adds to the strength and appearance of the item.

When talking to vendors or reading manufacturer's specifications, it is helpful to understand the following terms used in wood construction. (See Figure 4.)

Butt joint: The easiest method for joining two pieces of wood, by simply butting them together at a 90-degree angle, without intermembering the two pieces. This is not a very strong joint until it is reinforced in some manner.

Cleat: A block of wood used to support a shelf or other piece of wood.

Corner block: A triangular piece of wood, larger than a glue block, that is used to reinforce a corner joint in a chair or table where the legs and side rails meet.

Dado: A rectangular groove cut into the face of a piece of wood, and into which a second piece of wood can be inserted. In a through dado, the groove goes all the way across the face of the wood. In a blind, closed, or stop dado, the groove partially crosses the board. The dado is used to join parts of a cabinet or bookcase.

Dovetail joint: Essentially a mortise-and-tenon joint, in which the tenon is broader at the end than at the base. The two pieces of wood are joined like interlocking fingers. Dovetail joints are used mainly in drawer construction. Fine card catalog drawers are made with dovetail joints.

Dowel joint: Any joint that is reinforced by inserting dowels (round wooden pegs) into holes on the inside of the two pieces of wood to be joined. Dowel joints are used, for example, to join the rails of chairs to the legs.

Glue block: Small blocks of wood used to reinforce a frame that is supporting a horizontal surface, such as a chair seat or tabletop.

Miter joint: A joint in which the two pieces are cut at an angle. On a square corner, for example, each piece of wood will be cut at a 45-degree angle, to form a 90-degree angle. Mitered corners are used to give a finished look to a high-quality piece of furniture.

Mortise-and tenon-joint: A mortise is a hole or notch made in a piece of wood, into which a tenon, a piece of wood of the same dimension, is placed. The joint can be a blind mortise and tenon, which *looks* like a butt joint, or an open mortise and tenon, which is a strong, attractive joint used to join two parts of a chair arm or a chair rail to the leg.

Rabbet: An L-shaped groove cut along the edge of a piece of wood that then intermembers with the edge of a second piece of wood. It is used to attach the fronts to drawers, backs to cabinets, etc.

Spline: A narrow strip of wood used to join two pieces of wood, the edges of which have been grooved to receive the spline. These are used to reinforce a miter joint.

Tongue-and-groove joint: A joint used to join the *edges* of two pieces of wood. As the name implies, a groove is cut out of the edge of one piece of wood, so it will intermember with another piece of wood that has a tongue, or raised edge, of the same dimension.

Although several library manufacturers are capable of making high-quality furnishings, the attention to detail in a design and the overall workmanship apparent in a finished item distinguish some products from others. Many

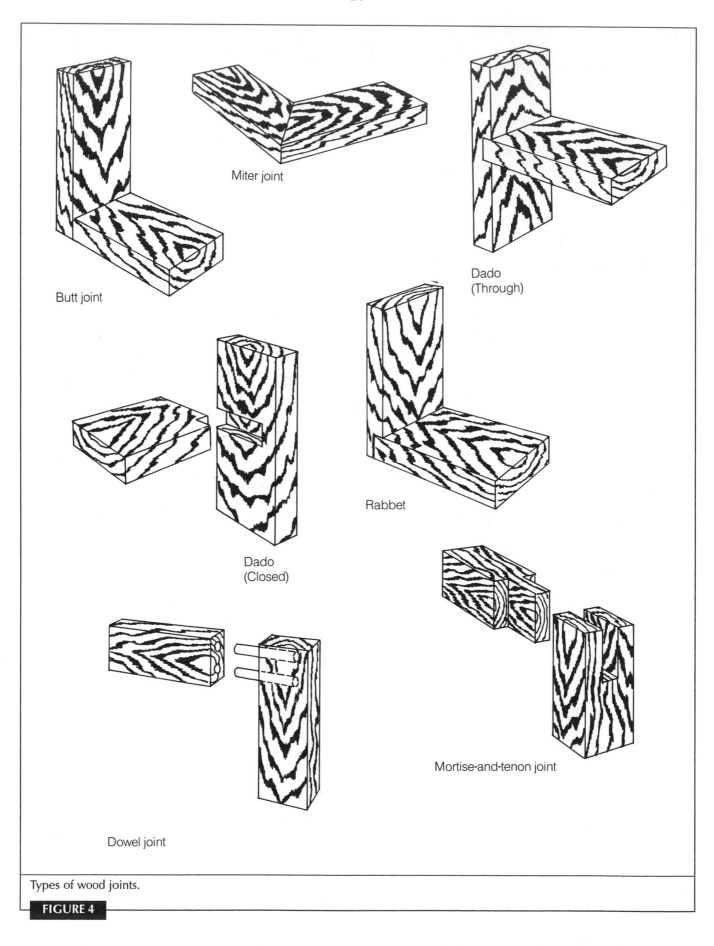

Miter joint

Butt joint

Dado
(Through)

Dado
(Closed)

Rabbet

Dowel joint

Mortise-and-tenon joint

Types of wood joints.

FIGURE 4

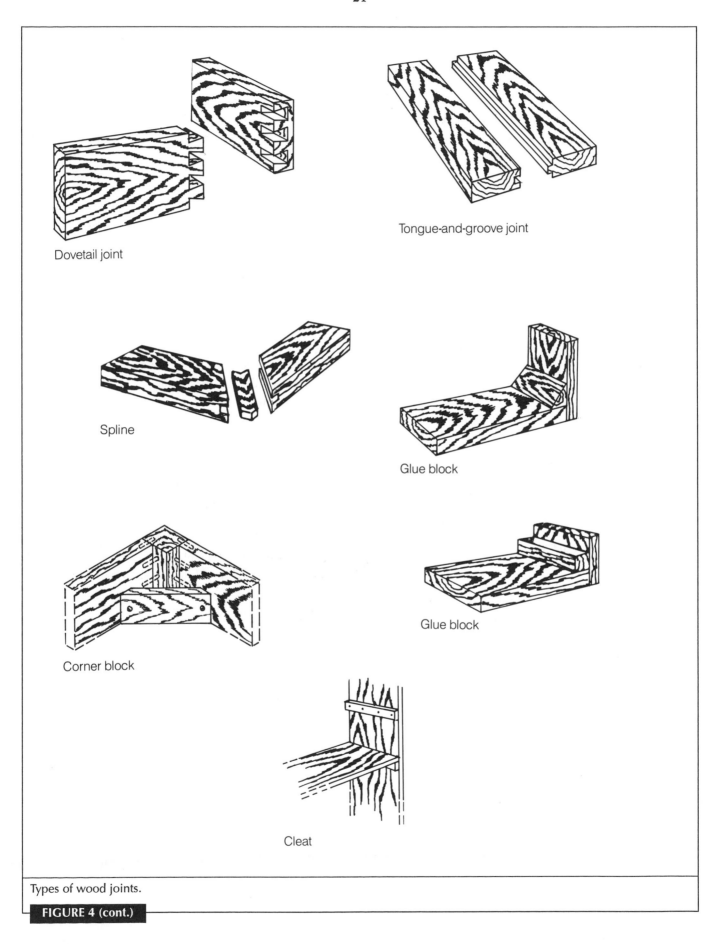

Dovetail joint

Tongue-and-groove joint

Spline

Glue block

Corner block

Glue block

Cleat

Types of wood joints.

FIGURE 4 (cont.)

consumers are so used to accepting less than the best that they do not know what can reasonably be expected from a reliable manufacturer.

When evaluating a line of wood furniture, a librarian or design professional can get a better idea of how an item functions by looking at furnishings in a library setting, rather than in a booth at a conference. Although many specific features of tables, chairs, and other furnishings will be discussed in the following chapters, here are examples of the kinds of general questions to ask, or details to consider, in evaluating wood furniture:

1. Do all of the parts of an item fit together snugly? There should not be a gap, for example, between the worksurface and the side of a study carrel, or between a shelf on a double-tiered index table and the end panel, or between the sections of a modular circulation desk.

2. Look at anything that contains a shelf. Is there any indication of the shelf bending in the middle from a load? Are empty shelves level, or do they appear to be warped slightly? Is the shelf pulling away from the sides? How is each shelf supported?

3. Consider how the edges are finished. Are there attractive wood edge bands that fit snugly against the sides and that are flush with the surface? Are wide edge bands mitered on the corners? Do the miters fit together snugly?

4. Are plastic laminates flush with edge bands? Do long worksurfaces (like those on a circulation desk) have continuous tops, so there are very few seams between pieces of laminate?

5. Are veneers matched in some fashion? Is the color of various items consistent? Has the finish remained in good condition, even on areas that receive heavy wear, such as on the edges of tables or the arms of chairs?

6. Do drawers open and close easily? Do cabinet doors fit well when they are closed?

7. Are there attractive details in the construction that indicate craftsmanship went into the design? For example, can you see open mortise-and-tenon joinery, dovetail joints in drawers, finished surfaces on the working, as well as public, side of desks?

Although furniture companies ordinarily have several standard lines of products, most manufacturers of wood library furniture are prepared to engineer and construct custom designs or custom features for their standard pieces. The furnishings for most library building projects include some nonstandard details needed because of a particular library function. Often customized features are desirable in order to make the furnishings and library distinctive.

Although modified or custom-designed products may be more expensive than standard products, the difference in price may be much less than expected. Discuss desirable custom features with a vendor, rather than assuming that items are not affordable. It is possible that someone else has already asked for, and received, the item or feature envisioned; once a company has completed the engineering and shop drawings for an item for one customer, it is less expensive to manufacture it for succeeding customers. Sometimes pieces of furniture that begin as custom items become standard products when a number of consumers express an interest in them. In a project that involves a number of pieces of custom furniture, consider requiring in the specifications that a person from the factory be on-site during installation.

In most library building and renovation projects, shop drawings for furniture should be required. A complete and thorough review of furniture shop drawings is absolutely necessary in order to ensure that furnishings are manufactured according to specifications. Shop drawings should illustrate exactly how each piece of furniture will be constructed. Plan views, elevations, and section drawings should be supplied by the manufacturer. Plans should show clearly how and where electrical systems and wire management channels will be placed in the furnishings.

Both the vendor handling the project and the person responsible for the specification of the furniture should review all drawings. In some cases, a third party (the library manager or the architect) will also be involved in the review process. During the first review, the library representative will compare the drawings to the written furniture specifications, mark any changes needed on the drawings, and note any necessary drawings that have been left out. The drawings are then returned to the manufacturer for revision. (The first set of shop drawings are rarely final.) Any drawings that have not been approved during the first review are returned to the specifier following revision at the factory. This process continues until all drawings have been approved. It is not unusual for some of the drawings to be reviewed and revised two or three times before they are finally approved. The furniture will be constructed in the factory according to the shop drawings that have been approved in writing by a member of the library planning team. If the drawings are unclear, ask for clarification. A manufacturer is accountable for making the furniture according to the approved shop drawings only.

A company can be evaluated by touring its factory. When a manufacturer is interested in a large library project, it is not unusual for some of the decision makers in the selection process to be invited by the company to visit the plant. Here are some observations to make and questions to ask when visiting a wood furniture manufacturer:

1. Notice how the raw materials are handled. Some companies are more involved than others in the quality control of the wood used.

2. Take a close look at the detail and craftsmanship of items being produced in the factory. The representative of a company that prides itself on quality will point out distinctive features of construction and appearance while you are touring the plant.

3. Notice whether the company is using several different types of materials, three-ply flakeboard and five-ply lumber core, for example, and whether custom as well as stock items are in production.

4. Look for evidence of quality control. Are finished items checked carefully before they are shipped? Are large pieces, such as circulation desks, assembled at the plant before they are shipped to make sure that the components of the finished product are constructed according to the drawings and that all of the parts fit together correctly? Are items packaged in a manner that will prevent damage during shipping?

5. Ask about performance testing of products and take a look at any in-house testing facility. Does the information given about products show evidence that the company has engineered its furniture to last?

6. Ask what steps are taken at the factory to control indoor air quality during the manufacturing process. How clean is the factory?

7. Is the management interested in getting input about new product needs from the librarian? Is the company involved in new product development?

8. Is the company interested in marketing and concerned about providing adequate support for its representatives in the field?

FURNITURE CONSTRUCTION AND INDOOR AIR QUALITY

Environmental concerns have become such a part of everyday life that both consumers and manufacturers are aware of the issues. Most people are familiar with the problems associated with outdoor air pollution; however, they are less familar with the issue of indoor air quality (IAQ). Although IAQ has been a concern for a segment of the design community for many years, the topic is only now emerging as a major issue to be considered by everyone involved in the construction and maintenance of buildings. Design professionals and other project decision makers should be familiar with the subject of IAQ in order to make informed decisions regarding facilities and furnishings.

Two of the factors that have contributed to a growing number of problems with indoor air quality are increased use of synthetics as construction and cleaning materials in buildings and furnishings and a dependence on mechanical systems in sealed buildings for heating, cooling, and ventilation. In an ALA presentation in 1993, Richard Silberman, technical representative for Healthy Builders International (a consulting firm based in Fairfax, Virginia), said that "there are literally thousands of pollutants found in today's libraries. New building interiors, common office supplies and equipment, furnishings, detergents, pesticides, paints and lacquers, and even humans themselves contribute to a mix of gases, fibers, dusts, compounds, dander, and microbial contaminants." (Silberman, 1993) When indoor pollutants reach a critical level in a building, the occupants may experience "sick building syndrome (SBS)," which refers to a variety of symptoms, such as headaches, nausea, breathing difficulties, and allergic reactions that are apparently caused by indoor air pollution.

The level of pollutants that can be tolerated by individuals varies, however. The issue of indoor air quality involves, therefore, not only maintaining indoor pollutants below a level that is satisfactory to prevent SBS among regular building occupants, but reducing the level of pollutants below a level that makes a building essentially "barrier free" to people with multiple chemical sensitivities (MCS). In response to a consumer's "right to know," some building owners are now requiring manufacturers to supply complete information regarding the materials used in making furnishings. The information is kept on file by the building owner and is made available to people who enter the facility and who ask whether particular materials to which they are sensitive have been used in constructing the building or furnishings.

The experience of the San Francisco Public Library in planning its new main facility serves as an example of how the issue of indoor air quality affects library planning. Concerns involving indoor air quality surfaced early in the planning of the new Main Library. In the initial stages of the project, the library administration and the architects conducted meetings with both staff and users to gather the opinions of interested parties prior to planning the library interior. Staff members expressed a great deal of concern over indoor air quality. Likewise, meetings with groups of users regarding compliance with the Americans with Disabilities Act (ADA) produced questions about indoor air quality from people with MCS.

As a result of these initial concerns, project planning for the San Francisco Public Library included IAQ as a major priority. During the planning process, the services of an indoor air quality consulting firm, Hal Levin & Associates, were enlisted. The consultant, architect, and staff developed a list of priorities for achieving a healthy building. The list included consideration of the heating, ventilation, and air conditioning (HVAC) system, particleboard use, carpet, adhesives, paints, furniture, and copy machines. The architects subsequently developed strategies for improving the HVAC system and established guidelines to minimize the off-gassing of volatile organic compounds (VOCs) from product materials and furniture. The IAQ goal of the San Francisco planning team was to reduce contaminants in the building as much as possible.

The design team for the San Francisco Public Library decided, therefore, that no particleboard would be used in the construction of the building and the furnishings. The specifications for furniture for the San Francisco library included emission standards with which furniture suppliers were required to comply. The San Francisco architects identified at least one core material, a medium-density fiberboard, that met the city's emission standards for the project. The bid specifications for furnishings did not include a specific product, nor a formula for a product, that had to be used as core material. Instead, the bid document for the furniture included a performance specification that required bidders to supply emissions testing data for the core material they proposed to use. Other requirements regarding furniture for the San Francisco

library included the use of low-VOC-emitting adhesives and finishes, "airing out" of the furniture prior to delivery, and the use of a solvent-free cleaning agent for cleaning office system components prior to delivery. (Information supplied by Anthony Bernheim, AIA, with the firm of Simon, Martin-Vegue, Winkelstein, and Moris, project manager for the San Francisco Main Library.)

The San Francisco Public Library experience is an example of just one library's approach to the issue of indoor air quality. Some particleboards emit levels of formaldehyde that are noxious *in some situations*. If the material is handled properly, however, some types of particleboard remain safe materials for constructing furniture for many situations. One library furniture company reports that even with large quantities of particleboard on the site, with proper ventilation, the level of formaldehyde emissions in the factory is below a noxious level and complies with all state and industry safety standards. In a library situation, if the furniture is correctly finished and installed carefully, all of the raw particleboard will be faced with another material (wood or laminate) that limits the emissions to a safe level. Because of increasing concern with IAQ, it is expected that formaldehyde-free particleboard and other types of low-emitting building materials will be used more extensively by furniture manufacturers.

With information about IAQ readily available, library planners can take a proactive approach to prevent poor indoor air quality and resulting building-related illnesses. A proactive approach involves considering all of the various factors in building design and construction that work interdependently to produce a healthy building. Richard Silberman refers to this as the "building systems approach," a holistic method analogous to the "systems" approach to furniture design mentioned earlier.

Using the building systems approach, preoccupancy studies for clients performed by Healthy Buildings International include the following five elements to ensure safe indoor air quality: (1) review of all parts of the original building design to ensure satisfactory air quality and compliance with local indoor air quality standards, (2) selection of materials and equipment that will remain durable and maintainable over time, (3) selection of products for the building that include consideration of Manufacturer's Safety Data Sheets, (4) on-site monitoring during construction to ensure that all air quality recommendations and standards are implemented and maintained, and (5) development of a baseline standard for indoor air quality in the building to serve as a reference point against which air quality and building systems can be measured in subsequent inspections.

Contract furniture manufacturers, such as Haworth, Herman Miller, and Steelcase have been addressing IAQ issues for several years. These and other companies concerned about IAQ have printed information (available from local vendors) about their approach to the problem. Prior to purchasing furnishings for a library building project, the issue of IAQ should be discussed with library furniture manufacturers to ascertain their level of knowledge and concern and their ability to comply with any applicable governmental regulations or industry standards.

Local, state, and industry standards and regulations for indoor air quality are changing continually. One result of the San Francisco experience is expected to be the development of an ASTM standard test for measuring emissions from building materials. On a governmental level, organizations such as the Business Council on Indoor Air are working toward legislation that will require the development of a national IAQ strategy.

Good air quality is maintained by eliminating the source of pollutants, removing pollutants where they accumulate, and providing adequate ventilation to dilute the concentration of pollutants. It is the responsibility of decision makers planning library buildings and selecting furnishings to be aware of indoor air quality issues and to make choices based on the latest information and all applicable standards and regulations. In general, the following suggestions can be used in making furniture selections:

1. Select core materials and finishes that limit the emission of VOCs to safe levels as established by local, state, and industry standards.
2. Select products made of durable, stable materials. Select products that can be cleaned using solvent-free cleaning agents and that do not require frequent painting or refinishing.
3. Ask vendors for Manufacturer's Safety Data Sheets. Select products from companies that are responsive to concerns about indoor air quality and that demonstrate an awareness of maintaining safe air quality in their manufacturing processes, shipping, delivery, and product installation.
4. Consider hiring an indoor air quality consultant to assist in designing the building and selecting the furnishings.

ADA AND FURNITURE CONSTRUCTION

Design professionals and librarians have all addressed issues related to compliance with the ADA, the Ameri-

cans with Disabilities Act of 1990, Public Law 101-336. In the chapters that follow, ADA concerns that relate to specific pieces of furniture or interior elements are discussed in more detail.

A succinct description of ADA was presented to librarians in an article by Christopher Lewis, library/media specialist at Indiana University's Institute for the Study of Developmental Disabilities, in *Public Libraries*, January/February 1992. Lewis stated,

> The Americans with Disabilities Act (ADA) of 1990, Public Law 101-336, is landmark legislation that mandates explicit civil-right protection to people with disabilities. The ADA is designed to end discrimination against persons with disabilities and bring them into the economic and social mainstream of American life. The law is an extension of the antidiscrimination legislation, originally included in Section 504 of the Rehabilitation Act of 1973. Whereas Section 504 made it illegal for federal agencies and other organizations receiving federal funding to discriminate against people with disabilities, the ADA extends the legislation to apply to private organizations and public entities not supported by federal funding. The act provides enforceable standards addressing all forms of discrimination against individuals on the basis of ability.

Prior to the 1990s, the matter of having wheelchair-accessible worksurfaces in a library was, unfortunately, apt to be an afterthought in preparing the specifications for library furnishings. Since the passage of the Americans with Disabilities Act, however, planning barrier-free access to library buildings and services has become a priority for both librarians and design professionals. Most libraries are service-oriented organizations; librarians are expected, therefore, to take action that supports both the spirit and the letter of the law. Furniture and shelving selections should reflect an awareness of the desirability of providing convenient access to all library users. Planning interiors with barrier-free access is concurrent with planning built-in flexibility. A library that has tables and computer stations with adjustable-height worksurfaces, service desks with tops at varying heights, and seating of several different kinds can easily provide access to people of differing abilities.

An excellent research summary entitled *Equal Opportunity Facilities*, prepared by contract furniture manufacturer Herman Miller, Inc., discusses the idea of "universal design" in furniture. The concept of universal design suggests that furnishings should have built-in flexibility. In other words, furniture should be designed for a life span and for a wide range of abilities rather than designed for an ideal person frozen in time. As the research summary states, "It's tempting to believe that disabling conditions will always be someone else's problem. But the hard fact is that they are inevitable for a large percentage of the population." (*Equal Opportunity Facilities*, Herman Miller, October, 1991, p. 21) The concept of universal design as applied to a library makes the facility more manageable for everyone, both staff and users, now and in the future.

The *ADA Accessibility Guidelines for Buildings and Facilities* (ADAAG) sets the standards for compliance with the ADA. Although the guidelines are applicable to many aspects of the design and space planning of library buildings, very few details of the document refer directly to library furniture and shelving.

Specifically, the guidelines state that circulation and reference desks shall have at least one service point that is at least 36 inches in length with a maximum height of 36 inches above the finished floor. In reading and study areas, at least five percent, or a minimum of one of each element of fixed seating, tables, or study carrels must be accessible to someone in a wheelchair. Accessible knee space must be at least 27 inches high, 30 inches wide, and 19 inches deep. The top of accessible tables must be 28–34 inches from the finished floor. Card catalogs and magazine displays should have a maximum reach height of 48 inches.

In the absence of extensive guidelines and, in order to ensure that a library interior complies with the spirit of the ADA, it is suggested that individual libraries hold open forums with interested users to collect information prior to planning a new or renovated facility. This is the approach that was taken in planning the new main facility for the San Francisco Public Library, where a series of public meetings were held to collect opinions from current and potential patrons. A consultant who specializes in ADA compliance was hired to assist with the project.

At the San Francisco Public Library public forums were conducted to gather suggestions from visually impaired, hearing-impaired, and physically disabled library users. At key points during the design process, representatives from the various user groups completed an exercise in which they "mentally walked through" the plans to study access all over the building. Doorways, aisles, and ramps were studied, for example, to ascertain whether all users could conveniently and safely travel from point A to point B throughout the facility.

Many concerns that were raised by the user groups were addressed in the final design of the new San Francisco Main Library. For example, wayfinding and signage were major issues that resulted in the development of new products designed to make the library barrier-free. (See chapter 9, p. 117 for a detailed discussion). Other issues that were raised included the selection of particular types of furnishings, assistive devices, clear paths of travel, special arrangements of furnishings needed for convenient use of the library, and the location of furniture in relation to natural and artificial lighting.

Currently, no ADA guidelines specifically relate to furnishings for children. Some information relevant to this topic is, however, available in a book entitled *Accessibility Design Guidelines for Public Facilities Serving Children*, published by People's Center for Housing Change located in California. (See p. 153 for address and telephone number). According to the guidelines included in the book, a counter in a library that is accessible to a child in a wheelchair should have the following minimum dimensions for a front approach: floor space beneath counter—minimum 24 inches high, 28 inches wide, and 17 inches deep; maximum height of counter—30 inches; minimum counter width 30 inches. In other words, a standard 36-inch-wide-by-30-inch-deep unit in a reference or circulation desk with a worksurface that is designed at an adult seated height of 29 inches should be accessible for a child in a wheelchair (provided a modesty or center panel in the unit is placed a minimum of 17 inches from the public side of the counter).

Organizations seeking further guidance are referred to the publication *The Americans with Disabilities Act: Its Impact on Libraries: The Library's Responses in Doable Steps*. (Crispen 1993) The publication includes a useful self-evaluation survey for public libraries based on ADAAG.

POWER AND DATA DISTRIBUTION IN LIBRARY FURNISHINGS

The selection of library furnishings that have a worksurface—tables, counters, desks or carrels—involves consideration of how the item will accommodate some type of computerized or other equipment safely, conveniently, and attractively. When one piece of equipment is used on a carrel, the solution may be as simple as specifying a grommet (a plastic or metal ring that fits into a hole to protect cords running through the opening) in the worksurface to allow dropping a single cord down to an outlet in the floor. When several pieces of equipment are used in one location or on one piece of furniture, however, multiple data cables and electrical cords make an unsafe mess hanging down under the furniture and lying on the floor. In response to the need for safe and attractive wire management and power distribution within furnishings, manufacturers offer a variety of products to accommodate the needs of electronic offices and libraries.

Products for Handling Power and Data in Furniture

Every customer-responsive company that claims to be a manufacturer of high-quality library furniture should offer a basic wire management system and an electrical system as standard products. The simplest wire management systems have grommets or cord slots in worksurfaces to provide access to plastic, metal, or wood J-shaped channels mounted below the worksurface for carrying cables and cords to the power/data supply. In furnishings that hold several pieces of equipment, such as a circulation desk, the J-channel has to be large enough to hold a data cable for each computer, telephone cables, cabling to connect computers to networked printers, and electrical cords. A J-channel with the dimensions four inches by four inches by four inches is the *minimum* size needed, for example, to handle the equipment used on a circulation desk in a small to medium-sized library. Additional or larger J-channels may be needed to provide adequate wire management for desks in larger libraries. J-channels may have metal septums or dividers to separate power and data.

Many library furniture manufacturers offer prewired, modular electrical systems that are similar to the electrical systems that have been used in office panel systems for many years. In library service desks and equipment tables designed to hold computers, four-circuit, eight-wire systems (three utility circuits and one isolated dedicated computer circuit) are used. Multicircuit systems must be hardwired to the building power by a licensed electrician. The availability of other possible circuit configurations should be discussed with furniture vendors. In addition to multicircuit systems, manufacturers also offer single-circuit systems that terminate with a 20-amp, three-pronged, grounded plug. A 20-amp offset configuration plug cannot be used in a standard 15-amp receptacle. Other electrical components for furnishings include power entry devices and columns, wood and metal chases to manage cords and cables from the floor or wall box to the J-channel under the worksurface, and a variety of power strips and columns that can be attached to the corners of carrels or under worksurfaces.

Adequate surge suppression should be supplied either for the entire building or in the library furnishings. Ide-

ally, surge suppression will take place at the main electrical panel for the whole building. Several kinds of surge protection are available for electrical systems in furniture also. In order to obtain the best kind in a given situation, the vendor should be asked to explain in layperson's terms how particular surge suppression devices will protect specific equipment to be used. It should be noted that some devices available on the open market that use the words "surge suppression" on their labels are really only temporary power taps and do not provide surge protection. A device that really does supply surge protection will be described as providing transient-voltage surge suppression and will include a voltage rating. The device may also carry a UL1449 label.

Determining What to Specify

For several years now, the question of what constitutes a safe and effective electrical system for library furnishings has been a topic of debate by interior designers, building consultants, and library furniture manufacturers. During the furniture selection process, consumers talking to several manufacturers will hear more than one point of view regarding safety and electrical systems. The following material is provided as background information for consumers to use in selecting furnishings that include electrical components. Discussions about electrical systems will include mention of Underwriters Laboratories (UL) and the National Electrical Code (NEC). Both are identified below.

Underwriters Laboratories (UL) is the most widely recognized independent testing agency. According to UL's descriptive literature, "UL's principal business is safety investigation of electrical and electronic equipment, products, and components; mechanical components; construction systems; fire protection equipment; burglary protection systems and equipment; and marine supplies." UL tests products to one or more of approximately 600 UL-developed and published standards for safety. The safety standards are developed and revised based on recommendations by safety and standardization experts, consumers, manufacturers, vendors, governmental authorities, inspection authorities, insurance interests, utilities, and other informed parties. A standard may also change as the result of litigation.

The National Electrical Code (NEC) is the most widely adopted code of standard practices and set of electrical safety requirements in the United States. According to the *NEC Handbook* (National Fire Protection Association, 1993), the code "is offered for use in law and for regulatory purposes in the interest of life and property protection." (p. 3) The code is adopted and approved by the National Fire Protection Association and the American National Standards Institute. Many state and local electrical codes are based on the NEC.

Electrical components in library furnishings are handled in several different ways.

1. Some design professionals typically specify service desks and equipment carrels made by local furniture makers or millwork houses that do not include prewired, modular electrical systems. Wire management raceways and electrical components (conduit and duplex outlets) are wired directly to the furnishings on-site by local electricians.

2. Several library furniture manufacturers offer prewired, modular systems that are composed of individual electrical components, each component of which has been safety tested as a separate entity and has received the "UL-recognized" mark. Components that are UL-recognized may not have been tested in regard to their safe use with any other components or in end-use applications. Each component has been tested according to a different UL standard; for example, electrical attachment plug and receptacles are tested to the UL 498 standard, and flexible cord and fixture wire are tested to the UL 62 standard.

3. Some manufacturers offer furniture that has been safety tested and "UL-listed;" that is, the entire piece of furniture, including its electrical components, has been safety tested as a *working unit* and is authorized to bear the UL-listing mark. Most library furnishings are tested to UL 1286, *Standard for Safety, Office Furnishings* (labeled as QAWZ). UL 1286 addresses electrical safety, the stability of furniture, and the flammability of furniture. Compliance in regard to electrical safety includes standards for the types and lengths of cords and conduit that can be used in particular situations, the manner in which outlets are mounted and in which cords pass through panels, the type of connectors and plug configurations to be used in certain applications, the materials that are used in the components, and the way in which power entry into the furniture is accomplished. A manu-

facturer who has a product that is listed is subject to quarterly inspections by UL after an initial investigation to ensure that the materials and construction continue to comply with the standards.

A UL-listed product is identified by the UL labeling on a specific piece of furniture, such as a carrel that states: "Office Furnishing by Company A For Use With Listed Office Furnishing Accessories by Company A." A second electrical label identifies any accessory, an electrical component, such as a raceway, that is intended to be attached in the field, or may be shipped separately. The label on an accessory states: "Office Furnishing Accessory by Company A for Use With Listed Office Furnishings by Company A." Both labels include the UL file number (beginning with the letter E), which identifies a particular manufacturer. Because the UL 1286 standard involves the use of components within a system, compliance requires a company to supply assembly manuals with its products. Both mechanical and electrical instructions are required to ensure that all of the elements can be put together correctly in the field. The status of a product can also be verified by calling Underwriters Laboratories. The American National Standards Institute adopted UL 1286 as its national standard for the use of electrical equipment in furniture.

In the debate about safety and electrical systems in furnishings, some manufacturers and vendors take issue with the necessity for testing and listing to UL 1286. In many situations, design professionals and furniture vendors who specify or sell library furnishings that are not UL listed, but that include UL-recognized components, assure consumers that electrical systems installed in their furniture meet all relevant local and state codes and the National Electrical Code. Individuals with this point of view believe that UL 1286, which was originally developed for office panel systems, does not apply to library furniture and that UL listing of library furnishings to UL 1286 is not necessary to ensure product safety.

Proponents of furnishings listed under UL 1286 and other UL standards make the case that the standards are relevant to library furniture and that, in many cases, they are necessary to ensure the safety of their products and to protect both the manufacturer and the library from possible liability suits that can result from improper use of electrical components in furniture.

Within this context of varying opinions about what constitutes a satisfactory electrical system for library furnishings, the consumer is faced with deciding who to believe and what system to specify. It is important to understand that all codes and standards are subject to interpretation and enforcement at the local and state level. For example, stating that an electrical system meets the National Electrical Code is inexact; what is more relevant is the manner in which the NEC and other local and state codes are applied *in the field at a specific library location.* Similarly, stating that furniture must be listed to UL 1286 may also be inexact; what is relevant is the application of the standard *in the field at a specific library location.*

The decision-making process in regard to electrical systems in furniture begins, therefore, with talking to the local electrical inspector who has jurisdiction over the project and who may eventually inspect the manner in which furnishings are wired to the building. Obtain a written "early determination" or policy statement from the local inspector about the relevancy or lack of relevancy of UL listing to the project. The information provided by the electrical inspector may determine the type of electrical system to be specified. Some jurisdictions require the UL 1286 listing on furnishings and will not allow nonlisted furniture items to be wired. As a result of the requirement, those with local jurisdiction may rule that UL-recognized components will not satisfy a local requirement for UL-listed furniture. In some large cities, such as Chicago, UL 1286 is irrelevant; all electrical components must be wired on-site by local electricians. In many jurisdictions, the UL listing may not be required because the electrical inspector makes the interpretation that UL 1286 is not relevant to library furnishings. In the latter case, the decision as to whether to specify listed furnishings falls back to the library manager or specifier. Remember that electrical systems that are not listed cannot be used in some jurisdictions; however, virtually all electrical inspectors will allow UL-listed products in their jurisdictions, if they are called upon to inspect a furniture installation.

In making the decision about what to specify, some additional information might be useful. The scope of UL 1286 is defined in the standard as follows:

> These requirements cover landscape office furnishing panels, study carrels, work stations, and pedestal-style systems that may be mechanically interconnected to form an office furnishing system in accordance with the National

Electrical Code. These may be provided with an electrical distribution system, including switches and receptacles, and may also provide channels for routing communication cables within system components separate from electrical raceways. These systems may include filing cabinets, desks, work surfaces, shelves, storage units, and the like, that have a particular electrical or mechanical function unique to an office furnishing system.

UL (Underwriters Laboratories 1988, p. 5) defines a furnishing system in UL 1286 as "an arrangement of interconnected or individual units, work stations, study carrels, and similar types of products." Although UL 1286 originally applied to open landscape office panel systems, its application has been broadened through use to include library furnishings. Study carrels, workstations, desks, worksurfaces, shelves, and storage units all refer to library-related furnishings. Anyone in doubt about the applicability of the standard to library furnishings (either consumer or manufacturer) should read the latest edition of the standard or call UL for information. (Consumers can ask a vendor to lend them a copy to read.)

Some library furniture manufacturers are simply not convinced of the desirability of compliance with UL 1286 and probably will not ever have all of their products listed. The initial cost of obtaining a UL listing is high; however, a company that has its products listed recovers the cost of the listing process in a relatively short time through savings in liability insurance. Currently manufacturers with the UL listing have achieved product differentiation; when proof of UL 1286 is required in a bid document, manufacturers without listed products cannot meet the specifications. It would be advantageous to library and design professionals specifying UL listed furniture to have more companies that can meet bid requirements for furniture tested to UL 1286. Library furniture consumers would benefit from lower prices in bid situations requiring UL 1286, and more choices would be available in regard to furniture manufacturers and styles.

The decision regarding which electrical system to specify in a library building project should involve consideration of more than codes and standards. The use of electrical systems and the distribution of power and data in furnishings are primary concerns in the electronic library. Most librarians and many design professionals do not have the technical knowledge and expertise necessary for making initial decisions about electrical requirements in furnishings, for writing accurate specifications that describe the interface of furnishings and building power and data, for reviewing shop drawings of furnishings with electrical components, and for installing the furnishings and electrical systems safely. The level of knowledge and experience of furniture vendors and manufacturers in regard to the use of electrical systems in furniture is very important to the overall success of a building project. Consider the following:

1. Representatives of a company should have a broad understanding of the use of computers in libraries. The company should understand the use of integrated computer systems and the use of local area networks (LANs) in libraries as they relate to furnishings that hold computer terminals and other equipment. Because of the interface of power and data in buildings and furnishings, representatives of a furniture company should be able to discuss power and data distribution systems in buildings and types of cabling used for data transmission now and in the future.

2. In their desire to be customer-responsive, a manufacturing company and its sales staff should view power and data distribution systems in furniture as one of their primary concerns. Product literature, exhibits at conferences, and their initial sales pitch should provide evidence of the company's interest in, and expertise with, power and data distribution.

3. The company should have the products and expertise needed to assist the library or the library planning team in specifying power and data distribution systems in furnishings that offer the highest level of safety and convenience available for library furnishings.

In summary, the following questions should be answered in regard to the electrical system to be used in tables, carrels, reference and circulation desks, and other pieces of furniture:

1. Has the system specified been discussed with local electrical inspectors and automation system managers?

2. Does the wire management system keep the worksurface free of cables and cords except at the point where the cords enter the wireway?

3. Does the system allow for cords to drop below the worksurface at several points along the worksurface, so that use of the space can be adjusted as needs change?

4. Does the wire management system keep the space below the worksurface as neat as the area above?

5. How adaptable is the system? Does it allow for neat and unobtrusive entry of power, data lines, etc., into the piece of equipment, regardless of the design of the furniture?

6. Is the system designed to be relatively tamper free if it is to be used in a public reading area?

7. Does each piece of equipment—for example, a double-faced row of carrels or a circulation desk—allow for powering the entire unit from only one point, or will cords be seen hanging down from several locations below the worksurface?

8. Does the system have or need built-in surge protection?

9. Does the system provide for special electrical needs, such as isolated dedicated circuits?

Coordinating Power/Data Systems in Furniture and Buildings

In a project involving a new or renovated library, coordination of electrical and data distribution *within the building* with electrical and data distribution *within the furnishings* is absolutely essential to ensure that the completed building is safe, attractive, and functional. Furniture selection and design should be done concurrently with building design to eliminate the need for costly change orders when the building is already in construction. Because furniture and building design are interconnected activities in a building project, the following discussion covers some aspects of building planning as well as furniture selection.

New buildings designed without proper coordination of electrical and data distribution in the building and in the furnishings can have the same problems as old buildings that have been automated: The outlets aren't where the library staff would like to place the furniture for the computers; not enough circuits are available at particular locations; unsightly cords and cables dangle from the furniture and lie in a mess on the floor; and every time furniture arrangements change, new electrical connections have to be rigged. In a completed building that has been designed correctly, computers and other equipment are conveniently placed for public and staff; equipment can be moved easily to other locations when changes are needed; and, except for power and data entry into a piece of furniture, no cords or cables can be seen lying on the floor or dangling underneath the furniture.

Because not all architects and designers have worked with libraries, it is important for librarians working on building projects to discuss the use of computers in the library with the design professionals early in the planning process. If a library building consultant has been hired to work on the project, the consultant should discuss the need for coordination of the building and furnishings with the architect. As the design process continues, the librarian and/or the consultant should make sure that the furniture and shelving layout coordinates with the electrical plans for the building and that power and data distribution throughout the building are adequate.

A number of decisions made about building design have an impact on how effectively furnishings and equipment accommodate the needs of the library over the lifetime of the building. For example, the type of system used for distributing power and data throughout the building should be carefully considered and discussed with all of the members of the library planning team.

Ideally, all libraries would be built with an extensive underfloor duct system or cellular deck to allow access to building power and data on a two-foot-by-two-foot grid. Unfortunately, the more flexible a distribution system is, the more expensive it is to install initially. Most libraries have to compromise with a poke-through system of carefully planned standard conduit or an underfloor duct system designed with a much larger grid than two feet by two feet. Additional flexibility can be achieved for limited-budget projects by using various kinds of distribution in different parts of the library. For example, standard conduit can be used in areas expected to hold bookstacks for many years to come, and a more extensive underfloor duct system can be specified in reference areas where equipment use will be heavy. (Flat wire systems used with carpet tile are not as popular as they were at one time, and they are illegal in schools and universities. Although flat wire can be used successfully for power distribution, library automation companies have generally discouraged its use for computer cabling.)

Power and data distribution systems should meet building criteria in regard to their capacity to accommodate current and future electronic and communication systems and their flexibility in regard to adding new outlets or taking out old ones. Librarians and design professionals should discuss the type of data transmission system that will be used, not only in the building and furnishings initially, but in the future as well.

As libraries employ faster computers and as the use of interactive data systems increases, libraries will be less likely to choose simple twisted pair (Category 3, typically used for voice and low-speed text transmission) systems like those commonly used for data transmission in libraries today and will be more likely to choose systems with wider bandwidths and greater speed that are capable of handling more data at a faster rate. Many libraries are now bypassing the use of Category 4 twisted pair systems and are specifying more sophisticated twisted pair (Category 5) systems, coaxial cable, or fiber optic systems. Each data transmission system has advantages and disadvantages that should be discussed with an electrical engineer. Category 5 twisted pair systems, for example, have 10 times the speed and bandwidth of Category 3 systems and nearly the same capacity and bandwidth of coaxial cable. Nothing approaches the capacity or speed of fiber optics, however. Light can carry approximately 1,000 times more information than current electrical communication systems. (Twisted pair categories result from standards developed by the Electronic Institute of America and the Telecommunication Institute of America.)

Often libraries use several types of data transmission within the same building. For example, sometimes fiber optic cable is used in the building as the "backbone" and copper (twisted pair or coaxial cable) is distributed throughout the building and the furnishings. Sometimes fiber optic cable is used both in the building and in the furnishings. The specific manner in which fiber optics can be used in buildings and in furnishings is determined by the nature of the fiber optic cable itself. The particular characteristics of fiber optic cable (single- or multimode) and the requirements for its use in furnishings and in buildings should be discussed with furniture vendors and with electrical engineers.

In order to help architects and electrical engineers plan a building with adequate circuitry and a satisfactory power distribution system, the library staff must supply information about the equipment to be used at particular locations when the library opens, and if possible, the maximum amount of equipment the library expects to use in the future on any one piece of furniture. A thorough inventory of all power and data needs should be prepared during the schematic design stage of the building project. All of the members of the planning team, both architects and interior designers, must then use the inventory as a guide in making final decisions about power and data throughout the building planning process. The inventory should include the following information, at a minimum:

the overall dimensions of each piece of equipment (to use in determining the size of a worksurface), the maximum power requirements (amps) of the pieces of equipment to be used at any one location or on any one piece of furniture, the number of receptacles that will be needed at each workstation, and any specific requirements in regard to the kinds of circuits needed.

Here is a real-life example of the activities involved in coordinating building power and data with electrical systems in the furniture: During the design of a branch library, it was decided that public access catalogs (PACs) would be housed on three six-place computer carrels placed at different locations around the building. Computers would also be used at CD-ROM (Compact Disc-Read Only Memory) workstations, two reference desks, the circulation desk, a two-place self-check station, and in numerous offices and work areas. The PAC is now provided on dumb terminals that take up a small amount of space; however, someday the library may use larger personal computer (PC) workstations at all locations, rather than dumb terminals. The number of pieces of equipment the library will have initially is only a small portion of the number of pieces that may be needed eventually.

After the initial furniture selections for the branch were made and the furniture and shelving layouts were completed, the library automation manager provided information about the maximum sizes and quantities of equipment, the maximum number of receptacles required at each workstation, and the maximum power needs for the equipment on each piece of furniture. One six-place PAC carrel, for example, would hold a maximum of six PC workstations, each drawing four amps of power, and six printers, each drawing two amps of power. A maximum of 36 amps, or three 20-amp circuits would be needed at the carrel. (The National Electrical Code indicates that a circuit for which the utilization of equipment is not known should be used at 80 percent of capacity. In this case the number of circuits was based on using 16 amps of each 20-amp circuit.) In this particular situation, the city automation manager required that all computer equipment be on an isolated grounded circuit. The furniture vendor, therefore, agreed to supply a special multicircuit electrical system that had three isolated computer circuits and one utility circuit, rather than the standard three utility circuits and one isolated computer circuit. The architect and the electrical engineer used the information collected by the library staff to determine how many and what kinds of circuits to bring to the power entry point of each table, carrel, or desk; the interior designer worked

with the architect to provide an electrical/data system in each furniture item that would interface correctly with the building power/data systems. The architect talked by phone to the engineer at the furniture factory several times to make sure that the building power and the electrical systems in the furniture would interface correctly.

In summary, the interior designer, the consultant, or the librarian specifying the furniture for a project must be familiar with the use of electrical systems in furnishings. In order to ensure the coordination of the furnishings and the building, the person responsible for furniture selection should supply the architect and/or electrical engineer with a detailed description of the electrical system that will be specified in the furniture and should serve as a liaison between the architect and the library to make sure that electronic equipment is housed safely and attractively on the furnishings. The following items should be reviewed prior to completing plans for both the building and the furnishings:

1. The exact locations on the floor plan of items or furniture configurations with built-in electrical systems that will require hardwiring to the building power. (According to the National Electrical Code, a cord connect must be within 12 inches of the source of power.)

2. The exact location of each power entry device in a piece of furniture in relation to where the power comes out of the floor or the wall.

3. The exact location of data outlets in the building in relation to power outlets. (Power and data locations should be coordinated.)

4. The number and kinds of circuits needed at each furniture location. (For example, a microform reader/printer draws 10–13 amps; a separate circuit is needed for each reader/printer. A laser printer may require seven or more amps.)

5. The number of receptacles needed at each workstation in a piece of furniture with a built-in electrical system. (For example, a single CD-ROM workstation with a central processing unit, a monitor, a printer, and a disc drive can require as many as four or more single outlets, depending on the configuration of the outlets. At a circulation desk, receptacles may be needed for a terminal, a printer, and a scanner at each workstation. Plan for more receptacles than currently needed to accommodate equipment changes in the future.)

6. The location of receptacles in the piece of furniture. Tables or carrels designed to allow library users to plug in their own equipment, such as laptop computers or calculators, should have outlets located above the worksurface. Furnishings that are designed to hold library-owned equipment should have receptacles below the worksurface.

7. The manner in which cords and cables drop beneath the worksurface. (A hole drilled in a worksurface without a grommet is unsatisfactory. A grommet is necessary to protect the cords running through the hole and to seal the core material in the worksurface. The size of the grommets should be carefully considered. A single grommet must be large enough to hold numerous cords and cables and to allow plugs and connectors—perhaps as wide as three inches or more—to pass through the work surface to the wire management channel. A two-inch slot across the back of an entire worksurface provides greater flexibility than grommets placed at intervals along a worksurface.)

8. The location of the wire management channel in the furnishings. (Wire management at worksurface height rather than near the floor provides more convenience in stowing cords and prevents the untidy appearance of cords hanging down beneath the worksurface.)

9. The size of the wire management channel in the furnishings. (Make sure that the furniture vendor understands that, in addition to accommodating all of the power and data cables in a piece of furniture, the channel may have to hold transformers that can be as large as 4½" x 3" x 2" in size.)

In summary, the selection of furnishings involves consideration of a number of elements that contribute to the quality of an item. These elements include overall engineering and design, as well as the kinds of materials, construction, joinery, and finishes used in manufacturing a product. The qualifications of manufacturers and vendors should be studied; performance- or field-testing information for possible selections should be obtained as evidence of the durability of the furnishings under consideration. Since 1990, the specification of some details of furniture design involves consideration of compliance with the Americans with Disabilities Act. Finally, because of the extensive use of computers in libraries, one of the primary concerns in choosing furnishings is the selection of appropriate electrical systems and the coordination of power and data in furnishings with power and data in buildings.

CHAPTER

3

Shelving

As long as books continue to be one of the primary information sources in libraries, shelving will remain an important item to be selected in a building or renovation project. Shelving is used to organize, store, and display the major product to be marketed in many libraries. For this reason, the decisions concerning what type of shelving to choose and which brand to purchase are crucial to the success of the building. The best shelving that is available for the amount of funds allocated should be selected and viewed as a long-term investment. High-quality bookstacks will last the lifetime of the library.

Although stability and strength are vital to a library planning to use the shelving for years, the liability factor involved in the safe use of shelving makes the selection of bookstacks even more critical. Librarians are well aware of the real possibility of lawsuits that can result if loaded bookstacks fall and injure, or even kill, someone.

Most libraries choose wood bookstacks, cantilevered steel shelving, or a steel shelving system with wood end panels. Most of the information given in this chapter will relate to the types of shelving most frequently used in libraries. Because all kinds of libraries also use compact movable shelving systems, the last part of the chapter will discuss some of these products.

In addition to the styles noted above, several other types of shelving are marketed as library bookstacks. Post-lock

or four-post shelving, for example, is sometimes used in compact systems in libraries. For the most part, however, post-lock shelving is used in industrial or warehouse situations. Multitier steel bookstacks and case-style shelving of steel, or a combination of steel and wood, are also sold to libraries. Multitier has typically been used in academic installations, where the quantity of book storage needed is so large that it is cheaper to purchase multitier shelving than to construct several floors with the load-bearing requirements needed for fully loaded bookstacks.

Case-style shelving is sometimes used by libraries that want the look of wood library shelving in a less expensive form. This shelving is more apt to be used in offices and special libraries than in public or academic libraries. For example, it is used in law libraries where the size of the volumes is fairly uniform and there is little need to adjust the distance between shelves or to interfile volumes of all different sizes on the same shelf.

When choosing shelving, one of the three selection factors (function, maintenance, or appearance) is likely to be an overriding consideration. For example, where large quantities of books are to be stored as efficiently as possible, with little concern about the aesthetics of the area, function will probably direct the decision toward some kind of steel shelving. Where a look of tradition or luxury is desired, appearance will enter into the decision, so wood shelving is more apt to be the choice.

Some libraries are forced to purchase steel shelving for budgetary reasons, even though wood shelving is their preferred selection; high-quality wood shelving is more expensive than steel. The combination of steel shelving with wood end panels can be a compromise; however, wood end panels designed with a lot of special detail can be very expensive also.

Shelving selection has an impact on space planning that should be noted early in a building project. The dimensions of a section of steel shelving as illustrated in a catalog are nominal, not actual. In planning for aisles between bookstacks that comply with the Americans with Disabilities Act (ADA), keep in mind that the actual width of a double-faced section of steel section is larger than the nominal width. For example, one company's nominal 24-inch-wide double-faced base is actually 25¼ inches wide. In order to have an aisle that is the ADA-required 36 inches wide along the length of a double-faced range of this particular shelving, the distance from the center of the upright on one range to the center of the upright on the next range will have to be more than five feet, or 60 inches. End panels also decrease the aisle at a point. Steel end panels may make the actual dimension of the end of a range of double-faced shelving 26–27 inches wide rather than the nominal 24 inches wide. Although an inch or two may not seem worth mentioning, knowing the exact dimensions of shelving in the planning stages of a building project can help prevent surprises during shelving installation.

Library Buildings and the Loma Prieta Earthquake Experience of October 1989 by David C. Weber provides graphic evidence of the need for proper design and installation of bookstacks in California and other seismic areas. Librarians in California now have standards for the installation of shelving. Ironically, in October of 1989, the Office of the California State Architect published its *Manual of Recommended Practice, Seismic Safety Standards for Library Shelving*, prepared by John A. Shelton, Supervising Structural Engineer. In his preface to the publication, Gary Strong, California State Librarian, states that "library shelving designed and installed in conformance with the practice recommended in this manual is expected to withstand the range of earthquakes commonly encountered in California . . . ."

Every librarian and library design professional working in an earthquake-prone area should be familiar with the manual and should use the practices described in it. Engineers and consultants who have expertise and experience with the successful installation of bookstacks in seismic zones should be employed to correctly interpret the safety standards for any building or renovation project.

WOOD SHELVING

Most of the manufacturers who sell library technical furniture also sell wood shelving. It is significant that these companies manufacture shelving that is designed specifically for library use. Many contract furniture companies and office supply houses sell "wood" shelving that is advertised as suitable for libraries; however, the specifications for these products should be studied in order to ascertain exactly what materials and what types of construction are used in manufacturing the shelving. Wood shelving constructed of particleboard shelves, end panels, and intermediate panels is not as satisfactory as that made with components of solid wood; particleboard shelves and upright panels are apt to sag or warp under the weight of books.

Wood shelving is of the starter/adder type; that is, only the first section of each range (the starter) has two vertical panels, while subsequent sections (the adders) have only one panel. Wood shelves come in standard 8-, 10-, 12- and 16-inch sizes with bookstacks 42, 60, 82, and 96 inches high. Back panels are available from all of the manufacturers, if desired.

Standard wood shelving designed for library use has the following general specifications (see Figure 5):

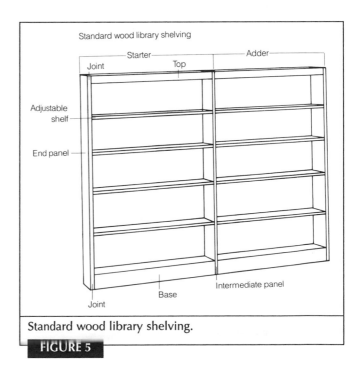

Standard wood library shelving.

FIGURE 5

End and intermediate panels. Panels, 1" to 1 ¼" thick, constructed of five-ply lumber core with a solid wood edge band, edge-glued wood panels, butcher block, or plank oak.

Top. Three-ply particleboard or five-ply lumber core with veneer facing or solid plank construction, ¾" thick.

Base. Five-ply lumber core or solid edge-glued wood panels, ¾" thick.

Shelves. Solid edge-glued wood panels with strips of wood less than 4" wide, sometimes with a solid wood nosing, or five-ply lumber core, ¾" thick.

Shelf support. Shelf pins placed at 1" increments in holes in the upright panels, or flush-mounted aluminum shelf standards (K-V track) to hold clips for adjustment at ½" increments.

Joinery. Metal-to-metal joining of panels to tops and bases with bushings, Rosans, or heliocoils used with bolts and washers.

In selecting wood shelving, compare the specifications of several products and talk to numerous vendors about the specific characteristics of the wood shelving that they are selling. Evaluation of wood shelving involves using the "systems approach" discussed in chapter 2; the level of quality depends on the engineering of the shelving as a whole as well as the construction of each individual component.

Generally, the thicker the upright, the stronger the shelving; however, the thickness of the upright has to be considered in relation to other details of construction, for example, the use of back panels or braces that add stability to the shelving. Because of the hygroscopic nature of wood, wood plank may be a poor selection for end and intermediate panels on wood shelving; the panels may split as the wood dries out. Wood shelving should be constructed of high-density hardwood for strength; however, the species of wood used in shelving may be determined by the end use of the product. For example, some oak contains tannic acid that causes paper to deteriorate; shelving constructed of oak with this characteristic should not be used for housing materials requiring careful preservation. As with any wood furniture item, the edges of the core material on all four sides of the end and intermediate panels and on the base should be banded or sealed in some manner to keep contaminants in and to keep cleaning agents out of the core.

Shelf support in wood systems is provided either by recessed metal shelf standards (K-V track) with slots to receive adjustable metal shelf clips or holes drilled in the panels to hold shelf pins. Once again, there are advantages and disadvantages from an engineering standpoint to both types, and the quality of the shelving support de-

pends on particular details of construction, for example, the material used in the shelf clips (steel or aluminum) or the particular hardware used in a pin-and-hole system. Many different kinds of pins and metal inserts for the holes are used satisfactorily. To prevent accidental removal of shelves, the pins should be self-engaging and should have some type of retainer to keep them from falling out easily.

STEEL SHELVING

For the last 25 years, there has been little stability in the steel shelving industry. Even long-established manufacturers have undergone a variety of changes. Factories have been taken over by new owners or managers, the same product has been marketed under more than one name, and plants have closed, only to be opened again several years later.

Some of the companies that sell steel shelving systems are BC Inventar (BCI), Biblomodel, Tennsco/Estey, Gaylord, MJ Industries, Montel/Aetnastak, Scania/BTJ, Spacesaver, and Borroughs/Wilsonstak. Several of these steel shelving products are manufactured in other countries: BCI is manufactured in Denmark; Biblomodel is manufactured in Mexico; and Scania/BTJ is manufactured in Sweden.

Products, as well as manufacturers, change as new library materials require different kinds of storage or display units, as better ways of manufacturing a product are developed, or as new trends are preferred by consumers for aesthetic reasons. Because fluctuations in the industry are likely to continue, a librarian or designer selecting steel shelving is best advised to consider the brands mentioned in this chapter *only as a starting point* for assessing possible steel shelving system options. Companies and products change so frequently that it is impossible to write about particular brands and expect them to be the same for years, or even months, to come. Specific products are discussed here solely to illustrate which qualities in shelving are satisfactory or unsatisfactory; the information can be used either to evaluate new lines of shelving or to reevaluate older products.

As is the case with other library technical furnishings, the major manufacturers of steel bookstacks exhibit at the American Library Association conventions and at state or regional conferences. Because these companies are primarily in the business of making bookstacks rather than other kinds of steel shelving, they are more apt to focus on serving the library market and, therefore, are more attuned to consumer demands.

There are many other steel shelving lines that are not specifically designed for libraries. These products are less likely to hold up when fully loaded with books, may not have easily interchangeable parts, and probably cannot store materials as effectively or as attractively as true library bookstacks.

The process of selecting library furnishings, as noted earlier, begins with deciding the function of the various items. Likewise, in the case of shelving, it is the responsibility of the librarian to decide what use will be made of the bookstacks and the level of quality needed in each particular situation. For example, a special library that stores mostly oversized, heavy volumes like law books may require different shelving than a small public library with a general collection.

Shelving products with the best features may not be (and often are not) the ones that are the highest in price. Also, because the steel shelving market is so changeable and bidding is so competitive, the high-priced product today may be a bargain tomorrow. Furthermore, the price may depend on conditions of which the librarian is unaware, such as the lack of qualified installers in the area, the closing of a factory, or a manufacturer's overstock of a particular product.

Performance Testing

Since its first testing of steel shelving in the 1960s, *Library Technology Reports (LTR)* has sought to develop a nationally recognized performance standard for library shelving. In 1985, a subcommittee of the American National Standards Committee on Library Equipment and Supplies, Z85, drafted a "Proposed American National Standard for Library Bookstacks, Z85.3 1985." The document never received official status. In 1990, *Library Technology Reports (LTR)* published "Library Bookstacks: An Overview with Test Reports on Bracket Shelving," by John F. Camp and Carl A. Eckelman. This report includes the results of the testing of 16 models of steel shelving using the 1985 proposed standard (with some changes), which were incorporated into the *LTR Performance Standard for Single-Tier Steel Bracket Library Shelving*. The 1990 *LTR* report describes testing methods and *LTR*-recommended standards for steel shelving that can be used by consumers to compare the products of competing manufacturers. The introductory material in the report provides information that supports the use of performance-tested products. In 1994, *LTR* will achieve its goal regarding a national standard for steel shelving. According to Howard

S. White, editor of *LTR*, the standard for library shelving has been passed officially and will be published as *ANSI/NISO Z39.73 1994, Single-Tier Steel Bracket Library Shelving.*

Every steel shelving product that enters the market should be tested by an independent laboratory using the LTR/ANSI methods, and, as changes are made in older products, manufacturers are encouraged to retest their shelving systems. Librarians and design professionals are encouraged to be familiar with the shelving performance tests and to discuss testing data with vendors prior to deciding which products to purchase.

LTR-recommended standards are intended to ensure that tested shelving meets three requirements: "(1) that it bear prescribed loads without sagging, bending, leaning, swaying, or collapsing; (2) that its finish endure normal use and cleaning for at least 30 years without signs of wear; and (3) that changing the position of adjustable shelves should be easily accomplished without tools or excessive effort." (*Camp*, 1990, p. 803) The *LTR* method includes tests of the following steel shelving attributes: lateral deflection of uprights under shelf loads, deflection of the shelves under load (shelf sag), longitudinal deflection of the uprights under horizontal pull, condition of the finish, hazards to books or people, gloss of finish, adhesion of finish (bending and impact tests), resistance of finish to abrasion, and resistance of the finish to acids and chemicals, resistance of the finish to a lighted cigarette, ease of changing unloaded shelves, and ease of changing loaded shelves.

The 1990 report includes the results of *LTR*'s testing of 16 shelving samples supplied by 11 manufacturers. Since 1990, many companies have submitted to additional tests of both newly developed and older products conducted under the same conditions. Because the market and individual products are constantly changing, the results of the 1990 report should not be the only source of information on which a shelving selection is made. In researching the best product to specify, decision makers should study the *LTR* 1990 report for background information and should ask shelving vendors for additional, more recent performance testing data.

General Description of Steel Library Shelving

Steel bookstacks consist of two upright, slotted columns that are connected at the top and bottom by other channels of steel (spreaders). The frame (uprights and spreaders) either intermembers with a base bracket or rests on a leg base. Cantilevered shelves are then held by brackets that hang from slots in the uprights. The slots are spaced one inch on center for the full height of the uprights, thereby allowing adjustment of the shelves in one-inch increments. The bookstacks may have a closed base or kick plate, canopy tops, end panels, and a number of accessories. (See Figure 6.)

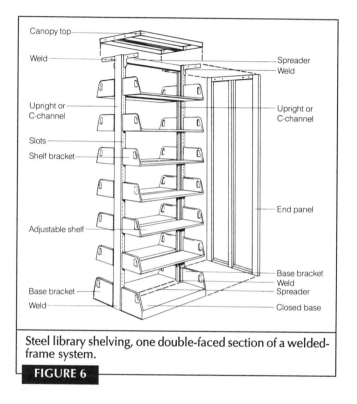

Canopy top

Weld

Upright or
C-channel

Slots

Shelf bracket

Adjustable shelf

Base bracket

Weld

Spreader
Weld

Upright or
C-channel

End panel

Base bracket
Weld
Spreader

Closed base

Steel library shelving, one double-faced section of a welded-frame system.

FIGURE 6

Double-faced (two-sided) sections of shelving are usually freestanding, while single-faced shelving must be anchored to a wall. In order to gain stability in the former's installation, the base of freestanding, double-faced shelving is often specified wider than the adjustable shelves placed above it; for example, with two 10-inch adjustable shelves placed on either side of a double-faced section, a 24-inch base shelf will be used. Shelves come in standard lengths of 30 inches and 36 inches. Standard heights for steel bookstacks include 42, 66, 78, 84, and 90 inches. Adjustable shelves are standard in depths of 8, 9, 10, and 12 inches; double-faced base shelves are 16, 18, 20, and 24 inches. The depth dimensions of the adjustable shelves are "nominal", that is, they indicate the depth from the front edge of the shelf to the imaginary centerline of the shelving frame. For adjustable shelves, then, the *actual* depth of the shelf is one inch less than the nominal.

Bookstacks designed specifically for libraries by the major manufacturers are constructed of the following gauges of steel:

Uprights:	#14–#16 gauge
Spreaders:	#14–#16 gauge
Shelves:	#18–#19 gauge
Brackets:	#16 gauge
Closed base:	#18–#19 gauge
Open-base feet:	#11–#14 gauge

Because there is nothing to prevent a manufacturer from changing the material used in shelving, it is best to purchase from a manufacturer of known reliability and verify the latest specifications, especially if a product has not been purchased by the library for several years.

Three kinds of paint are used for finishing steel shelving. Formerly, many companies used a process in which wet paint is electrostatically applied to the steel. Now, most steel shelving is finished either with dry epoxy powder paint or with polyester paint, both applied electrostatically. With any of the paints used, the final step in the finishing process is baking the enamel. In abrasion tests of paint finishes for steel shelving conducted by *LTR* and by individual companies in the last four years, both powder and polyester paints have performed better than wet process paints. The proponents of epoxy and polyester paints claim that shelving with these finishes has a better overall appearance, and the shelving is more evenly coated with paint. Although all manufacturers offer a few colors as standard, many additional colors are available for a small upcharge that applies to the entire job.

The Kinds of Steel Shelving Systems

Three types of cantilevered steel shelving are available: traditional starter/adder shelving that requires sway braces, "European-style" starter/adder shelving, and bookstacks with one-piece, welded-frame construction. Particular products of each of the three types of shelving have been performance tested and have passed the *LTR* standards. Each of the kinds of shelving is described here. By way of clarification, note that each range of a starter/adder system includes one initial starter section and one or more adder sections. The starter consists of a two-sided frame with the second column acting as the upright for that section, as well as serving as one upright for the next section. Adder sections have only one upright, so that once the starter is in place, all subsequent sections share one upright between them. With this type of shelving, starters and adders cannot be interchanged, and each range requires one starter. In contrast, welded-frame systems consist of uprights and spreaders that are welded together; each section includes one four-sided frame. Any section can be used anywhere in a range of shelving.

Traditional style starter/adder shelving: Until the 1970s, most double-faced, freestanding library shelving was of the older starter/adder type that is stabilized longitudinally along the range by the addition of sway braces—diagonal steel rods tightened by means of a turnbuckle—placed every few sections. Sway braces, if properly installed, add to the stability of the shelving. However, there is a safety factor to be considered: Because the sway braces are visible and easily accessible, it is possible for someone to tamper with them. Although this may seem a remote possibility, it has happened. If a library staff member or patron does not realize the vital function of the rods and loosens one of the turnbuckles on the braces, the whole range of shelving can fall horizontally. Some librarians who have been using starter/adder shelving with sway braces safely for many years continue to prefer to buy this type of shelving. Also, the bookstacks of the older design are often sold as additional pieces for existing installations.

Library Bureau's starter/adder shelving was considered its best-selling shelving product for many years. Adjoining sections of the bookstacks share an upright that consists of two C-channels back-to-back with an additional piece of steel called a web stiffener. These three components are welded together. The top spreader and base brackets are bolted to the uprights. The system has a one-piece closed base and does require sway braces. Estey also continues to manufacture and sell its starter/adder product, a Z-based system with a kick plate that gives the shelving a closed-base appearance.

European-style starter/adder shelving: This newer starter/adder style was introduced into the American market by the Danish company, BC Inventar (BCI). This style of shelving is growing in popularity, and the number of companies manufacturing and selling similar shelving systems has increased in the last five years. In addition to BCI, new style starter/adder bookstacks are sold by MJ Industries, Biblomodel, and Scania/BTJ. Because of competition in the marketplace, it would not be surprising if other manufacturers of steel shelving develop new starter/adder products.

The European-style shelving consists of a T-base constructed of #11–#14 gauge steel welded to an upright. Top and bottom spreaders are bolted to the uprights or

are attached to the uprights with a hook-in type assembly. Some systems add a center crossbar to every three to five sections for added stability. The shelving can be open-based or, with the addition of base panels or kick plates, can become a closed-based system. No sway braces are used with this style of shelving.

In public areas, other types of shelving are typically installed with end panels, the new style starter/adder shelving is sometimes used, however, without end panels. Rectangular shelf brackets, available in several heights and in both closed-plate and open-band styles, provide a finished appearance to the shelving and add to the desirability of using the bookstacks without end panels. Libraries are, therefore, saved the expense of purchasing end panels. Some consumers prefer the starter/adder systems with the hook-in type assembly because of ease of installation—adjoining sections do not have to be bolted together. (See Figure 7.)

Welded-frame shelving: During the 1960s and 1970s, the major shelving manufacturers began making bookstacks of one-piece welded-frame construction while they continued to produce traditional starter/adder shelving. Borroughs, Estey, Gaylord, MJ Industries, Montel, and Spacesaver are some of the companies that sell welded-frame bookstacks. As the name implies, welded-frame shelving consists of uprights and spreaders that are welded together, so that each section includes a four-sided frame. In their descriptive literature, all of the manufacturers of welded-frame shelving emphasize the strength provided by the welding of the uprights to the spreaders. There is more flexibility in the use of a welded-frame system, because there is no need for a starter section in each range: Any frame is interchangeable with any other frame. Each frame is shipped as one module, so the shelving is easier to install than bookstacks that require bolting the upright to the spreader. (See Figure 8.)

Under ordinary conditions (level floors, no special requirements for seismic zones, etc.), welded-frame shelving should not require sway braces or any other special bracing. A consumer would be wise to investigate carefully if a vendor claims to sell a stable, welded-frame product, but then refers the customer to several projects where cross-ties or sway braces have been added to the shelving following the initial installation.

There are some subtle differences among the frames of the various manufacturers. The number of bends in an upright, for example, varies from eight to 16 bends in differing products. There are also small differences in the size of the uprights from product to product. Estey's up-

M. J. Industries System 3000, a "European-style" starter/adder shelving system. *Photograph courtesy of M. J. Industries. Photo: Paul Colburn.*

FIGURE 7

Estey welded-frame shelving system. *Photograph courtesy of Estey Company/Tennsco.*

FIGURE 8

right, for example, measures 1¼ inch at the front and rear and 2½ inches on the sides, with a ¾-inch stiffening flange. Borrough's and MJ have an upright that is 1¼ inch by 2 inches, with a ½-inch stiffening flange. On some bookstacks, the closed side of the C-channel of the upright is bolted to the closed side of the adjoining upright. This design allows the spreader to fit inside and to be welded into the C-channel. Library Bureau welded the frame with the closed sides of the C-channel bolted together, but the spreader was welded over the top of the upright, and a web stiffener was bolted between adjoining uprights for extra strength. Some manufacturers bolt adjoining uprights together with the open side of the C-channels together. The spreader is welded to the flat side of the upright.

Some welded-frame systems have a one-piece base bracket and a one-piece base shelf, while others have two base brackets and two base shelves. On some brands of shelving, a one-piece base bracket fits tightly around the welded-frame upright, and has a 90-degree flange at the bottom that rests on the floor. With this particular one-piece base, the bracket of one section is bolted to the bracket on the adjoining section and can telescope up or down the upright to allow for leveling the shelving. Other brands of shelving have a one-piece base bracket that does not fit around the upright, but rather fits between the two uprights below a web stiffener. The base bracket is then bolted to the uprights.

Some bookstacks have a two-piece base bracket that is bolted to either side of the upright. Likewise, there is a separate base shelf on either side of the double-faced section, with the bottom spreader filling the space between the two base shelves. Although the one-piece, wraparound base bracket may add to the stability of the shelving, some two-piece designs have the advantage of allowing the user to convert the shelving from double- to single-faced: One-half of the assembly from a double-faced section (one bracket and one base shelf) can be used for a single-faced section and, conversely, the base assembly from two single-faced sections can be placed back-to-back to convert them to one double-faced section.

According to the trusted source *Planning Academic and Research Library Buildings* by Keyes Metcalf, canopy tops, steel end panels, and one-piece bases all contribute to the stability of steel bookstacks. Another major factor in stability is the capability that the user has for leveling the shelving. Obviously, all of the features that make the shelving stable as a unit are of little value if the stacks are listing one way or another on an uneven floor. Most shelving is leveled by adjusting built-in threaded levelers. This method has proven to be reliable. Shelving products vary according to the number and location of the levelers. Some systems provide four adjustable levelers on each double-faced section and other systems provide six per section.

In terms of performance for most libraries, testing has provided evidence that the extra bends or the extra parts of an inch of steel do not need to be determining factors in deciding which type of shelving to select. Although it is important to have a product that holds together and does not bend or break with use, the stability of the bookstacks as demonstrated in performance tests should be the primary consideration in selection.

In addition to flat shelves for books, all of the steel shelving manufacturers make a variety of specialty shelves and accessories that can be placed in standard frames. These include divider shelves with backs for picture books, plays, or pamphlets; hinged and fixed periodical display shelves; sliding or stationary reference shelves; phonograph record shelves; newspaper racks; storage lockers; and in-stack carrels. Many manufacturers sell shelves with an integral back 1¼–2 inches high. The integral back prevents materials from falling off the back of the shelf and provides a carrier for a wire book support that moves across the length of the shelf on a nylon or plastic runner. (See Figure 9.) Adjustable backstops are also available. Proponents of regular flat shelves note that a back on a shelf prevents a book from occupying the empty space that is between the two shelves on a double-faced section of shelving. In sections of the collections that contain both wide and narrow books, some of the wide books will stick out over the front edge of a shelf with an integral back. Shelving vendors offer several kinds of book supports: the wire supports used on integral back shelves, wire supports that attach to the underside of a shelf, supports that hook on the front of the shelf, and "findable" book supports.

Gaylord is one company that makes an excellent book support of heavy-gauge steel.

Steel shelving can be used with steel or wood end panels or with end panels faced with high-pressure laminate

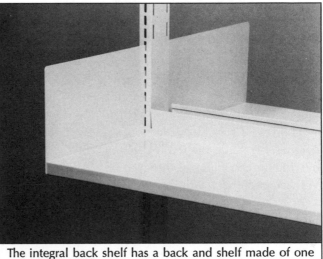

The integral back shelf has a back and shelf made of one piece of steel. *Photograph courtesy of BC Inventar.*

FIGURE 9

or fabric. Backs for steel shelving and fillers for corners and odd-sized spaces are also available. Shelving 42 inches high can be more effectively used as a display or worksurface if it has a laminate or veneer top. In public areas, 84–90 inch-high shelving is sometimes used without canopy tops. This is, of course, an economical choice; furthermore, it is easier to see the contents of the shelves when light from the ceiling is not blocked by the shelving tops. Shelving shorter than 90 inches is often used with canopy tops in order to give the shelving a more finished appearance.

In a library building project, wood end panels and custom wood tops for steel shelving are usually specified as part of a bid package for wood items. In this case, both the steel and the wood specifications should include the provision that successful vendors of both packages are required to coordinate their shop drawings to ensure that the end panels and tops fit the shelving.

Steel shelving vendors may not customarily provide shop drawings; however, shop drawings will be supplied upon request. Shop drawings of steel bookstacks allow the consumer to verify the actual (rather than the nominal) dimensions of the shelving, the number of sections of each kind of shelving included in the order, the number of shelves in each section, and any special requirements for the project.

Most shelving companies have responded to the public librarian's interest in merchandising library materials by providing a variety of kinds of specialty shelving systems and racks for housing books and multimedia. These display items are discussed in chapter 9, p. 117.

WOOD/STEEL SYSTEMS

As mentioned in the previous section, steel shelving systems can be used with wood end panels manufactured by a wood furniture company. Another kind of bookstack system, however, consists of steel shelves used with wood uprights; these are starter/adder systems. Brodart's Omega shelving, Bretford's LEGACY shelving, and Scania/BTJ's shelving are examples of this type of bookstack system. Wood/steel shelving systems are also sold by Worden, and BCI.

Brodart's product is essentially its solid wood cases used with steel, instead of wood, shelves. Bretford's shelving consists of veneer-faced particleboard panels and steel shelves. The system is available either with or without wood back panels. When the shelving is used without wood backs, sections are stabilized by the addition of #18 gauge steel tube frames that are installed at the back of each section. Shelving 42 inches high or less is installed with one frame. Taller stacks are installed with two frames. Scania/BTJ's shelving system also consists of upright panels used with steel shelves. Particleboard panels are veneer-faced and have a solid wood edgeband. The company's standard hardwood construction is beech; however, the shelving is also available in oak. The system can have an open base, or a wood kick plate can be added for a closed-base look. Sections without a back are stabilized by the addition of a 34-inch-square, #16 gauge welded-steel frame that is placed in each three-foot section. A range of shelving is strengthened horizontally by bolting the frame of one section through an intermediate upright and into the frame on the next section. Both the Scania/BTJ and Bretford lines include multi-media display units that are discussed in chapter 9.

INSTALLATION

Regardless of the bookstacks selected, shelving is only as good as the installation. Even if the best product available is purchased, it won't serve the intended purpose safely if it has not been installed in such a manner that it is stable. Once a librarian or designer has supplied a layout for the shelving, it is up to the supplier to see that the bookstacks are put together according to the manufacturer's instructions. It is the installer's responsibility to see that a shelving range is placed in a straight line and leveled for maximum stability. In some situations involving steel shelving, the installer may recommend the installation of crossties across the ranges of shelving, or the addition of sway braces.

Although it is important to let installers do their job, it is a good idea to watch how a couple of sections are put together. Installation is often subcontracted to another company by the supplier, so it is possible that the subcontractor will try to cut corners on hardware and labor. Reliable manufacturers and salespeople want the job to be properly installed.

Once the installation is complete, check the shelving for stability. When the shelves are shaken, there should be very little movement, either horizontally along the range or laterally from side to side. Wall shelving should be anchored securely to the wall. The installer should have touched up nicks and scratches in the finish; these are the natural result of shipping and installing the shelving. Bent or badly marred shelves, end panels, and tops should be replaced by the supplier. Manufacturers know that there will almost always be some small amount of damage in shipping steel shelving; therefore, more than the required number of shelves and other items are usually sent in the initial shipment.

If shelving is not stable, the librarian or designer should not give in to the argument that once shelves are fully loaded, the stacks won't sway. When shelving has been filled with books, any instability becomes a real danger. Check the shelving again when there *are* books on it, and insist that it be leveled properly.

The industry standard is a one-year warranty on steel shelving; however, manufacturers may provide a warranty of longer than one year, if it is requested. The manufacturer and vendor have a responsibility to live up to their warranties on parts and labor. Once a job has been accepted as satisfactory, however, it is unreasonable to expect a supplier or installer to come back, free of charge, to correct a situation that is the result of a defect in the building, such as uneven floors or walls, and not a problem with the product or installation.

Over the years, shelving that was once properly installed may become unstable, as bolts loosen or a building settles. Go back and check older installations occasionally. If the shelving has become unstable, ask a local vendor for the name of a qualified installer who can be hired to do whatever is necessary to improve the stability of the bookstacks. Occasionally a librarian will inherit older shelving that was not installed properly initially. The fact that none of the shelving has fallen in several years (luckily!) should not deter a responsible person from going to the expense of having the situation corrected immediately.

COMPACT MOVABLE SHELVING

The following discussion is limited to movable shelving systems that are essentially mobile ranges of shelving (similar to traditional stationary units) that make more efficient use of space by eliminating the need for most aisle space. The compact shelving business is as unstable as the steel shelving industry. Thus it is quite likely that during the time it has taken for this information to be published, the industry will have changed again and new companies will be selling compact systems. Some of the manufacturers currently selling movable shelving systems are Kardex, Spacesaver, TAB Products, Spacemaster Systems, White Office Systems, and ASRS (Automated Storage & Retrieval Systems of America, selling its product under the name of Elecompack).

There are essentially two components to a movable shelving system: the carriage, with some kind of wheel that runs on a metal track, and the shelving that rests on the carriage. Some companies sell a movable shelving system that includes their own steel shelving product placed on a carriage manufactured by another company; some companies manufacture a carriage, but not the shelving that goes on it. These companies use standard steel shelving from another manufacturer for a library situation. Some companies manufacture both their own library shelving line and the carriage for the movable shelving.

Because of the variety of products that are sold as compact shelving, consumers should research products carefully before purchasing a movable system. A company may do something as simple as placing standard shelving on wheels and then claim that this is a movable system, but with several satisfactory, well-tested products on the market, there is no need to consider a jerry-built system. It is also very important when developing specifications to consider the details of the construction and materials of the product. Most manufacturers sell several different grades of movable shelving. Some vendors have been known to say they can meet specifications, because they do make a top-of-the-line product that can match the specs. Unfortunately, however, when they bid, their less-expensive product is substituted for the better one. If unsuspecting consumers do not go over the details of a bid very carefully, but assume that the product will meet specifications, they may find out too late that the level of quality desired was not received.

The advertising literature of the various companies is sometimes confusing. Also it may be difficult to look at three or four company brochures and find very much to compare. One company, for example, includes detailed discussions of several systems in its literature, while another company explains very little in its advertising brochures. In selecting a movable shelving system, therefore, work with a reliable vendor, check with previous users, and, above all, know the right questions to ask. (See p. 49 for a list of appropriate questions.)

Because of the frequent changes made in shelving and the variety of products available, information about specific brands of movable shelving may not be useful for very long. For that reason, it will be most helpful here to discuss generally the components of movable compact systems and the details of material and construction that should be considered when selecting a particular product.

Compact movable shelving was once used mainly in academic and special libraries where access was limited to staff or special users. This is no longer the case. Many public libraries are now adding compact systems to older buildings and installing them in new buildings in order to make the best use of limited space.

Compact movable shelving systems should be designed to be in compliance with ADA guidelines. Jim Muth, director of Engineering, Spacesaver Corporation, has written an excellent brochure that discusses a number of ADA concerns that relate to movable shelving systems. The publication, entitled *Achieving ADA Compliance with Mobile Storage,* can be obtained from a local Spacesaver dealer. Several options are available for making mobile shelving accessible to library users and staff in wheelchairs:

1. A person in a wheelchair can back out of a single-access aisle between *short* ranges of shelving relatively easily.

2. The shelving can be planned with dual-access aisles (aisles that can be accessed from either end) so that people using wheelchairs can enter one end of the aisle and exit from the other end. (Aisles at the end of the ranges must be a compliant width also.)

3. The mobile system can be designed to allow for a 60-inch aisle (sufficient turnaround space for a wheelchair) between ranges. The wide aisle,

in effect, creates two 30-inch aisles for people not using wheelchairs.

Movable shelving systems, especially those added to existing structures, require ramping. Ramps are required by the ADA when there is a change of level greater than one-half inch. The length of the ramp will, of course, depend on the height of the mobile system in relation to the surrounding floor. Spacesaver calculates that with a low-profile system that extends one inch above the floor in an older building, a ramp of at least eight inches long will be needed for accessibility. The contractor supplying a movable system should provide calculations and specifications for required ramping. Other applicable ADA guidelines that should be discussed with movable system vendors include the height and type of controls to be specified and signage for the system.

Function and maintenance are obviously the prime considerations when selecting compact movable shelving. Although appearance may be considered in some situations, it definitely should not be the determining factor in selecting which brand to purchase. Important considerations when selecting a compact movable system include the following:

1. Who will be the major users of the shelving? Will they be able to operate the system easily and efficiently?

2. How often will the system need to be accessed and by how many users at one time?

3. What kinds of materials will be stored in the shelving? Is this the most efficient way of storing these items?

4. Will service be readily available if repairs are needed on the system?

5. In a new building, is movable shelving that is included to save space less expensive than adding more square feet to the size of the facility?

6. High-density storage requires a floor or foundation that can hold more weight per square foot than standard shelving. In an older building, has an engineer verified the load-bearing capability of the floor? In a new building, is the greater cost of building the area to carry the additional weight of compact shelving justified? Would it be less expensive to add more square feet of space to the building and include more standard shelving?

(Recommendations regarding the load-bearing capability of floors beneath compact systems range all the way from 200 to 450 pounds per square foot, depending on the materials to be stored. For this reason, always get the opinion of a reliable engineer before purchasing compact shelving.)

There are three kinds of movable systems: (1) strictly manual compact shelving, which is moved when the user pulls or pushes the ranges along a track; (2) mechanically assisted manual systems, which use some kind of crank to operate a chain, gear, and sprocket system to turn a drive shaft; and (3) electrically operated systems. Both cantilevered and four-post or post-lock types of shelving are used on movable systems. In addition, a wide variety of other storage units can be placed on the carriages for use in museums, hospitals, banks, data processing institutions, etc.

Different brands of compact movable shelving vary according to the load-bearing capabilities of their carriages, the maximum length of a range that can be moved satisfactorily, and the number of tracks needed for each range. For this reason, it is necessary to decide what size system is needed by the library, and then to talk to reliable suppliers about the specific manner in which the system can be designed to fit into the space available.

Manual systems are used in areas needing a limited amount of high-density storage that does not need to be accessed frequently. The ranges are usually no more than six feet long. Even with this limit on the range length to restrict the weight to be moved, some people would have difficulty moving the shelving. Because the ranges are moved strictly by hand, there is also a limit to the number of ranges that can be used efficiently.

Mechanically assisted and electrically operated compact systems can include more, longer ranges than manual shelving, and can still be moved easily. The decision regarding which of the three kinds of movable shelving to select may be based to some extent on the funds available for the project. Electrically operated compact shelving is more expensive than either of the manual systems. On the other hand, the electrical systems have better safety systems, can include built-in lighting, provide faster access, and can be operated with less physical effort. Also, such systems can be designed so that the material stored there can be accessed by computer.

It is possible to place standard steel shelving already owned by the library on movable carriages. This should only be done, however, if the shelving is a high-quality product that is strong and stable in spite of previous use. Take the advice of a reliable vendor. If the vendor says the existing shelving is not suitable for use on a carriage, take this advice seriously; if necessary, get a second opinion. The preceding information about quality in steel shelving can also be used by librarians in forming opinions on compact movable shelving systems.

Many of the problems to be overcome in designing a satisfactory compact movable shelving system can be understood with an elementary knowledge of the physical forces involved in moving several fully loaded ranges of library shelving. Force, of course, is needed to overcome inertia and get the shelving moving and—more important from the standpoint of safety and stability—also to stop it. The more that is stored on the shelving, the greater the effect of momentum once the shelving is moving, and the greater will be the force needed to stop the movable range from slamming into a stationary range and rebounding in the opposite direction.

In terms of use, then, once the shelving is moving, there can be a problem stopping a range gently enough to keep it from bouncing back against a person or object between the ranges. The shelving should be designed to minimize wear on the system caused by the constant heavy jolts when the ranges start or stop. From a safety standpoint, there must be some means of preventing someone from closing an aisle that is already in use, and some way of ensuring absolutely that the range will not tip over. The track must be level and designed in such a manner that the wheels of the carriage do not "jump the track." On long ranges, problems can also develop with the drive shaft that moves the shelving, if the shaft is not designed with the tolerance necessary to withstand the twisting motion that occurs as several sections of shelving are moved along by wheels on several different tracks.

Starting from the floor, consider the various elements that make up the compact movable shelving system. (See Figure 10.) The rails or track can be used in either new or old buildings. In seismic areas, a heavy-duty track is essential. Most systems allow for recessing the track in the floor, so that the rails are flush with the finished floor. (See Figure 11.) This allows for easier use with book trucks and safer entry by the staff. Ideally, the system will be part of the building program, designed along with the facility. The architect should work directly with the shelving supplier, so that the building is designed to accommodate the movable system with regard to the track, the load-bearing capabilities of the floor, and the availability of adequate power for electrical systems.

In older buildings, the system must be placed on a plywood deck that may be anywhere from ¾–1½ inches above the floor. Some systems are always installed on a deck. The disadvantage of having to add a deck, of course, is that ramping is necessary to enter the aisle. The deck is also an additional expense.

In order to have the shelving run smoothly and correctly, the track must be level. Some systems use shims at regular intervals—every 10–12 inches—under the track in order to level it. The advantage to this method is that the shims can be easily adjusted as the floor changes, without having to remove the deck. Other systems level the track by placing the rails on a surface of grout or quick-dry cement that is added to the floor. This method can cause problems if the grout breaks down and crumbles along the edges of the system, or even under the track. The process of leveling as the floor shifts in the future may also be more complicated, if the decking has to be removed for releveling. In addition, the grout must be removed in order to restore the floor, if the system is moved. Some systems installed on a deck have built-in levelers that allow for leveling the track without removing the deck.

The wheels of the movable systems range in size from 2¾–5 inches in diameter. Heavy-duty systems have steel wheels that are 4½–5 inches in diameter. The wheels must be designed so that they will stay on the track. Most of the systems have a double-flanged wheel; others have a wheel with a center flange that fits into a groove in the track. (See Figure 12.) On the better systems, there is a double flange on every wheel in the system, and every wheel helps to drive the system. On other systems, only some wheels are flanged and help to drive and guide the shelving; the other wheels are there just to support the carriage. These other wheels do not help to keep the system on track, but are dragged along by the drive wheels without helping to move the shelves. All wheels should be permanently lubricated and sealed.

The wheels are mounted on a drive shaft made of either tubular or solid steel. The proponents of the tubular shaft claim that solid steel is more apt to break from the torsional movement of the system but that the tubular shaft is more flexible and, therefore, has a greater tolerance for twisting motions. The high-quality systems all have a continuous drive shaft that runs the full length of each range of shelving. The carriage of the movable system acts as the base for the shelving. There is some disagreement among the manufacturers as to the best material for the carriage. Most of the systems have welded-steel

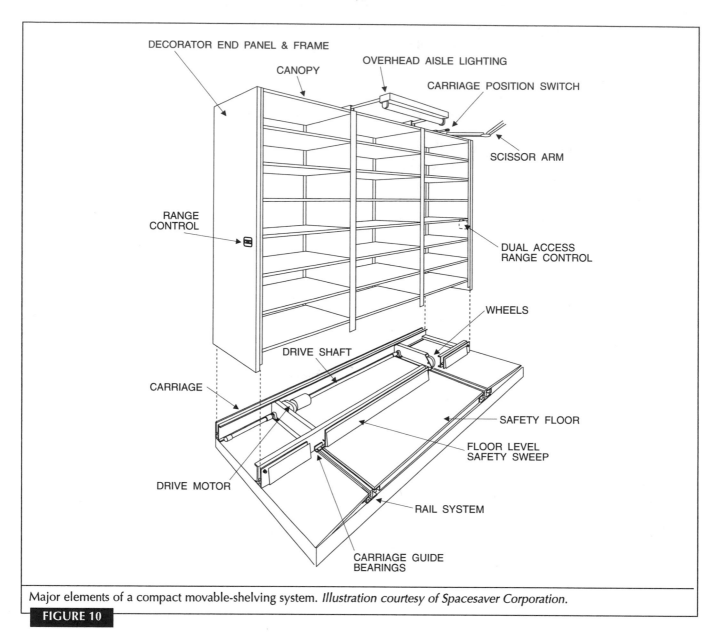

Major elements of a compact movable-shelving system. *Illustration courtesy of Spacesaver Corporation.*

FIGURE 10

frames; the manufacturers claim steel is needed for strength. The most reliable steel systems have welded rather than bolted frames. One company has an aluminum frame that the company claims is strong enough to carry the system and has the advantage of being lighter weight.

On mechanical-assist systems, the gear-and-sprocket assembly is essentially the same from system to system. (See Figure 13.) Likewise, all are operated by turning some kind of crank or wheel located on the end panel of the ranges of shelving. Several ranges can be moved by cranking the system at one location.

The well-known, electrically operated systems have a motor on each carriage that turns the drive shaft for that range. The motors should have automatic thermal-overload protection. In the earlier discussion about electrical systems in furniture, a distinction was made between those products that contain UL-recognized components and those that have their entire electrical system UL-listed. A similar situation exists with compact movable shelving: Although all of the systems include components that are UL-recognized, only some of them have their complete electrical compact system UL-listed. This is a distinction that can be important in writing specifications and in setting the level of quality desired. Another elec-

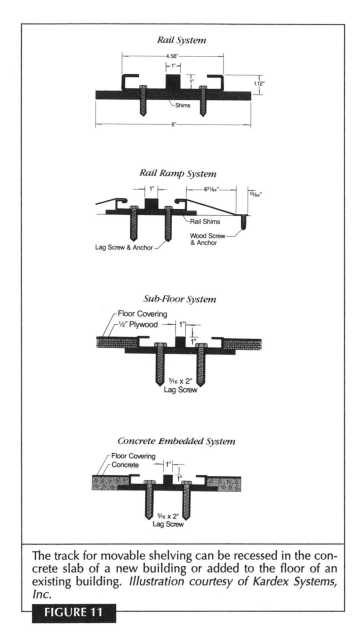

Rail System

Rail Ramp System

Sub-Floor System

Concrete Embedded System

The track for movable shelving can be recessed in the concrete slab of a new building or added to the floor of an existing building. *Illustration courtesy of Kardex Systems, Inc.*

FIGURE 11

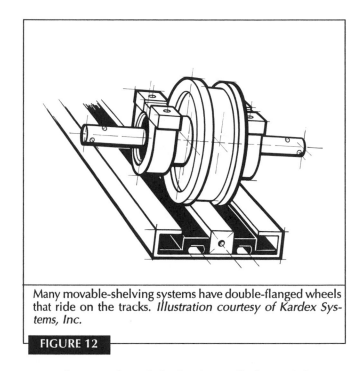

Many movable-shelving systems have double-flanged wheels that ride on the tracks. *Illustration courtesy of Kardex Systems, Inc.*

FIGURE 12

trical consideration is how the system will be powered. Some require a receptacle at the end of each range into which the cord for that one carriage is plugged. This means that as the shelving moves, the cords from each range are dragged back and forth. In the better systems, the entire unit (up to a maximum size) can be plugged into one power source. In the event of power failure, it is best to have a system equipped with mechanical override, so that the shelving can still be operated.

A mechanical-assist system should have some kind of safety feature that locks the aisle in use. Several of the systems have a locking device on the end panel. On one system, for example, a safety knob on the end panel must be depressed by the user entering the aisle. The carriage cannot be moved until the knob is pulled out. Other systems employ a pin that is engaged in some fashion in order to lock the range in use.

Safety systems on electrical compact shelving are extremely important. The well-known companies offer both a primary and a secondary system to protect users, and to prevent an aisle from closing on other objects, such as books, stools, etc. The primary system is typically one that is activated in some way when the user opens an aisle and prepares to enter. In some systems, this may mean pressing an "open" button on the end of the range to activate the secondary safety systems. Access to the aisle in another system is gained by a wave of the hand over the sensor control at the end of the range. In the less sophisticated and, certainly, less convenient systems, aisle access may be limited by such things as a rope that must be moved from one side of the aisle to the other in order to allow entry, or by warning lights or sounds indicating aisle use. Another system uses a safety "eye" that activates the safety system when someone enters the aisle. When a user leaves an aisle, the primary safety system on most movable shelving is reset either automatically or by the depression of a safety switch.

Secondary safety systems are typically a toe-level bar running the full length of the range that stops the system when hit by a person or an object and a waist-level bar that will likewise stop the system when hit. Be wary of safety devices that are attached by no more than double-stick tape and can easily fall off. All of the manufacturers

Mechanical-assist systems move when the user turns a handle that operates a gear-and-sprocket assembly. *Illustration courtesy of Kardex Systems, Inc.*

FIGURE 13

offer some kind of safety floor, at least as an option. The floor prevents an aisle from closing if there is as little as 15 pounds of pressure on it. Although some customers insist on the floor, it is not necessary if the other safety systems mentioned above are well designed and included in the shelving system.

Recently, passive electronic safety systems that require no secondary systems have been developed as an option for electrically operated movable shelving. For example, Spacesaver's ZFS™ (Zero Force Sensor, patents pending) is a completely electronic system. The passive safety system is considered ideal for public areas because it automatically sets and resets itself during use; no action is needed by the user as aisles are entered or exited. ZFS is a microprocessor-controlled infrared photoelectric system with three sensing components: (1) an infrared safety shield with cross aisle sensors along the full length of the carriage that prevents movement of the carriage whenever a beam is broken or when the sensors are in a tracking mode; (2) two infrared photoelectric sensors at the entrance to each aisle that sense both presence and direction of movement; and (3) a photosweep system that scans the length of the carriage and prevents movement of the carriage whenever the beam is broken by the pres-

ence of a person or object. Because of the electronics involved, the ZFS system is, of course, more expensive than the standard mechanical safety systems offered by Spacesaver.

Another useful feature that is available on some movable shelving systems is a safety bypass that allows the operator to bypass the safety systems in a range, in the case of a malfunction in that one range, without shutting off the entire system. On one system, for example, a bypass key is inserted into the range that is affected, and a chime sounds as a reminder that the safety system is not activated when that range is operated.

Another safety consideration in compact movable shelving is the availability of anti-tip devices on the system. Ideally, the system should have two kinds of anti-tip protection: an overhead system, such as the scissor arms between the ranges, and anti-tip devices built into the track and carriage. In seismic areas, an anti-tip device at the level of the track and carriage is mandatory. Because of the problem of one range slamming into another, an anti-tip system should have some kind of limit switch or braking system that softens stopping.

There are some other features that can make a compact system more convenient; these are offered as options on some systems, but may be standard on others. As an example, overhead lighting, available on several systems, is turned on when the button is pressed to activate the safety system for the aisle to be entered. Another feature allows for multiple-aisle access in systems that will be used frequently. Other options available on some systems are the capability for temporarily converting a movable range into a stationary range and the capability for restricting access to any number of ranges while permitting access to others. Most of the compact movable shelving can be locked to prevent access to the system.

Although the carriage-and-track assembly is vital to a movable system, the quality of shelving desired should be clearly specified. The shelving that goes on a movable system should be the same high quality as that selected for use in the rest of the library. The same selection considerations regarding construction and materials that were discussed previously for standard steel library shelving should be applied here. In earthquake-prone areas, the connection of the shelving to the carriage should reflect the same kind of attachment used to secure standard stationary shelving to the floor of the building. (The California State Library *Manual of Recommended Practice, Seismic Safety Standards for Library Shelving* includes sample specifications for movable compact library shelving.)

A one-year warranty is fairly standard for compact movable shelving. The installers of the shelving should be factory-trained. The systems should be easily expandable and should allow for dismantling and moving to a new location. If an electrically operated system is to be used in an area where service is not readily available, it is important to select a system with controls that can be easily accessed and that has some self-diagnostic capabilities.

In summary, there are many questions to consider when selecting a compact movable system. The following can be used as a guide in working with a vendor:

1. Can the rails be recessed, or will there be some kind of deck for the system? If there is a subfloor or deck, how high will it be?

2. How will the rail or track system be leveled?

3. How are the wheels designed and how do they fit into the track to prevent misalignment on the rails?

4. How is the carriage designed for strength?

5. Is there a full-length drive shaft? How is it constructed? Are all wheels drive wheels?

6. What safety systems are available on the system? Are they convenient for the user? Are both primary and secondary systems included for movable shelving that employs mechanical safety systems?

7. If the system is electrically operated, is the entire system UL-listed? Can the system be plugged into a single power source?

8. Does the electrical system have a mechanical override?

9. Does the system have both overhead and carriage-level anti-tip devices? Does the system have limit switches or a braking system?

10. What kind of shelving can be used on the system? Does it meet the criteria for strength and stability needed in any library shelving?

11. Does the system have features such as multiple-aisle access, safety bypass of individual ranges, lighting, locks, and the capability for temporarily making a moving range stationary?

12. What is the warranty on the system?

13. Who will install and service the system?

14. Can the system be expanded or moved?

Additional information about movable systems can be found in *Planning Academic and Research Library Buildings* and *Planning for a Movable Compact Shelving System* by Franklyn F. Bright (LAMA, Occasional Papers No. 1, ALA, 1991). The latter publication includes a model request for quotation that can be used in preparing bid specifications or a request for quotation for a movable shelving system.

In closing, it must be reiterated that the specific shelving products discussed here may no longer be manufactured by next year or even next month. Products with the same or similar features to those discussed will be available, however, and the specifications can be compared with regard to construction and materials. Libraries should select high quality steel shelving that has been performance tested to the latest ANSI standards. Properly installed, high quality shelving should last the lifetime of the library. Compact movable shelving systems should hold the same high quality steel shelving that is used in the stationary bookstacks of the library.

CHAPTER

4

Service Desks

Two stereotypical assumptions about librarians continue to prevail in spite of the efforts of library professionals to dispel them. First is the assumption that everyone who works in the library is a "librarian," and the second is that everyone who is a librarian loves to read and spends time reading on the job. Contrary to this distorted view of the profession, library work requires staff with a wide variety of expertise, experience, academic credentials, and knowledge. And, although many librarians love to read, most of the active members of the profession do well to find time to read off the job, much less during the work day.

The active, varied nature of library work is evident in the planning of service desks, those areas in the library that are the location of most staff/user interactions. Although desks are designed on the basis of the functions to be performed there, a subjective element to the planning is related to the philosophy of the librarian or the goals of the library. Librarians with several years of experience usually have considered or observed what they think makes a satisfactory reference or circulation desk.

It is doubtful that there is one ideal service desk. What works in one location won't necessarily work in another; there are just too many variables to consider. With this in mind, let us review some of the many possibilities available for planning attractive, functional service locations in the library.

Both reference and circulation desks should be designed in such a manner that their function is obvious to the user. Signage may simply announce "Information," "Reference," "Check Out," or "Return." On the other hand, the shape (half-circle or U) and height (38–40 inches rather than 29 inches) of the desk may indicate that it is a service location. In a library or department with several desks, the material or finish may distinguish the service desks from the furnishings for the user. Or, the service desks can be "color-coded" with a finish that is different from any other in the library.

Circulation and reference (or information) desks can be part of a building contract and, therefore, part of the millwork or cabinetry designed by the architect. Or they can be part of the furnishings purchased for a building. The purchase of a desk outside the building contract does not need to be a problem if the desk is designed right along with the rest of the building. General plans for the desk are determined in discussions with the architect early in the preliminary design phase of the building project. As planning continues, the architect is informed of the power and data requirements for the desk and given additional details about the desk as the design is refined. Finally, the supplier of the desk is required to make field measurements while the library is under construction. The vendor then passes on to the factory any required adjustments to ensure that the desk can be assembled correctly on-site.

Although "built-in" desks can work satisfactorily, there are some advantages to selecting units manufactured by a library furniture company. The latter are more likely to be modular in construction, that is, built of standard modules that can be disassembled and relocated if major changes in the building are needed in the future. The desks are likely to be constructed of an outer "shell" that can be seen from the public side. Standard modules are then placed into this shell on the working side of the desk. The modules are designed to include specific interior elements (shelves, file drawers, knee space, etc.) that will allow the staff to accomplish certain transactions effectively.

Another reason for purchasing a desk as a piece of furniture is that the better library and contract furniture manufacturers have already addressed the need for effective power distribution and wire management in service desks. The library can take advantage of this experience and expertise by purchasing desks that have electrical systems designed into them. One of the primary considerations in selecting a manufacturer for these items is the electrical system that can be provided. The information and criteria presented in chapter 2 concerning electrical systems in library furnishings should be applied to the selection of desks.

In planning the interface of a desk and a building, the point of power and data entry into one end of the desk from an adjacent wall or from the floor should be determined with the architect early in the building design process. Ideally, power and data entry from the building to the desk will occur within a locked space that provides easy access if changes are needed. Entry points located in locked space are out of the way of staff working at the desk.

Wire management channels, large enough for stowing all of the cords and cables easily, should extend the full length of the desk. Likewise, the electrical system should extend from the power entry point through all modules of the desk. The electrical system should provide the number of outlets needed in each workstation for powering equipment to be used now and for powering the maximum number of pieces of equipment that might be used in each module in the future. On a desk with a single flat surface, cords and cables drop through grommets placed in the worksurface. The location and number of grommets should be carefully planned to allow flexibility in moving equipment as library needs change. On a desk

with a transaction top, cords and cables can drop through grommets or through a slot located at the back of the worksurface. The slot allows flexibility in the placement of equipment and is hidden by the transaction top.

ADA guidelines require at least one lane or area at each service counter (both circulation and reference desks) to be accessible. The lane(s) should be located on an accessible route, should be at least 36 inches wide, and should have a maximum height of 36 inches above the finished floor. These guidelines seem to contradict the standards for fixed seating that mandate countertops between 28 and 34 inches above the floor with knee spaces 19 inches deep and an under-worksurface clearance of 27 inches from the floor. These varying guidelines can be applied in two different situations: 36-inch height maximum for a side approach to a desk; 28–34-inch height for a desk unit with a front approach that allows a user to pull up under the worksurface. In either case, the unit must be a minimum of 36 inches wide.

In applying the principle of "universal design" discussed in chapter 2 and in consideration of the spirit of the ADA, an accessible counter should follow the guidelines for fixed seating. A desk unit that falls within the guidelines of 19 inches deep and 28–34 inches high will conveniently serve not only patrons in wheelchairs, but also any library user who wishes to sit down while transacting business at the service desk. (The 19-inch deep guideline should be considered a minimum. A regular San Francisco Public Library user pointed out that a knee space that is deeper than 19 inches is preferred.) A 36-inch-wide module is not really large enough for an accessible workstation at a desk in an automated library. The staff member seated behind the equipment at a 36-inch unit may be hidden behind the computer. With a wider module, for example 48 inches wide, the staff member can sit to one side of the equipment in order to make eye contact and speak more attentively to a user.

The design for a service desk that has an accessible workstation for both the staff and the user has additional considerations. A 30-inch deep workstation that is 36 inches wide will not allow for a 19-inch-deep knee space on both the public and staff sides of the desk. A desk module that is 72 inches long, 30 inches deep, and 28–34 inches high can accommodate two 36-inch knee spaces: one that opens to the public side of the desk and one that opens to the staff side. The staff member and user can easily communicate across the adjoining accessible modules.

PLANNING CIRCULATION DESKS

Flexibility of design is essential in planning circulation desks. All desks should be designed so that they can accommodate different kinds of equipment and varying functions in the future. In small to medium-sized libraries, circulation desks often have a rectangular shape that allows for the flexibility of performing a number of functions within the same relatively small space. Angles in the desk, or zigzag and stair-step configurations of the modules, add some interest to the shape of the desk, delineate workstations, and establish the beginning of a queue for users. (See Figure 14.) In a library with a very small staff, the shape of the desk and its placement in a particular location may be determined by the fact that this is the only control point in the building. The desk may serve as the reference as well as the circulation desk.

In large libraries, a circulation area often has several desks, each designated for a particular function, such as check out, return, and registration. In some libraries, the check out of books takes place at individual stations (like check-out lines at the grocery store). At the new San Francisco Public Library, for example, individual check-out stations will be staffed with circulation personnel initially; however, the stations are designed to operate as self-check stations in the future. Planning for new and renovated libraries should include consideration of self-check stations. Many libraries are including plans for self-check stations near the main library circulation area, as well as in various bookstack locations around the library. The first self-check stations placed in a library should be near the circulation desk so that staff can offer help to first-time users, but the stations should be out of the way of people

Custom circulation desk with Worden Diametrix™ accents designed by the author for Frankford Village Branch, Carrollton Public Library, Carrollton, Texas. *Photograph courtesy of The Worden Company. Photo: Paul Colburn.*

FIGURE 14

waiting in line to check out materials at the traditional circulation desk.

A circulation desk worksurface has to be long enough to accommodate the maximum number of staff members who may need to be assigned there and deep enough to hold the equipment to be used on it. At the same time, it must not be so wide that staff members cannot comfortably pass books across to the user. The desk height will be determined by the functions to be performed there. A standing height of 39 inches for desks is considered standard. Worksurfaces to be used by staff seated in a task chair are at the usual office desk height of 29 inches.

Most desks designed for manual operations are built of components corresponding to other standard library furniture sizes: modules 36 inches wide and desks 60 or 72 inches long. It is not unusual, however, for a library to require one or more units of another size, such as 24 or 30 inches, in order to have the desk fit correctly into a particular space. The conversion from manual to automated systems has, however, changed the size of modules needed for circulation desks. In busy computerized libraries, the

traditional circulation desk built from standard three-foot modules is inadequate. A fully computerized check-out station with a monitor, keyboard, scanner, printer, and peripheral hardware takes up most of a 36-inch space. In planning a circulation desk for an automated library, consider whether the check-out stations should be 48, rather than 36 inches wide. A 48-inch wide unit will accommodate all of the equipment needed for circulation and will provide plenty of space next to the computer to place several stacks of books and other materials for check out or return.

In libraries where circulation staff sit on high stools to check-out materials, knee space under the worksurface should be kept free of drawers and shelves. In order to accommodate needed supplies, such as forms, a 24-inch module between each 48-inch wide check-out unit can contain slots, drawers, and shelves.

The depth of both circulation and reference desks in an automated library should also be carefully considered. In many situations, the 30 inch depth typically used now is no longer sufficient. In planning the depth of a

Worden's CRI desk is an example of a desk designed using a modular-systems approach. *Photograph courtesy of The Worden Company.*

FIGURE 15

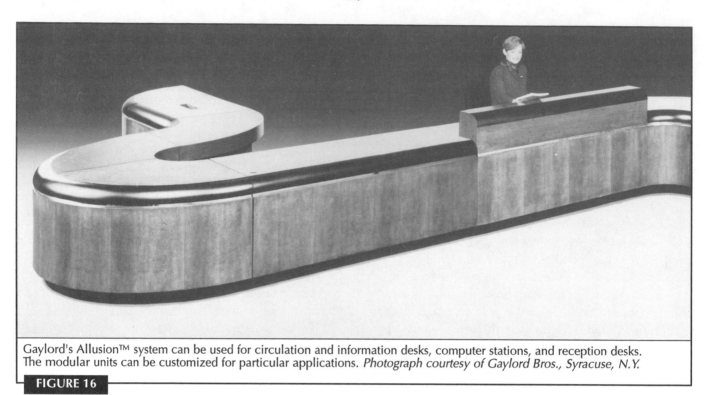

Gaylord's Allusion™ system can be used for circulation and information desks, computer stations, and reception desks. The modular units can be customized for particular applications. *Photograph courtesy of Gaylord Bros., Syracuse, N.Y.*

FIGURE 16

worksurface, take into account the maximum size of any equipment that might be used there and the space needed to accommodate dropping cords and cables through slots or grommets into a wire management channel. For example, in a typical library, computer equipment (terminal and keyboard) will require 24 inches of counter space from the working side of the desk to the back of the equipment; two inches of space will be needed at the back of the equipment to accommodate the cords coming out of the equipment; three inches of space will be needed to accommodate a grommet for dropping cords into the J-channel; and another one inch of worksurface will be needed to finish off the desk at the public side. The total depth of the worksurface for this desk is 30 inches, which is the minimum depth that should be planned for any automated library. Circulation or reference desks that must accommodate PC workstations may need to be 36 inches deep.

The tops of circulation desks are sometimes built with wells cut out for equipment or with the worksurface at one height and a transaction top at another height. A single-height countertop provides maximum flexibility when changes are anticipated in the future. Equipment can be used anywhere on the surface, and both the user and the staff member can slide stacks of books or other materials across the counter instead of having to lift them

to the height of the transaction top. A circulation desk with a transaction top does, however, provide a solution to the problem of shielding exposed cords from public view and from tampering. Another solution is to devise an equipment screen that fits on the desk behind the piece of equipment, such as a terminal. Ideally, the screen can be moved as the equipment is moved. The screen should be large enough to keep the public from tampering with the cords, but small enough to be unobtrusive. Inexpensive, ready-made screens in neutral colors can be purchased from several library supply companies.

Prior to working with designers, consultants, or vendors, a library staff can plan the basic requirements of a circulation (or reference) desk and draw some simple sketches to illustrate their ideas. Using, for example, 36-, 48-, or 60-inch modules as building blocks, the staff can decide what will be included in each module. Here is a sample planning scenario:

In a fictitious public library, the circulation desk will face the front entrance. People working behind the desk will see users enter the door directly in front of them. The main adult reading room will be visible to a circulation assistant looking to the right. The children's area will be visible to the left. The wall that separates the public area from the circulation workroom will be behind the desk.

Considering the desk from the working (staff) side and planning from left to right: two self-check stations, each 36 inches wide, will be located near the end of the circulation desk. At least one of these stations will be 34 inches high and have a knee space 19 inches deep. The main part of the circulation desk will have five workstations. The first station on the left will be designed primarily for returning books and collecting fines. The unit will include a book return slot and space for a depressible book truck. A cash register will be placed on the worksurface. The other four stations will be designated for check out and registration. The return station and three of the check-out stations will be 39 inches high. The fourth check-out station, the one on the far right, will be a maximum 34 inches high with a 19-inch-deep knee space on the public side. Each of the five circulation stations will be 48 inches wide in order to accommodate a terminal and keyboard, a printer, and a scanner. Because the staff sits at high stools at each station, no drawers that will obstruct the knee space will be placed under the worksurface at the 48-inch-wide units. In order to accommodate needed forms and supplies, a 24-inch storage unit will separate each check-out station. The storage unit will have slots for forms, drawers for pencils and small supplies, and a bookshelf for other materials. Because of the equipment used on the desk, the top should be a minimum of 30 inches deep. Depending on the final design, the overall depth may be larger than 30 inches. Books reserved for users will be stored on shelves located on the wall behind the circulation desk.

The same kind of planning described here can be done for a reference desk: determine the basic requirements, decide what size modules are needed and what should be included in each section, and draw some simple sketches. These basic ideas can then be discussed with the design professionals or vendors who will assist with the final specifications for the desk.

PLANNING REFERENCE DESKS

The configuration of a reference desk presents an interesting design problem. In small libraries, reference service may be provided by staff seated at one or more standard office desks. In larger libraries, the shape and configuration of the desk may reflect particular services offered or the reference philosophy of the organization. The task of designing the basic shape, size, and configuration of a reference desk should involve the library staff. Decisions regarding the desk can include consideration of some of the following: the location of the desk in relation to the library's collections, both paper and electronic; the location of the desk in relation to the reference workroom; the maximum number of people who will be working at the desk at any one time; the kinds of ready-reference files and materials that will be stored at the desk; the kinds of equipment that will be placed on the desk (computers, printers, fax machines, microform equipment); and the kinds of questions that will be answered at the desk (questions resulting in short answers or long consultations regarding research topics).

The planning of a reference desk involves different considerations for each library staff and each buiding. For example, in a public library with a user-oriented reference philosophy, the shape of the desk may be particularly important. If the shape is a "U", or a "fenced" square, the function of the unit is obvious, but the staff is seen as being less approachable. Sometimes staff members tend to stay within the confines of the desk instead of approaching the user and are less apt to go with the user to the catalog or shelves to provide extra assistance. The tendency to stay close to the desk may be incompatible with the reference philosophy of the library. In this situation, the reference desk may represent a compromise between the two extremes of having a reference location that is a standard desk and having the staff fenced in by the desk. A service desk can be designed so that it has a straight, approachable front section, and two sides that are separated from the front by corner units at, for example, 30-degree angles. More than one staff member can face approaching users and can easily get out from behind the desk.

The height of a reference desk must be determined by the library staff. Some library managers insist that reference staff be standing or seated at high stools behind a 39-inch high desk in order to achieve eye contact with approaching users. Other managers believe that reference desks at a seated height of 29 inches are satisfactory and that librarians will rise when necessary to greet a patron. Some libraries compromise with a height of 36 inches for the entire adult reference desk. Children's reference desks are usually built at lower heights of 29–36 inches . For an excellent example of the problem-solving approach to planning the height of a desk, see "Designing a Reference Desk," by Hugh Macdonald in the Fall 1986 *Texas Library Journal*. The article outlines the manner in which Texas Christian University Library staff went about defining their requirements for a desk and then specifying a design that would fulfill their needs.

The kinds of transactions that will take place at a reference desk may affect a decision regarding the height of the desk. For questions that require quick answers or moving to the catalog, the patron usually remains standing. A desk at standing height of 39 inches is, therefore, appropriate. A reference desk that is 29 inches high on the staff side and has a transaction top that is at standing height (36–39 inches) on the public side of the desk may be a satisfactory compromise. The library user can set books or other items down on the top while talking to the librarian, and the librarian can place a reference book or other information on the transaction surface in order to help the user. Sometimes a library staff may also want a transaction top in order to hide some of the paraphernalia that accumulates at any busy desk.

In a situation where the staff/user interaction is a long consultation about a research or technical topic, the user, as well as the staff member, will want to sit down. A flat surface between them is desirable for passing information back and forth. Both the librarian and the user will require knee space under the desk. In small to medium-sized libraries, the accessible module of the desk may serve as the sit-down unit for research consultations.

The library user's right to privacy is another concern that must be addressed in planning reference desks. A user should be able to speak privately (or semiprivately) to a librarian without having to step to another room. The position of staff members stationed at a reference desk with a rectangular, U, or L shape can identify one side of the desk as the "public" side that most users approach first in seeking assistance. A person who wishes to speak privately, or indicates hesitancy in asking a question, can step with the reference librarian away from the "public" side of the desk to a consulting area on another side of the desk that allows for more privacy.

A library that was concerned about privacy and that had been providing reference service from standard office desks in an older building did not want a new building to have a reference desk with a single counter. The information desk that was designed for the new library, therefore, included individual reference workstations in a stair-step design that allows a user to approach a single librarian to ask a question. Each librarian has individual equipment and information at the workstation, and also has convenient access to shared information in the overall configuration of the reference desk. (See Figures 17 and 18.)

Another approach to take in designing a reference desk is to use components of a panel or open-office system manufactured by a contract furniture company. One ad-

vantage of these systems is that they provide excellent wire management and power and data distribution systems. The use of office panel components for the reference desk allows for coordinating the design of the desk with other pieces of furniture, such as study carrels and tables for computers, constructed from the same modular system. (See Figure 19.)

The planning process for designing a reference desk sometimes involves addressing the special needs of a particular library. A brainstorming session with the staff who will be working at the desk will help to determine the detailed requirements of the design. For example, in one genealogy library, the main service desk is strictly an information location; none of the material circulates. The design of the desk was especially important because many people coming into the building have not done genealogical research before and stop at the desk to be instructed by the staff on how to begin researching their family history. Part of the instruction involves giving a new user several information sheets and forms for filling in a family tree. A special desk module was designed to accommodate these special materials at the desk.

The desk was designed to allow two librarians to work at the front. Immediately to the side of the work space for each librarian is a section of the desk that includes shelves for holding the giveaway materials. These sheets are usually 8½" x 11" and will never be larger than 8½" x 14". The 8½-inch width, therefore, allowed for placing enclosures, three across, in a 36-inch module. In order to keep the items from getting lost by being pushed too far back on the shelf, a strip of wood was placed approximately 15 inches from the front of the shelf. It was determined that it would not be necessary to have a stack of any single flier available at any one time more than two inches high; therefore, the retaining strip was designed to be two inches high. In order to make the space flexible for other use in the future, however, the shelves were made adjustable. It will be possible in the future, for example, to remove the shelves and place several reference books in the space. (Similarly, circulation and reference desks are sometimes designed to have pigeonholes or slots to hold smaller items that are used by the staff or given to the public.) (See Figure 20.)

SERVICE DESK CONSTRUCTION

Tops of service desks are constructed of wood, stone (marble or granite), and solid surfacing materials. Wood tops are approximately 1¼ inches thick and are typically

Custom reference desk with Worden Diametrix™ accents designed by the author for Frankford Village Branch, Carrollton Public Library, Carrollton, Texas. *Photograph courtesy of The Worden Company. Photo: Paul Colburn.*

FIGURE 17

constructed of three-ply flakeboard or lumber core. Because the worksurface must withstand hard wear over a long period of time, wood tops are usually faced with high-pressure laminate rather than veneer. Wood tops faced with laminate sometimes have a solid wood edge band

Atlas stand, custom-designed as part of the reference desk for Carrollton Public Library shown in Figure 17. *Photograph courtesy of The Worden Company. Photo: Paul Colburn.*

FIGURE 18

that can be used to coordinate the look of the desk with the other wood furniture in the library. Tops made of solid-surfacing materials do not require wood edge banding; the surfacing material itself is formed to create a finished edge.

Laminate tops are typically specified to be continuous over several modules and as long as possible, considering the materials used. Because there are fewer seams on the worksurface, the desk has a more finished appearance. The individual pieces of a wood top are splined and held together with joint fasteners. Tops for individual units can also be specified, if desired.

The vertical surface on the front of service desks can be faced with a variety of materials: high-pressure laminate, wood veneer, vinyl, painted steel (some panel systems), fabric, and polyester resin. A desk is an expensive item to purchase, so the customer should expect high quality in the materials and construction. Wood veneer is frequently used on the front of the desk. The veneers should be carefully matched by color, grain, and sequence. The seams between panels should be tight.

The interior units of a desk are usually constructed of three-quarter-inch plywood or three-ply particleboard. The major library furniture manufacturers offer a variety of standard modules for service desks. These include knee space units, card files, open storage units with adjustable shelves, book return units, typing desks, machine well units for manual operations, discharge units, cabinets, and triangular or square corner units.

Herman Miller's Ethospace® Interiors used for a library information desk and adjacent offices and conference areas. A Newhouse Group® table desk and Equa® chairs are also shown. *Photograph courtesy of Herman Miller, Inc. Photo: James Terkeurst.*

FIGURE 19

A desk module, custom-designed by the author and built by Worden, to accommodate giveaway materials at Clayton Library, Center for Genealogical Research, Houston Public Library. *Photo: David J. Lund.*

FIGURE 20

A high-quality desk will be finished on the interior of the units, as well as the exterior. The interior of the cabinets and the shelves should be faced with veneer or laminate. The working-side edges, as well as the edges on the public side, should have wood edge banding or be self-edged with laminate. No exposed core material should be seen anywhere on the desk.

Standard desk modules should be viewed as the building blocks from which a desk can be designed to fit the particular needs of the library. It is common practice for a library to specify some customized features that can be built into standard modules. Box, file, pencil, cash, or card file drawers, for example, can be added to a basic unit. Drawers are usually constructed with five-ply lumber core or solid wood fronts and sides. Well-made drawers have the fronts and backs dovetail joined or rabbeted to the sides. Drawers are mounted on steel, ball-bearing, and nylon full-extension slides. Service desks are finished off with end panels constructed of three-ply particleboard or five-ply lumber core faced with the material used on the desk front.

In order to make a desk flexible, knee space units can be specified with flush-mounted aluminum shelf standards (K-V track) and adjustable/removable shelves. The knee space can then be converted to shelving, if it is needed in the future. A desk can be built to accommodate the addition of steel storage files for specialized items such as compact discs or audio cassettes. Special storage units for cassettes, compact discs, or videotapes can also be built into the desk.

The major library furniture manufacturers have addressed the fact that computers will be used at every desk—reference as well as circulation. Companies offer various components that can be purchased as part of individual workstation units or added to circulation or reference desks. These components include below-worksurface terminal units, mobile and stationary printer stands, pull-out printer shelves, special accommodations for printer paper, keyboard trays and articulating keyboard arms, central processing unit (CPU) and disc-drive storage units, and turntables.

Don't assume that the library cannot afford a special or custom feature for either a reference or a circulation desk. Discuss desired possibilities with a vendor. Another library may have asked for the item before; therefore, the manufacturer will have already addressed your need, or a similar one.

In summary, circulation and reference desks must be designed to support the needs of the staff and users of a particular library. Although most desks are designed using some standard desk modules, such as shelf units and kneespaces, most desks also include some customized features. It is essential in planning for the present needs of the library, however, to design a desk with built-in flexibility so that the desk can be adapted as library staff, procedures, equipment, and philosophy change.

CHAPTER

5

Chairs

No furniture item in the library receives more use and abuse than the reading chair. In a few quiet libraries, the chair may be used only for its intended purpose: to provide a place for the user to sit while reading or studying. It is not uncommon, however, for a reading chair to be dragged around the floor, to be used as a stool for reaching high places, and to serve as a temporary rocking chair for those who are more comfortable leaning back. The arms of chairs are great for those who enjoy sitting with their legs draped over something. Arms also provide a handle for the person who wishes to grab a chair and move it to a different location. In addition to allowing the traditional kind of use, the reading chair can provide seating for those who wish to sit facing the back of the chair, for those who like to sit on the backrest with their feet on the seat, and for those who prefer to sit close to the person *in* the chair, by sitting on the arm. Finally, the library reading chair can be a source of amusement for young people who like to tip backward the chairs containing their friends. Obviously, it is essential to select a chair that is strong enough to withstand heavy and varied use, especially because it is often expected to last for 20 years or more.

In addition to being sturdy, a reading chair has to be comfortable. For many years, libraries were furnished with sturdy-looking wood- or metal-framed chairs with little style. (From an aesthetic standpoint, it is unfortunate that some of these have proven to be almost indestructible!) Now that librarians are interested in marketing their services, however, it is also desirable to select a chair that is designed to enhance the appearance of the library. If the funds are available, many libraries will choose a chair that does not look "institutional."

When selecting a reading chair for the library, keep in mind that there are a variety of kinds from which to choose: standard wood-framed library chairs, a variety of styles of chairs manufactured by contract furniture companies, wooden captain's or Windsor chairs, chairs with metal frames, stacking chairs designed for meeting or classroom use, chairs originally intended to be used as office side chairs, etc. A library chair does not necessarily have to be one that is marketed or designed for library use. A satisfactory chair may be one that is made by a contract furniture company with a much wider market than libraries. (See Figures 21–26.)

PERFORMANCE TESTING

Regardless of the manufacturer, however, it is essential to gather information about the *performance* of a chair considered for purchase. The qualities that make a chair satisfactory cannot usually be determined just by looking at it; the librarian must obtain some evidence that it can withstand heavy use and abuse over a long period of time.

Thos. Moser reader's side chair. *Photograph courtesy of Thos. Moser Cabinetmakers ©1986.*

FIGURE 21

Steelcase® Snodgrass chair. *Photograph courtesy of Steelcase®, Inc.*

FIGURE 22

Danko Bodyform™ chair. *Photograph courtesy of Peter Danko and Associates.*

FIGURE 24

Lombard Harold Washington side chair. *Photograph courtesy of F. W. Lombard Company.*

FIGURE 25

Thos. Moser continuous arm chair. *Photograph courtesy of Thos. Moser Cabinetmakers ©1976.*

FIGURE 23

Buckstaff® side chair, 6781–333. *Photograph courtesy of Buckstaff®.*

FIGURE 26

The price of a chair does not necessarily reflect its strength; sometimes the price may be more a reflection of the kinds of materials used to make the chair or of its perceived value from an aesthetic standpoint. Furthermore, the reputation of the manufacturer does not necessarily provide a good indication of the reliability of the chair for use in the library.

Information about the capability of particular chairs to withstand heavy use can be obtained in two ways. First, the consumer can contact other libraries to inquire about the reliability of the chairs they have purchased. (The vendor or manufacturer should be willing to provide references to other libraries.) Second, the librarian or designer should obtain the results of any performance tests done on a particular chair. Ideally, *both* performance data and the service history of the product will be available to the consumer.

Consumers can use the results of performance testing to determine whether they are purchasing the level of quality desired in furnishings and to ensure that the most functional, durable, and safe product available will be obtained for the money. When several chairs are considered, test results can be used to justify the purchase of a more expensive chair, if performance tests have demonstrated a longer life for the item with the higher price tag. In other words, the results of performance testing can be especially helpful in using life-cycle costing (also known as cost-benefit evaluation) to justify purchasing a particular level of quality.

Systematic performance testing and labeling of chairs and other furnishings have been done in Europe for several years. In the United States, however, performance tests for chairs are not done on a regular basis by all manufacturers. Librarians will, however, soon have nationally accepted performance standards and testing criteria for library chairs.

In the 1960s, the American Library Association began a testing program for chairs as a first step toward developing standards. The formative studies of Dr. Carl A. Eckelman (professor of Wood Science in the Department of Forestry and Natural Resources at Purdue University), published in 1977 and 1982, were a continuation of these early efforts by ALA. Eckelman's past and current research provide a foundation for the development of systematic performance testing of library chairs in the United States. In 1994, the staff of *Library Technology Reports* once again worked with Eckelman to formalize existing chair performance data into national standards for library chairs. The resulting standards will be similar to GSA performance standards that are currently used for lounge furniture, that is, the standards will indicate the test results needed to designate a chair as light, medium, or heavy-duty. The completed standards will be published in *Library Technology Reports*.

Performance testing is now done by manufacturers in in-house laboratories and by independent testing agencies at the request of manufacturers. As noted above, GSA specifications provide standards that can be used for comparing the relative strength of various lounge chairs. Manufacturers who bid on GSA projects with these specifications are required to certify that the product to be supplied has been tested, and that it can meet the relevant GSA performance standards. The American National Standards Institute (ANSI) and Business and Institutional Furniture Manufacturers Association (BIFMA) also have standards for chairs. These are based on pass/fail-type-tests that essentially establish only minimum standards. The tests are neither as stringent as the performance testing required by GSA specifications for lounge chairs nor the upcoming *LTR* performance tests for reading chairs.

Although performance testing information is not available for some chairs, it is important that librarians know about performance testing and compare any available results, in order to make informed purchasing decisions. Most manufacturers who test their products do not include this information in their literature. The librarian or designer should, therefore, ask vendors or manufacturers for performance testing data. As Eckelman states, "Performance tests will be conducted only if buyers and specifiers use them and only if manufacturers are assured that purchasing decisions will be based, insofar as possible, on the results of such tests and not on sudden whim." (1982, p. 557) In other words, librarians can affect the market by basing purchasing decisions on the performance data now available, thereby forcing all library manufacturers to do testing on a regular basis.

The following discussion summarizes the points of Eckelman's reports that are most relevant to the process of selecting library reading chairs. Readers who want further background about the development of performance testing in the United States and other countries, as well as those who want to study the test results in greater depth, are encouraged to read the complete reports.

Eckelman's studies, in effect, describe what happens to a chair when it is subjected to the many kinds of use noted at the beginning of this chapter. He identified eight forces that are applied to a chair by a user:

1. *Vertical seat forces* are applied to the seat of a chair when someone sits down and remains seated.

2. *Horizontal seat forces* are applied when a user pushes a chair backward, pulls it forward, slides it sideways, or tries to tilt the chair in any direction.

3. *Torsional seat loads* are forces caused by a user's changing position or twisting around in the chair.

4. *Horizontal forces on back rests* are those placed on the back rest when the user leans or tilts the chair back, when the chair is pushed forward, or when it is pulled backward and falls to the floor.

5. *Vertical forces on back rests* occur when a user slides down in the seat, tilts the chair back, or sits on the top of the back rest with her/his feet on the seat.

6. *Horizontal arm loads* are forces caused by a user pushing out on the arms of the chair when sitting down or getting up, and forces that occur when a chair is pushed or pulled sideways by the arms.

7. *Vertical arm loads* occur when a user pushes down on the arms when sitting down or rising from a chair, or when a user sits on the arm of the chair.

8. *Horizontal longitudinal arm loads* are forces that are applied along the length of the arms as someone pushes on the arms of the chair when changing positions or when sitting down or getting up from the chair. (1982, pp. 509-520)

Tests that simulate these forces in the laboratory have been developed for studying the performance of chairs. Testing demonstrates how the joints and members of a chair are affected by use and identifies the components of the chair that will eventually fail. The quantitative data obtained in the tests describe the amount of force the chair can withstand without breaking. When different brands, styles, production runs, etc., are subjected to the same test, the resulting data can be used to compare the relative strength of various chairs.

Usually, the simulated action is repeated 25,000 times at a speed of 20 times per minute with the force applied at a certain load level. The force/load is then increased for the next cycle of 25,000 times, with the force continuing to increase through a certain number of cycles, or until the part of the chair to which the force is applied fails.

Eckelman's research provides some interesting performance data. One of the most important tests for chairs is the front-to-back-load test of seats. Generally, the test determines the resistance of a chair to back tilting and how well the joints were manufactured. In this test, for example, Eckelman found that chairs of the same style, but made by different manufacturers, were able to withstand amounts of force varying by as much as 200 pounds: Some sled-base chairs failed at loads as low as 225 pounds, while others withstood amounts of force as high as 475 pounds. In the same test, stool-type seating (like captain's chairs) varied in strength by withstanding from 175 to 275 pounds. Four-legged chairs withstood amounts of force from a low of 300 pounds to a high of 400 pounds. In other words, among the products tested by Eckelman, a good four-legged chair was found to be almost as strong as a sled-base one; but none of the stool-type seating was as strong as the best four-legged or sled-base chairs.

Another interesting result was found in the side-thrust-load test on arms (which evaluates the resistance of chair arms to side-thrust forces), where chairs withstood forces ranging from a low of 150 pounds to a high of 350 pounds. As Eckelman reported, "These values are of considerable significance because they were all obtained with 'high quality' furniture. They suggest, therefore, the differences in strength that must be expected even from furniture presumably of the same quality." (1982, p. 552)

The Worden Company is one company with a well-developed program of performance testing; its data will be combined with Eckelman's results in establishing standards for library chairs. Worden's 1100 series chair (sled-base with front and back stretchers), for example, completed the front-to-back-load test at the 400-pound level and the vertical-load test on seats at 1,000 pounds. Similarly, the Academy chair (a slat-back, four-legged chair with two side and three cross stretchers and a solid wood seat) completed the front-to-back-load-test at the 400 level and the vertical load test on seats at 1,100 pounds. In its testing, Worden has found that chairs that cannot withstand more than 200 pounds in the front-to-back-load test are not strong enough for library use. On the other hand, chairs that can withstand 300 pounds in the test have not failed in 10 years of library use. The *LTR* tests will establish more precisely the amount of force a chair must withstand in order be classified as light, medium, or heavy-duty.

Buckstaff also has a complete program of in-house performance testing. Its laboratory has the capability for certifying products to meet GSA specifications. Buckstaff reading chairs are currently tested to meet an international standard, ISO 7173:1989.

EVALUATING LIBRARY CHAIRS

According to Eckelman, the evaluation of library chairs involves the consideration of three factors: (1) the overall structural characteristics or design of the chair, (2) the strength of the joints, and (3) the design and strength of the various members or components of the chair. All of these factors should be considered together when selecting a chair. (See Figure 27.) In addition to providing valuable quantitative data, Eckelman's research has generated a body of useful information for comparing the relative merits of various products.

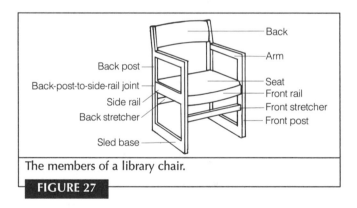

The members of a library chair.

FIGURE 27

Joints

A chair has joints where any two parts or members are joined, such as where the rails are attached to the legs or where the stretchers join the legs. Front-to-back-load tests on the seats of chairs demonstrate that the relative strength of one chair over another is determined more by the joints than by any other component. Similar results were found in side-thrust-load tests on seats: "In chairs of essentially identical construction, chairs with well-made joints were found to be as much as twice as strong as those with poorly made joints." (Eckelman, 1982, p. 540)

Eckelman's research found that the joint most critical to the strength of the chair is the back-post-to-side-rail joint. The testing done by Worden and Buckstaff has sub-

stantiated this. By way of illustration: Buckstaff makes a four-legged, multipurpose stacking chair that has no stretchers; however, the chair tests to meet level five of the international standards primarily because of a patented joint used to join the back post to the side rail. This joint consists of a unique combination of one dowel and a wedge, secured by three screws. The chair is further strengthened by the joints on the front of the chair. The front leg and rail are joined by double dowels and a bolt that threads into a slug embedded in the front rail. Mitre-corner finger joint construction reinforces the front leg and side rail connection.

Most chairs are constructed with glued dowel or mortise-and-tenon joints. The particular construction of the joint is more important than the kind, however. Either a dowel or a mortise-and-tenon joint is satisfactory, if it is constructed correctly. Proper construction can be ensured by having an adequate number of dowels that are the correct size in proportion to the rails, by having enough glue that is well applied, and by having the dowels spaced correctly. In his research, Eckelman found that satisfactory joints on a library reading chair consist of two dowels, each of which is $3/_8$ inch in diameter and two inches long, and which are spaced 1½ inches apart. A well-glued joint is one in which "the walls of the dowel hole have been adequately covered with glue. Simply shooting a small amount of glue into the bottom of the hole in the hope that somehow it will work itself up around the dowel cannot be expected to give adequate glue coverage." (Eckelman, 1982, p. 536)

In addition to the primary joints (dowel or mortise-and-tenon), some chairs also have a bolt-and-dowel nut added where the side rail meets the back post. (See Figure 28.) In his 1977 and 1982 studies, Eckelman considered this a supplemental construction to ensure that the joint will remain sound even if the primary dowel joint fails. Some chairs are also reinforced with glue blocks where the rails and legs are joined. Like the bolt-and-dowel-nut assembly, Eckelman considered the glue blocks as secondary joints to provide added strength to the chair in the event that the primary joints (dowel or mortise-and-tenon) fail. Since 1982, however, testing has demonstrated that both of these types of reinforcement increase the potential for strength of the chair.

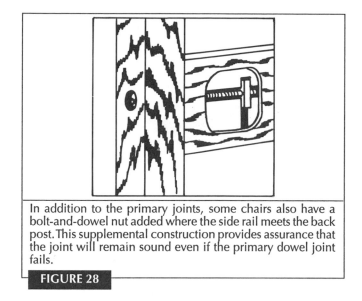

In addition to the primary joints, some chairs also have a bolt-and-dowel nut added where the side rail meets the back post. This supplemental construction provides assurance that the joint will remain sound even if the primary dowel joint fails.

FIGURE 28

Rails and Stretchers

The relative strength of a chair is affected by the size of the rails. The wider the front rail is the greater the potential for strength because the rail allows for wider spacing between the dowels. The number and size of the stretchers used also affect the strength of the chair. According to Eckelman's research, a chair with side stretchers is twice as strong as one without them, and a chair with a large stretcher is stronger than one with a small stretcher. In addition to side stretchers, front and back stretchers help to strengthen a chair, especially when it is subjected to sideways forces. On a sled-base chair, a single stretcher placed in the middle, from one side of the base to the other, helps to keep the two side frames from spreading, but does not provide the *sideways* strength of two stretchers, one on the front and one on the back.

Arms and Posts

An arm on a chair serves to strengthen the chair in somewhat the same manner as a side stretcher. The arm adds to the strength, however, only if it is joined correctly to the frame of the chair. If dowel joints are used, the size and spacing of the dowels and good glue coverage are important. At the back of the chair, an arm that is attached to the front or top of the back post is stronger than an arm attached to the side of the back post. Mortise-and-tenon joints are sometimes used to provide a strong, attractive alternative for joining the arms of the chair to the front post.

An armchair with a continuous front post (that is, the stump of the arm and the leg are constructed of one piece of wood) is stronger than a chair with an arm that requires a joint. In the latter case, the stump of the arm is attached to the side rail and the leg is a separate piece of wood.

The strength of the back post of a chair is determined by the size of the post and the wood used there. The post has to be large enough to remain strong around the area of the dowel joints. The critical back-post-to-side-rail joint can be adversely affected if the back post is constructed of a piece of wood so small that the dowels from both the side and back rails meet at the same point; that is, when a relatively large amount of wood is removed in this one small area where both dowels must meet. Also, a chair with steam-bent curved back posts should be stronger than a chair with back posts cut from straight grained wood. Eckelman explains this as follows:

> "If a part is steam bent from straight-grained stock, the grain of the wood tends to remain parallel to the longitudinal axis of the piece . . . . If a curved part is cut from straight stock, however, the grain of the wood tends to 'run out' of the piece . . . . This condition of the wood is commonly referred to as 'cross grain,' and parts made of cross grain wood are much weaker than parts in which the grain follows the contour of the piece. Back posts of cross grain are more likely to break if the chair falls backward, for example." (1977, p. 410)

Chair Style

Many different styles of chairs can be used satisfactorily in the library. The examples noted earlier illustrate that sled-base, four-legged, and other chairs can be used, if they are well constructed. Performance testing has, however, produced some enlightening information about particular styles.

Eckelman considered a well-constructed sled-base chair to be potentially one of the strongest available. Also, testing of four-legged chairs showed that failure occurred primarily in chairs having relatively small, square back legs. The relative strength of the chair with the stool-type seat was found to depend on several factors: the size of the pins on the ends of the legs; the thickness of the seat and, therefore, the depth to which the end of the legs (the pins) could be inserted into the seat; the number of spindles on the back of the chair; and how well the spindles are glued.

In the testing of Breuer-type chairs with bent metal frames, it was found that cost was not a reliable indicator of the strength of the chair. The strength of this type of chair was found to be dependent on the diameter of the tubing used to construct the frame, the wall thickness of the tubing, the yield strength of the steel used in the tubing, and the location of the holes for the screws that are used to join the seat and back to the metal frame.

In testing its metal-framed Diametron chair, Worden found that the gauge of steel and the type of weld used determine the strength of the chair. Although a brazed joint is more attractive than one that is welded, the strongest joints are those that are MIG (gas metal-arc) or TIG (gas tungsten-arc) welded. (Brazing is similar to soldering in that the heat used in the process does not melt the base metal as welding does. Brazing is done, however, at higher temperatures than those used in soldering.) (See Figures 29–31.)

Based on Eckelman's conclusions, theoretically, the strongest wooden-framed library chair would be constructed with dowel or mortise-and-tenon joints. The dowels would be correctly sized in proportion to the rails, stretchers, and posts and would be placed properly in relation to the other dowels used to join the parts of the chair. Specifically, the dowels would be at least $^3/_8$ inch in diameter, 2 inches long, and spaced 1½ inches apart. The chair would have rails at least three inches wide attached directly to the front and back posts. The chair would have a sled base, as well as front and back stretchers. The arms of the chair would be formed from a continuous front post and would be attached to the front of the back post. If the back post were curved, the wood would be steam bent. For added reinforcement, the chair would have a bolt-and-dowel-nut construction, as well as double dowels at the side-rail-to-back-post joint and glue blocks where the legs and rails join. If it were well constructed, this ideal chair would probably be stronger than what is needed in most libraries. The description can, however, serve as a model when evaluating existing chairs.

SELECTING A LIBRARY CHAIR

Salespeople representing the major library furniture manufacturers all sell a standard reading chair; however, not all of their companies manufacture chairs. Some companies that do not operate chair factories market chairs that have been designed and manufactured to be sold exclusively by them. Some companies operate factories that make chairs for libraries, as well as for other markets. Still other companies sell chairs made in their own factories, as well

Worden Diametron™ chair. The chair is also available in children's sizes. *Photograph courtesy of The Worden Company.*

FIGURE 29

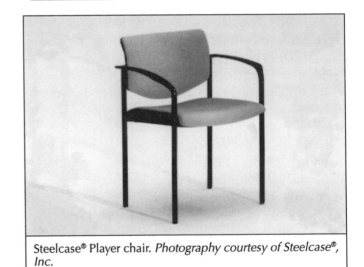

Steelcase® Player chair. *Photography courtesy of Steelcase®, Inc.*

FIGURE 30

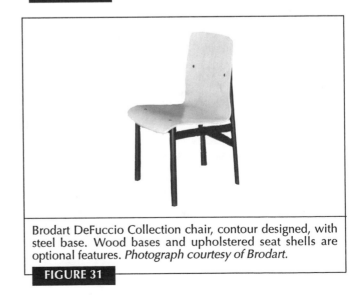

Brodart DeFuccio Collection chair, contour designed, with steel base. Wood bases and upholstered seat shells are optional features. *Photograph courtesy of Brodart.*

FIGURE 31

as styles purchased from other manufacturers. It may be difficult to determine which company is actually manufacturing a chair; however, if a chair has been performance-tested or has a satisfactory service history, that information may not be relevant to the selection decision.

The "standard" reading chair sold by library manufacturers is available either with or without arms, with a sled or four-legged base, with an upholstered seat and back, or with a wood seat and back. The chairs vary in the number of stretchers used, the placement of the stretchers, the size of the backrest and other members, and the manner in which the parts are joined. Some of the chairs have a straight back post, while others have a slight angle at the top of the back post and in the base frame. The seats and backs of fully upholstered chairs are typically made of bent or formed plywood. Wood seats (not upholstered) are constructed of edge-glued pieces of solid wood or of formed plywood covered with a wood veneer.

Upholstered furniture may not be as long-lasting as the all-wood chairs; however, fabric adds warmth to the environment and enhances libraries that are seeking to avoid looking "institutional." In selecting an upholstered chair, it is necessary to consider how easily the chair can be reupholstered. Seats and backs that can be easily removed for reupholstering are an advantage. In some situations customers purchase some extra upholstered seats and backs and additional material. The extra seats and backs can be used to replace worn components on-site, and the worn pieces can be sent out with the additional fabric to be reupholstered. (Upholstery selection is discussed on page 70.)

There is one final consideration when selecting a chair—one that cannot be emphasized enough. When selecting a chair with an arm, it is absolutely essential to make sure that the arm will fit easily under the worksurface of any carrel, table, or other piece of furniture with which it might be used. Knowing the worksurface height of that piece of furniture is not enough. The thickness of the table, desk, or carrel top and the depth of any rail or apron under the worksurface must be taken into consideration. The purchase of stylish arm chairs that do not fit under a table can be an embarrassing and costly error for a librarian or designer.

Generally, the cost of a chair is determined more by the way it looks than how strong it is. Attractive details in the styling, such as open mortise-and-tenon joints on the arms or bent wood frames, add to the cost of the chair. Most chair manufacturers are willing to customize a chair

on request (e.g., add an arch to a standard straight backrest). That distinctive touch will, however, add to the price of the product. In bid situations requiring a sample of the item specified, it is possible that a small, local manufacturer will produce a chair that looks very similar to one made as a standard by a larger company. It is doubtful, however, that the chair will have been performance-tested or have a service history. It is also not unusual for several companies to produce their own version of a chair that is popular. For example, several companies manufacture a chair that is frequently specified for dormitories. The chair allows the user to sit in two positions: flat on the floor or leaning back. Likewise, several companies make A-frame chairs that are similar in appearance.

Many chairs designed specifically for the contract market (rather than the library market) should also be considered for use in the library. When these chairs are considered for purchase, however, it is especially important to study relevant performance testing data or check references of long-term library (or similar public) use.

Dozens of both steel- and wood-framed chairs with sled and leg bases in a variety of styles are appropriate for use in a library. For example, Breuer, Windsor, captain's, and other styles of wood chairs made by a number of different companies are used as library reading chairs. Another choice is a steel-framed chair with a steel, wood, or molded polypropylene seat, designed to be a stacking meeting room chair. These might be used in a library where chairs will have to withstand heavy student use. A high school librarian on a limited budget justified this selection sensibly by reasoning that the advantage to this type of chair is that it is made to be strong, and, if the teenagers manage to break one, it is relatively inexpensive to replace.

In areas where someone is expected to sit for short periods of time, such as at a computerized catalog or at an index table, a bench or stool without a back is often used to discourage the user from occupying the position for long-term reading or studying. Stools, either leg- or sled-base, that match the frame of the reading chair are one choice. If the stool is not a standard product, it should be designed so that its members are proportioned attractively when the basic design chair is scaled down for use as a stool. On the other hand, the construction details necessary for making a chair strong must also be present in the stool. Most companies that make chairs also manufacture stools.

The selection of reading chairs and stools should include consideration of the need to move items out of the way at a table or workstation in order to accommodate a wheelchair. A person in a wheelchair should be able to pull a chair out of the way easily and quietly. A reading chair or stool should be neither so heavy that it cannot be moved with relative ease, nor so light that it falls over when it is pulled.

Dozens of office and contract furniture companies, as well as library manufacturers, make lounge and side chairs that are suitable for libraries. Lounge furnishings are available with either wood or steel frames, with open wood or steel arms and upholstered cushions, with upholstered side panels and cushions, and with butcher block side panels and upholstered cushions. Armless lounge furniture is also available. Waiting areas in libraries often include benches made by contract or library furniture manufacturers. Benches are available with or without arms and with or without backs. (See Figures 32–37.)

The same details of construction that affect the strength of a reading chair determine the strength of the frame of a lounge chair. Performance tests similar to those for reading chairs are done on lounge furniture: back frame tests, backrest foundation tests, arm strength tests, seat load foundation tests, side-thrust leg tests, and leg strength tests. The most stringent standards are those established by the heavy-duty rating for GSA Specification FNAE-80-214. This rating is equal to three 281-pound people sitting on a sofa simultaneously (a total load of 843 pounds) every 25 minutes, 24 hours a day, 365 days a year for 10 years.

With lounge seating, selection involves greater concern for the construction of the seat and back cushions than is necessary when choosing reading chairs. A common problem with a lounge chair is the tendency for the seat to sag or puddle in the center while the rest of the chair still looks fine. Seat cushions are typically constructed of a spring unit covered with some type of foam. The cushions fail either when the springs break or the foam collapses.

Although a particular lounge chair is often selected for aesthetic reasons, the design or style of the item is also very important in determining the ease of maintenance. For example, the arms of fully upholstered chairs or sofas are likely to get soiled quickly. Better choices in areas with heavy public use are chairs with a butcher block panel that serves as an arm, or those with an upholstered side panel that have a wood strip or cap on the top of the arm. For the same reason, a chair with an upholstered seat and back on a bent-steel or all-wood frame might be used. It is also important to consider how easily a chair can be reupholstered. Some furniture designed for offices was designed to be replaced, not reupholstered.

The design of a chair may also have something to do with how it is used. For example, librarians in facilities where a well-known style of swivel chair with a steel frame has been used have reported that children made themselves dizzy and sick by twirling around in the chair. Also, a lounge chair should not be so low or deeply cushioned that getting up is difficult. In public areas, it might also be wise to choose a chair with few cracks and crevices where dirt can collect. In libraries where there is a large transient population, the possibility of body lice infestations should be considered when choosing an upholstered chair rather than an all wood chair.

Before making the final selection of a chair, one or more vendors should be asked to supply samples for the staff to try out. (This is a common practice in the contract and library furniture business.) The staff then has a chance to provide valuable input and to participate in the selection process. In summary, the selection of chairs involves answering some of these questions:

1. Has the chair been used successfully in similar library or other public situations for several years, and/or, are performance data available to attest to the durability of the chair?

2. Does the chair have dowel or mortise-and-tenon joints?

3. Are the chair rails (for a reading chair) wide enough to accommodate double dowels approximately $3/8$" in diameter, 2" long, and spaced $1\frac{1}{2}$" apart? How has the glue been applied?

4. Does the chair have side stretchers, or arms and a sled base that serve as stretchers?

5. Does the chair have front and back stretchers to add strength for sideways forces?

6. Does the chair have a bolt-and-dowel-nut construction at the back post and rail joint and glue blocks to add secondary reinforcement to the chair?

7. Is the chair comfortable? Are the backrest and seat deep enough? Is there enough or too much padding? Is the back at a comfortable angle in relation to the seat? (Obviously, there will be several different opinions about the comfort of a particular chair. It is a good idea, therefore, to have several different people, of varying heights and weights, try out a chair.)

Metro Rossmoor lounge. Designed by Joe and Linda Ricchio. *Photograph courtesy of Metro Furniture. Photo: Steve Burns.*

FIGURE 32

Worden Regis lounge. *Photograph courtesy of The Worden Company. Photo: Julie Line.*

FIGURE 35

Metro Rossmoor bench. Designed by Joe and Linda Ricchio. *Photograph courtesy of Metro Furniture. Photo: Steve Burns.*

FIGURE 33

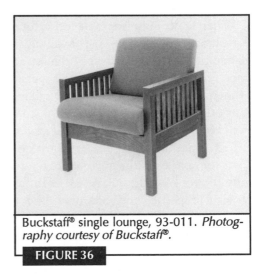

Buckstaff® single lounge, 93-011. *Photography courtesy of Buckstaff®.*

FIGURE 36

Metro Monterey lounge. Designed by Brian Kane. *Photograph courtesy of Metro Furniture. Photo: Steve Burns.*

FIGURE 34

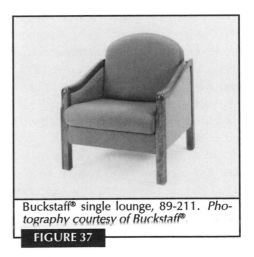

Buckstaff® single lounge, 89-211. *Photography courtesy of Buckstaff®*

FIGURE 37

8. Does the chair design and the kind of upholstery or finish used allow for easy cleaning? Can the chair be easily reupholstered or refinished?

9. Do the construction materials used meet applicable flammability standards?

10. If the chair has arms, will the arms fit comfortably under worksurfaces?

SELECTING UPHOLSTERY

Manufacturers typically offer a limited, standard line of fabrics, leathers, and vinyls for upholstering chairs and lounge furniture. Most companies also sell items "C.O.M." (Customer's Own Material). Selecting material that is not part of a manufacturer's standard line allows for the consideration of a wider variety of upholstery products; however, upholstering C.O.M. may add to the cost of a completed item.

When fabric upholstery is selected for a library project, the librarian or designer can take advantage of performance guidelines developed by the Association for Contract Textiles (ACT) in choosing a specific material. The 34 member companies of the ACT sell more than 90 percent of the textiles specified for the contract market in the U.S. The performance guidelines are a result of the ACT's commitment to industry education, providing standards for textiles in the areas of fire retardancy, colorfastness to wet and dry crocking, colorfastness to light, physical properties, and abrasion. Fabrics that have passed the performance tests required in the guidelines will be identified by the icons on their sample tags that symbolize compliance with specific tests: a *flame* for fire retardancy, an *artist's palette* for colorfastness to wet and dry crocking, a *sunburst* for colorfastness to light, a *star* for physical properties, and a letter A for abrasion (capital "A" for heavy duty and lower case "a" for general contract). The five icons "give architects, designers and end-users a vast amount of performance information in a succinct visual way." (Zelinsky, August 1993) A useful chart developed by the ACT lists the required tests that must be passed to meet the performance guidelines for specific end uses, shows an illustration of each of the five icons, and explains each of the five test categories. According to an article about the performance guidelines, "Specifiers may remain confident that each icon has a thick file full of technical information to explain the testing methods and standards of criteria." (Zelinsky, August 1993, p. 57)

ACT performance guidelines are provided for upholstery, direct glue wall coverings, panels and upholstered walls, and drapery. The guidelines that pertain to upholstery are as follows:

Fire Retardancy: Flammability testing determines a fabric's resistance to burning. (Identifying icon is a flame.)

> Upholstery meeting the performance guideline passes California 117.

Colorfastness to Wet and Dry Crocking: Colorfastness to wet and dry crocking refers to the rubbing off of color from the fabric onto cloth, hands, or other materials that can occur under wet or dry conditions. (Identifying icon is an artist's palette.)

> Upholstery meeting the performance guideline passes AATCC 8-1974 Dry Crocking, Class 4 minimum; Wet Crocking, Class 3 minimum.

Colorfastness to Light: Colorfastness to light refers to the degree to which fabric will retain its color when exposed to light. (Identifying icon is a sunburst.)

> Upholstery meeting the performance guideline passes AATCC 16A-1974 or AATCC 16E-1976, Class 4 minimum at 40 hours.

Physical Properties: Three physical property tests include: brush pill test to determine a fabric's pilling; breaking/tensile strength test to determine the ability of a fabric to withstand tension without breaking or tearing; seam slippage test that relates to the pulling apart of fabrics at the seams. (Identifying icon is a star.)

> Upholstery meeting the performance guideline passes Brush Pill ASTM D3511, 3-4 minimum; Breaking strength ASTM D3597-D1682-64 (1975) 50 lbs. minimum in warp and welt; Seam slippage ASTM D3597-434-75 25 lbs. minimum in warp and welt.

Abrasion: The ability of a fabric to withstand damage from wear and rubbing. ACT has a general contract specification as well as a heavy-duty specification. (Identifying icon is a letter "A" or "a.")

> Upholstery meeting the performance guideline for General Contract Upholstery passes ASTM 3597 modified (#10 cotton duck), 15,000 double rubs Wyzenbeek Method.

> Upholstery meeting the performance guideline for Heavy Duty Upholstery passes ASTM 3597 modified (#10 cotton duck), 30,000 double rubs Wyzenbeek Method or ASTM D4966 (with 21 oz. weight), 40,000 rubs Martindale Method.

The ACT guidelines can be used by anyone specifying fabric for library seating. In regard to the abrasion test, many libraries should consider upholstery meeting the heavy-duty performance, rather the general contract, guideline. In most libraries, upholstery selection will include consideration of the ease of cleaning a particular fabric.

The ACT guidelines refer to the most widely accepted upholstery flammability regulation for furniture, the State of California Standard. (Technical Bulletin 117) More stringent standards, such as the Port Authority of New York and New Jersey and the Boston Fire Department regulations, may also be applicable to fabric selection for a particular area. BIFMA standard F-1-1978 (Rev. A80) includes an ignition test that the GSA requires in its specifications. Check with local and state fire marshals to obtain information about any applicable regulations that will affect your choice of upholstery. (For a list of flammability regulations, see Reznikoff, p. 50.)

California Technical Bulletin 133

Specifiers must be familiar with another flammability regulation known as CAL 133 (California Technical Bulletin 133). CAL 133 is a full-scale fire test for seating furniture manufactured for use in public buildings. The California legislation was enforced March 1, 1992. Cal 133 has gained recognition as a nationally accepted fire safety standard. The American Society for Testing and Materials (ASTM) officially accepted Cal 133 as a voluntary standard in 1993 and published it as ASTM E1537. CAL 117 (mentioned in the previous fabric discussion) was initially developed to provide flammability standards for furniture for buildings with residential occupancy (although it has been applied, through use, to contract furnishings in public buildings as well.) CAL 133 was developed to address the specific fire problems of furnishings in public buildings and public assembly areas. The specific types of buildings to which CAL 133 and similar regulations apply vary from state to state.

A full-scale fire test involves an actual piece of furniture, or a furniture mock-up, that includes all of the essential features of the finished piece. CAL 133 "does not call for tests of small samples of component materials. It requires that a complete seating furniture product be exposed to a large open flame in a specially designed test room. It then measures what happens when the components are used together." ("Technical Bulletin 133: Questions and Answers," p. 3) CAL 133 specifies how the furniture must be tested and how it must perform. Each article of furniture that passes CAL 133 carries a flammability label that states that the item meets the requirements of the standard.

Legislation based on CAL 133 has been passed in the following jurisdictions: Illinois, enforced January 1, 1993; Minnesota, enforced March 1, 1993; New York/New Jersey Port Authority (adopted CAL 133 in early 1993 for buildings and airports under its jurisdiction); Ohio, enforced April 10, 1993. Some of the states in which CAL 133-based legislation has been introduced include the following: Louisiana, Massachusetts, New Jersey, New Hampshire, Washington, and Wisconsin. (Note: Do not rely on this list to determine applicability to a project in your area. Contact the fire marshal in your state to determine what flammability regulations apply to your furniture specifications and which specific furniture items must meet particular standards.) Additional information about CAL 133 can be obtained in a "Questions and Answers" brochure published by the State Department of Consumer Affairs, Bureau of Home Furnishings and Thermal Insulation, State of California; in architecture and interior design magazines; and from furniture vendors and manufacturers.

Tables, Carrels, and Computer Workstations

Several kinds of furnishings with worksurfaces are provided by a library to meet the varied needs and desires of its users. Most libraries supply tables, as well as individual study carrels, for reading and study. Appropriate workstations for computers and other equipment must also be selected for a library. Like chairs, well-made library tables, carrels, and workstations should be serviceable for many years. If the library can anticipate using a table or other worksurface for 30, 40, or even 50 years, a substantial initial investment can be justified. A table must be strong enough to hold equipment and books without sagging, and it must remain stable in spite of being shoved or dragged from place to place.

At least five percent or a minimum of one of each element of fixed seating, tables, or study carrels in the library must comply with the Americans with Disabilities Act (ADA) in regard to dimensions, space allowances, and reach ranges. Accessible worksurfaces for people seated in wheelchairs should have knee spaces at least 27 inches high, 30 inches wide, and 19 inches deep. The top of accessible tables and counters should be 28–34 inches above the finished floor.

These guidelines should, however, be considered minimum requirements. Stanley Pauer, a regular patron of the San Francisco Public Library, provided input to the library staff regarding the needs of wheelchair users for its new Main Library. Pauer stressed that clearance under a worksurface is particularly important. Tables with as much as 32 or 33 inches of clearance are more convenient than tables with only the required 27 inch clearance. Also, tables without an apron and with no legs in the middle are preferable. Pedestals on tables, according to Pauer, get in the way and make worksurfaces less accessible.

When furnishings are selected for a new building, an adult reading table can be specified that includes the required dimensions to make all tables accessible. Or, the basic table or carrel design can be modified to make some worksurfaces wheelchair-accessible. Furniture manufacturers have been constructing tables and carrels with worksurfaces 31 or 32 inches high for years. Special-height accessible tables and carrels should be identified with attractive signage.

Adjustable-height worksurfaces should also be considered for the library. Height adjustment systems, such as Suspa's Movotec hydraulic lift, can be specified for a table to allow users access to an infinite number of height adjustments within a particular range. Both crank-operated and push-button motor-driven mechanisms are available. (See page 153 for Suspa address and telephone.)

Marti Goddard, Deaf Services librarian, San Francisco Public library, recommends oval or round tables for hearing-impaired library users. Because the hearing impaired rely on visual cues for communication more so than other users, tables should be placed in locations that prevent windows from backlighting the face and hands of individuals seated at the tables. Everyone needs to see the face of everyone else, and nobody wants to look around another person to see the face of someone else in the group. Goddard also suggests that tables should not have task lights on them that block the view across a table. Likewise, comfortable lounge chairs should be arranged to facilitate communication. It is especially important that study carrels designed for hearing-impaired users have full panel sides to block visual distraction. In a meeting or conference room, curved tables should be provided to allow for creating a large circle for meetings.

TABLES

Different kinds of tables serve different purposes in the library; however, the elements of design and construction that result in high quality are the same, regardless of the intended use of the tables. The size and number of its members, the construction of the joints, and the strength of the materials used determine a table's durability. For the sake of clarity, the various elements of table construction are discussed separately in this chapter. When evaluating a table, however, it is important to consider all of its components as they relate to each other. The quality of a table depends on engineering that reflects the need for balanced construction; that is, each of the components must be as strong and as well made as any other so that the table does not fail because of one weak element.

Performance testing of tables involves applying forces/loads in the laboratory to simulate use in the library. There are no nationally accepted tests or standards, but library tables, like chairs, can be classified according to their ability to perform under certain conditions, or when acted upon by particular forces. Tables can be compared, for example, in terms of the vertical loads they are expected to carry, their resistance to deflection (stiffness), and their resistance to sideways and front-to-back loads.

Eckelman (1977) recommends that tables be classified as appropriate for light, medium, heavy-duty, and extra heavy-duty usage by comparing data collected in testing various tables. He suggests that vertical loads applied to a tabletop be measured in terms of pounds per square foot. The ultimate load that can be supported by a tabletop, then, must be calculated to take into account the dimensions of the top. For example, a table 60" (5') long x 30" (2½') wide has a top with an area of 12½ square feet (5' x 2 ½' = 12½ sq. ft.); a top 72" (6') long x 30" (2½') wide has an area of 15 square feet (6' x 2 ½' = 15 sq. ft.). If a

heavy-duty table is defined as ultimately holding between 9,000 and 10,000 pounds, a table 60" x 30" would be considered heavy-duty at 850 pounds per square foot (12½ sq. ft. x 850 lbs. per sq. ft. = 10,625 lbs.); while a table 72" x 30" would be considered heavy-duty at 650 pounds per square foot (15 sq. ft. x 650 lbs. per sq. ft. = 9,750 lbs.).

Resistance to deflection can be tested by measuring the amount of sag, or center span deflection, in a table. One criterion used frequently is that the deflection should be no more than $1/360$ of the table's span. This criterion is based on the amount of deflection that can actually be *seen* (rather than measured). Sideways loads are tested in terms of the ability of the legs to withstand floor reaction forces.

Performance tests are obviously valuable in comparing the relative strength of various tables. In order to have more reliable information, however, the performance data should be related to actual use in the library. It would be helpful, for example, to know that a particular model of table 60 inches long by 30 inches wide, with an ultimate load-carrying capacity of 850 pounds per square foot, has been successfully used for five to 10 years in a busy library.

Eckelman identifies four types of four-legged table construction: a simple two-member cantilevered table with a top and legs, a three-member table with a top, legs, and rails; a three-member table with top, legs, and stretchers; and a four-member table with a top, legs, rails, and stretchers. (See Figure 38.) Many different combinations of rails and stretchers are used, such as rails on two sides and stretchers on two sides, or stretchers on two sides and one center stretcher. Eckelman cites four factors that should be taken into account when evaluating the strength of tables.

1. The general nature of the total structural support system.
2. The strength and stiffness of the legs and other supporting members.
3. The strength and stiffness of the top and its reinforcing members (side or center rails), if any.
4. The strength and stiffness of the joints and attachments. (1977, p. 367)

When evaluating tables, several factors about the structural support systems should be kept in mind. For example, on a simple, four-legged table, only the cantilevered legs hold up the top; there are no other supporting members. The strength of the table, therefore, depends entirely on the joints—the attachment of the leg to a steel mounting

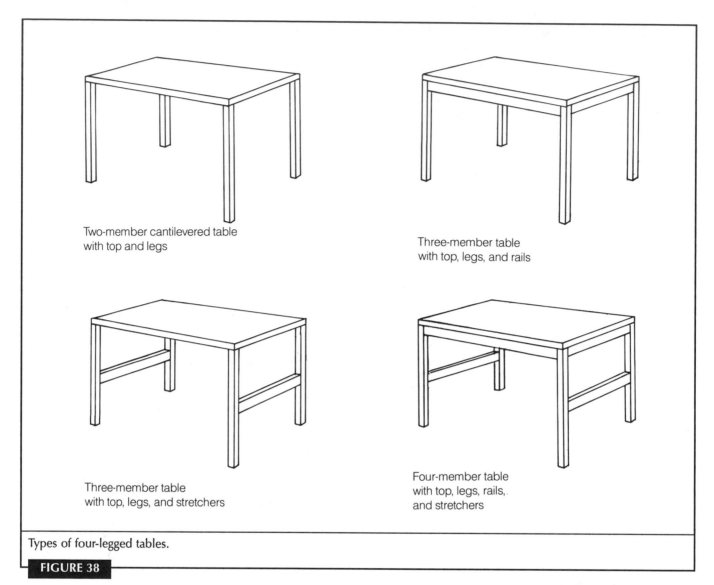

Two-member cantilevered table
with top and legs

Three-member table
with top, legs, and rails

Three-member table
with top, legs, and stretchers

Four-member table
with top, legs, rails,
and stretchers

Types of four-legged tables.

FIGURE 38

plate and the attachment of the mounting plate to the tabletop. Obviously, the construction of these joints should be studied carefully when selecting a table of this type. Furthermore, if a simple cantilevered table is considered for the library, references of use should be obtained and checked.

Although some leg-base tables have *only* side or *only* front and back rails, full leg-and-rail construction (rails on all four sides) provides the best support for a tabletop. The leg-to-rail joints provide resistance to both sideways and front-to-back forces. If the joints are well constructed and the members correctly sized, a table with rails on all sides is an excellent choice for a library. Likewise, a table with full stretchers resists both sideways and front-to-back

forces. A table that has both full rails and stretchers is an extra heavy-duty table. The rails and stretchers resist both sideways and front-to-back forces. Furthermore, the rails support the top well, while the stretchers help to distribute to all four legs the weight applied to the top.

Other table support systems that may be used include the following (see Figure 39):

Leg with wooden header: The header can run either the length or width of the table. The strength of this construction depends on the quality of the leg and header assembly.

Leg with side rails: The legs are joined in pairs rather than individually. The leg-to-rail joints provide strength and rigidity to the table, but do not aid in

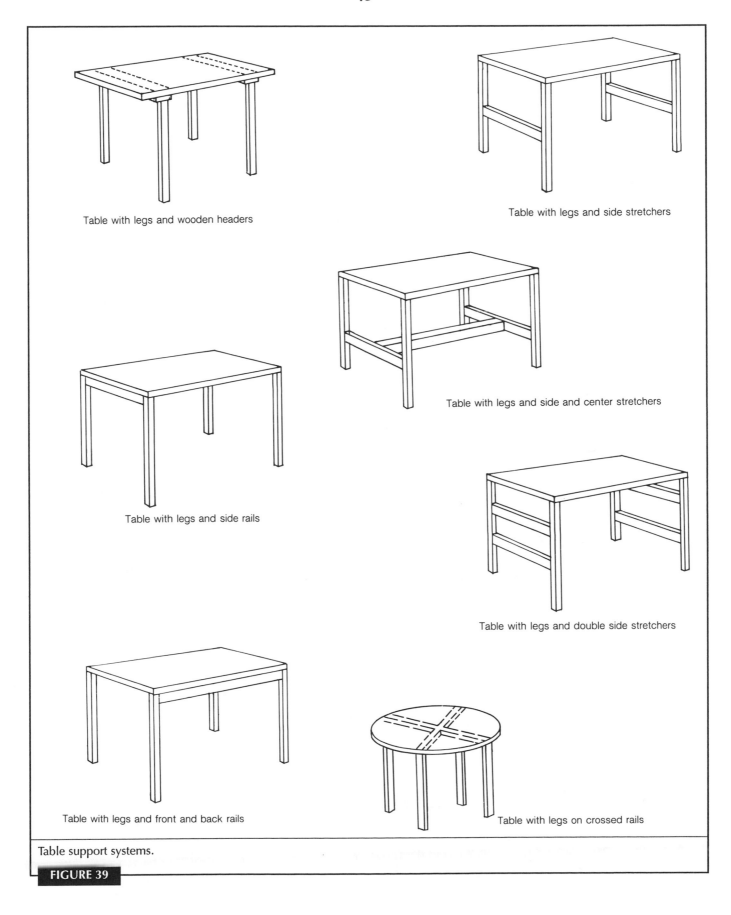

Table with legs and wooden headers

Table with legs and side stretchers

Table with legs and side and center stretchers

Table with legs and side rails

Table with legs and double side stretchers

Table with legs and front and back rails

Table with legs on crossed rails

Table support systems.

FIGURE 39

resisting sideways forces. The durability of the table depends on the thickness of the mounting plates and how well they are attached.

Leg with front and back rails or legs with front and back stretchers: These tables may lack front-to-back strength, so they are sometimes reinforced with panel ends. The rails provide good support for the top along the length of the table. Again, the strength of the table depends on the quality of the joints. Tables of this type that have tubular steel legs should have welded stretcher-to-leg joints to resist sideways forces. Also, the mounting plates should be of substantial size and should be strongly attached to the top.

Leg with side stretchers: Because this construction resists front-to-back, but not sideways, forces, the mounting plate must be particularly strong.

Leg with side and center stretchers: The center stretcher provides some sideways bracing, but does not provide as much strength as a stretcher-to-leg or rail-to-leg connection.

Leg with double side stretchers: The lower stretcher may actually be a sled base. This construction provides good front-to-back strength, but requires bracing for adequate sideways strength.

Leg with crossed rails or leg with crossed stretchers: These support systems are used on round or square tables and should be considered appropriate only for light duty.

The strength and stiffness of a table leg depends on its size and shape and the materials used to construct it. Wood, for example, is not as strong or as stiff as steel, and values for strength and stiffness vary according to the wood used. (See Eckelman, 1977, p. 372, for a table of stiffness values.) The strength of a table leg can be calculated in terms of the amount of floor reaction force it can resist; however, it is unlikely that most consumers will do these calculations themselves. The service history of the product and/or performance data supplied by the manufacturer should be used to evaluate the quality of a leg.

The evaluation of a tabletop must include the considerations concerning wood core material discussed in chapter 2. The strength and stiffness of a top depend on the material and type of construction used. Eckelman notes the advantages of a lumber core over a particleboard top: greater load-carrying capacity, more long-term loading strength, and less possibility of deflection. He does not, however, say that particleboard should not be used in tabletops. Rather, he notes that the thickness of the top should be determined by the strength requirements of the

table. It is important to know that the strength of the particleboard top is proportional to its thickness squared, so a small increase in the thickness adds greatly to its strength. For example, a top $1^3/_8$ inches thick is nearly twice as strong as a one-inch thick top. The advantage of the stiffness of lumber core does not eliminate particleboard as top material; however, when particleboard is used, it should be reinforced with side or center rails along the length of the table. In addition to lumber and particleboard cores, plywood or veneer cores are used for some tabletops. These materials are not as strong as lumber core, but they are stronger than particleboard.

Three types of joints affect the strength of a table: (a) the leg-to-top joints, (b) the rail-to-leg and stretcher-to-leg joints, and (c) the understructure-to-top joints. Leg-to-top joints usually involve the use of an intermediate component, a mounting plate, to which the leg is attached. With steam-bent wooden legs or steel legs, part of the leg may be bent to become the mounting device.

Sometimes the mounting plate is attached to the leg by an anchor screw that is screwed directly into the leg. All of the major library manufacturers, however, supply a stronger leg-to-top joint that is described as being metal-to-metal. This means simply that the primary fastener (bolt or screw) does not go directly into the wood, but rather joins the top and leg by screwing into a secondary metal fastener that is placed in the top or leg.

In the simplest metal-to-metal joint, the mounting plate is attached to the top and leg with bolts or screws that thread into a metal insert. The metal insert is threaded into the wood itself. An even stronger construction (used by all of the major library furniture manufacturers) involves attaching the plate to the tabletop with bolts threaded into metal inserts as described above, and then strengthening the joint by attaching the mounting plate to the leg with one or two machine bolts that pass through the plate and thread into a steel dowel nut (or barrel nut) embedded crosswise in the leg, about 1¾ inch below the plate. (See Figures 40 and 41.)

Metal legs are often welded directly to a mounting plate. The quality of the weld and the thickness of the plate determine the strength of the joint. Eckelman suggests that the plate be at least ¼-inch thick. The leg-to-top joint of a metal table illustrates well the need for balanced construction in a table: each part of the table must be constructed for maximum strength, so it does not fail because of one weak component.

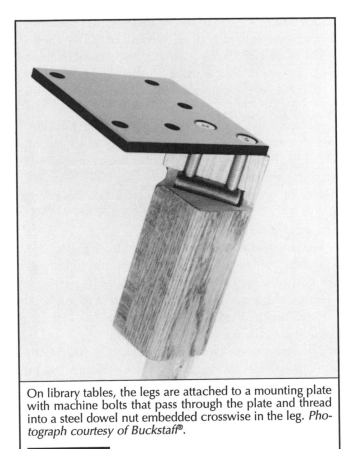

On library tables, the legs are attached to a mounting plate with machine bolts that pass through the plate and thread into a steel dowel nut embedded crosswise in the leg. *Photograph courtesy of Buckstaff®.*

FIGURE 40

The mounting plate is attached to the table top with bolts threaded into metal inserts embedded in the top. *Photograph courtesy of Buckstaff®.*

FIGURE 41

Several different constructions are used for the rail-to-leg and stretcher-to-leg joints. One of the most common is a dowel joint. The factors that affect the strength of a dowel joint in a table are the same as those that are important in chair construction. The strength depends on the size of the dowels, the spacing between the dowels, the kind of wood used, the type and coverage of the adhesive, and the tightness of fit of the dowel. The size of the dowel should be in proportion to the size of the members. The larger the size of the dowels and the wider the spacing between dowels, the stronger the joint will be. One standard that is often used is that the dowel should be at least half as thick as the thinnest of the two members that are joined together. The width of the rail or stretcher is also important: the wider the rail, the stronger the joint.

As with chairs, mortise-and-tenon joints are also used for tables. The tenon must fit snugly into the mortise and the amount of glue used must be adequate. When properly constructed, the mortise-and-tenon joint is slightly stronger than a dowel joint.

Wood corner blocks or metal anchor plates are also used to attach legs to rails. The wood or metal piece is attached to the leg with an anchor bolt. The block or plate is made to fit tightly to the rails by grooves cut into the rail, dadoes cut into the rail, or a full dovetail that joins the block to the rail. When used as the only joinery to attach legs to rails, this type of construction is not considered heavy-duty. Sometimes, however, corner blocks are used as secondary joints to reinforce the primary dowel or mortise-and-tenon joints in the leg-to-rail assembly. This construction can be considered heavy-duty.

In metal tables, legs are joined to the rails by welded miter or butt joints. The larger and heavier the metal tubing of the legs and rails, the stronger the joints. A miter joint is stronger than a butt joint. Also, full welding around the members results in a stronger joint than spot welding. In light- or medium-duty tables, metal legs are also bolted to rails in a type of construction that could be considered comparable to the dowel or mortise-and-tenon joint in wooden tables. The strength of this type of joint depends on the thickness of the metal used in the rails, the quality of any welds used in the joint, the thickness of the rail, the size and spacing between the bolts, and the strength of the leg itself. Anchor plates with anchor bolts are used in the leg-to-rail joints of both metal and wooden tables. The strength of this construction depends on the thickness of the metal anchor plate, and the number and spacing of the welds used to join the anchor plate to the rail.

Stretchers are attached to the leg of a wooden table in much the same manner in which rails are attached. Dowel, mortise-and-tenon, or turned-pin joints (in which the end of the stretcher is turned to form a dowel) are used. As with mortise-and-tenon joints, the strength of the turned pin joint depends on the diameter of the pin, the strength of the wood, the depth of the insertion of the pin end into the leg, the snugness of fit of the pin into the hole, and the amount and coverage of the adhesive used. Stretchers are also attached to the legs with screws or with through bolts and dowel nuts. Screws and through bolts and dowel nuts are also used along with dowels to reinforce a joint.

On metal tables, stretchers may be welded to the legs or attached by some combination of screws and welded plates or tabs. The strength of the joints depends on the quality of the welds and the thickness and strength of the materials used.

Understructure-to-top joints are as important as the leg-to-mounting-plate joints in cantilever leg construction. In order to be considered heavy-duty, cantilevered tables should have steel mounting plates at least ¼-inch thick. Plates $^3/_8$-inch thick are even better. The number of fasteners used and their spacing are also important in determining the strength of the mounting plate-to-top joint.

Metal-to-metal construction, rather than screws placed directly into wood, is desirable in joining the mounting plate to the top. The plate may be joined to the top by machine bolts that go through the mounting plate and into threaded metal inserts in the top, or by bolts threaded into dowel nuts (or bar nuts) embedded horizontally in the top. Another type of construction involves placing bolts through the plate into metal "T-nuts" (metal inserts) embedded in the upper side of a table. The T-nuts are then covered by high-pressure laminate. Eckelman notes that this type of construction is particularly effective with

particleboard. "When installed in this way, the pullthrough strength—actually the failing strength of the nut itself—would be expected to be over 2,000 pounds. As a result, when T-nuts are used in particleboard, during laboratory tests, the corner of the table will likely break off before the T-nuts fail." (1977, p. 396)

Although the primary joints described above are critical to the strength of a table, many library tables are reinforced by the use of U- or V-shaped metal rails or solid wood keels that run the length of the table. This reinforcement is especially important on index, microform, or computer tables, which must sustain heavy loads for long periods of time.

Metal-legged tables appropriate for libraries are made by several manufacturers of both library and contract office furniture. Both Brodart and Gaylord, for example, offer metal-legged tables. Brodart's Quantum table is a cantilevered design. A strip of metal is welded inside the top of the leg, which is attached to the mounting plate by a bolt that passes through the plate and into the metal strip. Worden's metal-legged Diametron table has a metal rail or apron. The mounting plate includes a round hub into which the table leg fits. The leg is held in place with set screws. The rails of the table fit over "tongues" that are also part of the mounting plate and are secured with screws. Metal-legged tables made by contract furniture companies have been used satisfactorily in the library for many years. Kinetics, Fixtures, Protocol, and Group Four are just a few of the contract furniture companies that offer metal-legged tables. (See Figures 42 and 43.)

Another possible option is to select a tabletop made by one company and specify a base from a manufacturer that specializes in selling table components, such as Berco or Johnson Industries. Bases come in a variety of styles—T-base, cylinder, disc- or trumpet-shaped, four- or five-point—and are available in colors, as well as in standard metal finishes. Select a base of an appropriate size to support the top, in order to reduce the danger of the table turning over. Although it will probably not be a major concern, when choosing a table with a pedestal or T-base, keep in mind that users will naturally rest their feet on the base. For this reason, consider how well the base will hold up under this abuse.

Panel-base (or panel-end) tables, as well as leg-base tables, are used in libraries. Panel ends are attached with some form of metal-to-metal joint. Most manufacturers use a wooden cleat that runs the width of the table at each end. Bolts pass through the cleat and into bushings

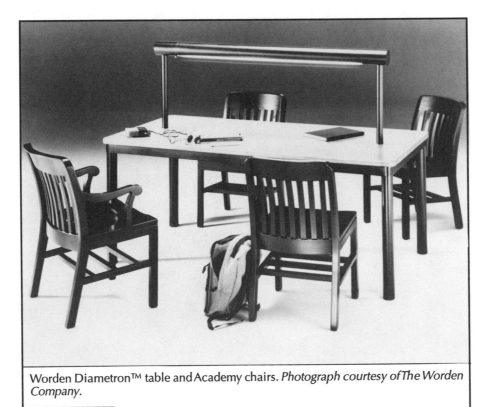

Worden Diametron™ table and Academy chairs. *Photograph courtesy of The Worden Company.*

FIGURE 42

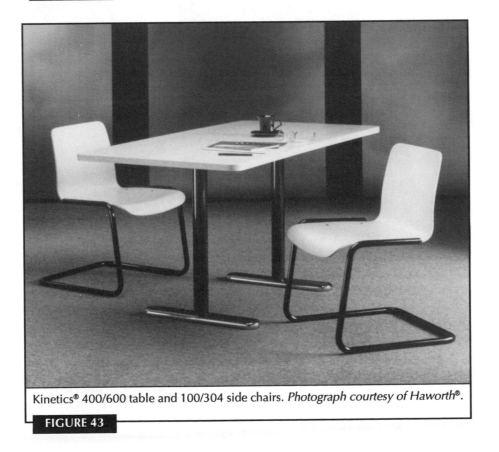

Kinetics® 400/600 table and 100/304 side chairs. *Photograph courtesy of Haworth®.*

FIGURE 43

embedded in the tabletop. Other bolts, placed at a right angle to those screwed into the top, pass through the cleat and into bushings that are mounted on the inside of the panel end. Buckstaff attaches panel ends with a "tight" joint. (The company's standard material is lumber core.) A large "T," approximately three inches long, is routed out on the underside of the tabletop on either side of the keel. The rout holds a bolt that threads into a bushing embedded in the end panel. The joint includes a heavy strip of metal, approximately 1½-inches wide, through which the bolt passes in the cross portion of the "T." As the bolt is inserted, the strip of metal tightens against the lumber core in the cross portion of the T-shaped rout to

hold the top firmly against the end panel. The long bolt provides support for the top, as well as joining it to the panel end.

Panel-end tables must be reinforced with a solid wood keel or brace, 8–12 inches wide, that runs the full length of the table and attaches to the panel ends. Two keels should be used on tables that are 48 inches wide, or more. The size of a table alone, however, does not determine the number and size of the keels needed. How the table is used is also very important; a table that will be used to hold heavy equipment will need more than one keel and, possibly, a center support panel. Keels are attached in much the same manner as end panels. Wood cleats are

Worden Academy-style table (modified design by the author) and Academy chairs, Pitkin County Library, Aspen, Colorado. *Photograph courtesy of The Worden Company. Photo: Paul Colburn.*

FIGURE 44

Table, chairs, and bookcase from Metro's Manhattan Collection of Library Furniture. Designed by Brian Kane. *Photography courtesy of Metro Furniture. Photo: Steve Burns.*

FIGURE 45

placed on either side of the keel. Bolts are then threaded through the cleats into bushings in the underside of the tabletop and other bushings in the keel. Worden reinforces this joinery with a metal L-bracket that attaches to the end panel and to the underside of the keel at either end of the table. The attachment of the keel should involve inserting fasteners into the keel perpendicular to the grain of the wood. When a keel is attached only at the end, where fasteners are inserted parallel to, rather than across, the grain of the wood, there is a greater possibility of the fasteners pulling out or becoming loose.

Tabletops are usually faced with laminate or veneer. When a high-pressure laminate is used on a worksurface, the customer has a choice of using a color or a wood grain laminate that matches the wood used on the frame or base of the table. Although some manufacturers claim that tables with plastic laminate surfaces are preferable in busy libraries, high-quality wood veneer or butcher block tops have been used successfully for years in many libraries. Different tables in the same library can have different surfaces. Wood veneer, for example, might be used on reading tables, while high-pressure laminate is used on tables

Thos. Moser round reader's table (Series 30). *Photograph courtesy of Thos. Moser Cabinetmakers © 1993.*

FIGURE 46

holding microfilm or computer equipment. Or, wood might be used on the tables for adults and laminate used on the tables for children.

Tabletops can be edged with laminate, vinyl, or a strip or band of solid wood. Laminate edges cannot be shaped like wood or vinyl, and are apt to chip or break. In most cases, a vinyl edge band can be splined to a table edge in place of a wood edge band that is standard on a particular table style. Several contract furniture companies market tabletops as a standard product with edge bands made from highly impact-resistant plastics that are fused to the core.

Wood edge bands can be either "internal" or "external." Internal edge bands, used less frequently than external edge bands, are pieces of solid wood that are applied to the core material before the veneer or laminate and backer are attached to the surface. An internal edge band is, therefore, attached to the core material and is held in

Worden's DeGilde® is a modular system of tables, carrels, and shelves available in a wide range of options, including the reference/index unit shown here. Designed by James Bubb. *Photography courtesy of The Worden Company. Photo: Bill Sharpe.*

FIGURE 47

place by the face veneer or laminate and the backer placed over it. The internal edge band is milled to the specific shape desired after the face and backer materials have been applied. Tabletops constructed of 19-ply wood core material, such as Gaylord's Informa® series, require no edge band. Like an internal edge band, the 19-ply core material itself can be shaped to form a finished edge.

External edge bands are pieces of solid wood that are applied to the core material after the veneer or laminate and backer are attached to the surface. External bands are available in many different shapes, ranging from a square to a full radius edge. The bands can be as thin as $\frac{1}{8}$-inch or as thick as needed. Narrow bands, ¾-inch or less, are usually attached to the table edge only with glue, while wider bands are splined or tenoned and glued to the core material. The splining ensures that the edge band will be positioned correctly and allows more surface for glue coverage. (See figure 48.)

The same library manufacturers who make wood shelving and circulation desk units also make tables. Most of them make leg-base as well as panel-end tables, which are available in several different styles and at several different prices. Although each company uses a particular core material as its standard, most of them will manufacture in either lumber core or in particleboard faced with either wood veneer or high-pressure laminate. Some also make tables with a butcher block worksurface. In addition to leg-base and panel-end tables, library and contract furniture manufacturers make trestle-style tables and tables with metal or wood pedestal bases. A library often has more than one style of table in order to make the interior more interesting, to provide users with a choice of reader stations, and sometimes, to make more efficient use of space. More round than rectangular tables, for example, can fit into a given space because the chairs of one table do not have to be placed back-to-back to the chairs at the next table.

In summary, the following questions should be answered when selecting a table:

1. Can the manufacturer or vendor provide performance data and/or information about the service record of the table? Can the supplier justify the design and construction of the table? (In other words, has the table been engineered to withstand vertical loads and sideways and front-to-back forces?)

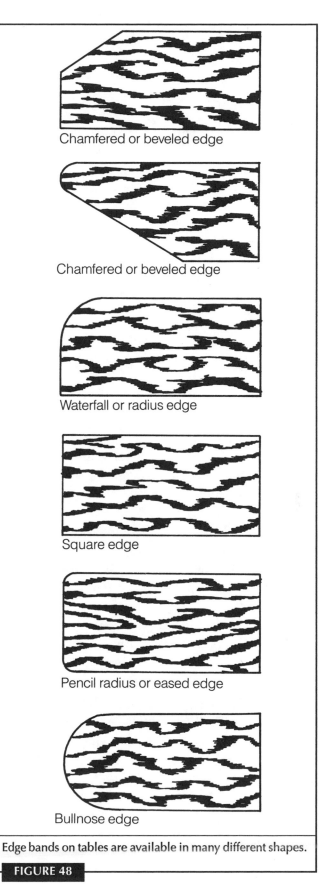

Chamfered or beveled edge

Chamfered or beveled edge

Waterfall or radius edge

Square edge

Pencil radius or eased edge

Bullnose edge

Edge bands on tables are available in many different shapes.

FIGURE 48

2. If the table is a simple two-member, cantilevered design, are references available to verify that the critical joints are constructed well enough to keep the table from racking or wobbling?

3. Does the table have additional members—panel ends, rails and/or stretchers—to add strength to the table?

4. Are the components of the table appropriately sized to accommodate the size and number of fasteners used? For example, are the legs and rails large enough?

5. Are the joints well constructed? Are metal-to-metal joints used to attach the leg to the mounting plate, and the mounting plate to the top, and to attach panel ends to the top and keels? Are dowel, mortise-and-tenon, or pin-end joints used to attach rails and stretchers to legs?

6. Are the number and kinds of fasteners used appropriate for the core material? Is the core material thick enough to provide good screw-holding power?

7. Are particleboard cores reinforced along the edge with solid wood bands where necessary?

8. Is the table braced or reinforced along its length with metal rails or wooden keels of the appropriate size and number?

9. Does a very long table have center support added to keep it from sagging?

10. Is the worksurface material appropriate for the use anticipated? Can the worksurface be easily maintained?

11. Does the table have any special accessories needed, such as task lighting, or electrical outlets?

STUDY CARRELS, WORKSTATIONS, AND OTHER LIBRARY TECHNICAL FURNITURE

The elements of construction that result in high-quality library tables are the same ones that should be used in making other pieces of technical furniture including: index and stand-up reference tables, computer and microform tables or workstations, audiovisual stations, carrels and carrel tables, and atlas and dictionary stands. Although this chapter's discussion of study carrels and workstations focuses on computer furniture, the information covered is relevant to the selection of any piece of furniture that will hold equipment.

Careful planning of all furnishings with worksurfaces in the library—study tables and carrels, computer and microform workstations—will ensure that use of the items can change as the library changes. Following such an approach, study carrels can become computer carrels; pieces designed as computer carrels for the future can be used as study carrels now. A library designed with maximum flexibility includes study tables that can be adapted to allow for convenient use of equipment on the worksurface, both equipment that is provided by the library and equipment that is brought to the library by users (laptop computers or calculators). In fact, all of the adult reading table designed for the new San Francisco Main Library can provide work-surface-level access to power and the library's computer network.

Large computer tables or carrel configurations should include electrical systems and wire management channels similar to those described for service desks. Furniture items designed to hold library-owned equipment should have power and data outlets below the worksurface. Items designed to hold user-owned equipment should have power and data outlets conveniently located above the worksurface.

Study Carrels

Many library users prefer individual study carrels rather than tables. Leg- and panel-base carrels are available in several styles: with full panels 48-inch high on three sides, with 48-inch-high panels that extend along the back and about halfway across the sides of the carrel, or with a rail four to six inches high around three sides. Carrels with panels often have a shelf placed above the worksurface on the back panel, with task lights mounted under the shelf. The carrels are then equipped with electrical components to provide power for the task light and/or for equipment to be used there. Individual carrels are available in double-faced units, with two study areas back to back or as single units. When ranges of either single- or double-faced carrels are constructed, the units are purchased as starters and adders, with each range requiring one starter. Four-place carrels are also available in a pinwheel or swastika arrangement.

The attachment of the worksurface is as critical to the construction of a carrel as is the joining of a top to the panel end of a table. In many cases, the joinery is similar—bolts through wood cleats into bushings in the top and sides of the carrel. Buckstaff uses the same tight joint on carrels that it uses on panel end tables. Worksurfaces are also joined to carrels with metal brackets that serve the same purpose as the wood cleats. (See Figures 49-51.)

Workstations for Computer, Microform, and Audiovisual Equipment

All of the library furniture manufacturers offer workstations, tables, and carrels to accommodate computers, CD-ROMs, microform readers and reader/printers, and audio-visual equipment. Often the same basic design can be modified to accommodate varying kinds of equipment. A wide range of styles of furniture can be used to hold electronic equipment. Although many standard products are available, library furniture manufacturers offer a variety of options; they expect to-make modifications to standard pieces to accommodate the needs of a particular library. (See Figures 52-56.)

Several different kinds of furnishings are used to hold computers within a single building: single carrels, mul-

tiple workstations in starter-adder configurations, double-faced carrels in starter-adder configurations, single- and double-faced equipment tables with two to six workstations, and round or hex-shaped (or half-hex) stations that can be used in an open area or around a building column. (Round or hex-shaped workstations have an advantage in that power and data entry from the building can occur

BCI's Living Library modular table system is available in a wide range of configurations. *Photography courtesy of BC Inventar.*

FIGURE 50

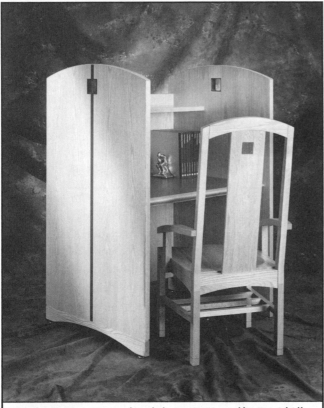

WordenTempus™ carrel and chairs. Designed by David Allan Pesso. *Photograph courtesy of The Worden Company.*

FIGURE 49

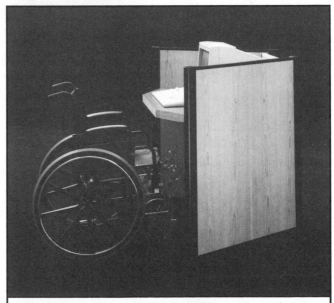

Brodart computer carrel with wheelchair-height worksurface from the DeFuccio Collection. *Photograph courtesy of Brodart.*

FIGURE 51

Modified Worden Academy-style computer stations custom-designed by the author for Pitkin County Library. Aspen, Colorado. Used with Worden stools. *Photograph courtesy of The Worden Company. Photo: Paul Colburn.*

FIGURE 52

in the center of the furniture where the wiring is not exposed to view.) Double-faced pieces of furniture with several workstations are very large and may be out of scale in a small building or space. In a small building, therefore, single-sided workstations 30–42 inches deep may be more desirable than double-sided workstations that may be as large as 60–84 inches deep.

It is a challenge is to design a workstation that is functional and attractive for the items used now, but is flexible enough to allow for using different equipment in the future. Although computers and other equipment can be placed on leg-base tables and carrels, a piece of furniture

with panel ends does a much better job of accommodating wire management channels and power/data distribution. On a leg-base table, power and data cords can enter the furniture through a hollow leg or through a chase attached to the leg; however, because the area under the table is exposed, the floor box containing the building power and data, the power entry device in the furniture, and the wire management channel are visible and often unattractive. On a piece of furniture with panel ends, power and data entry devices are usually placed at the end of the table, in the middle of an end panel, where they are partially hidden by the end panels. Also, on panel-

Modified Worden Diametron™-style computer stations, custom-designed by the author for Frankford Village Branch, Carrollton Public Library, Carrollton, Texas. Used with Steelcase® Snodgrass chairs. *Photograph courtesy of The Worden Company. Photo: Paul Colburn.*

FIGURE 53

base furniture, the wire management channel can be hidden between two keels in the center of the table or behind center panels.

Furniture for computers may have worksurfaces divided by panels that create individual workstations, or the furniture may have one single shared worksurface that holds several pieces of equipment. One long shared tabletop may offer more flexibility by allowing the use of larger equipment or more pieces of equipment on the worksurface in the future. Computer workstations can be at a sit-down height of 29 inches, wheelchair-accessible height of 31 or 32 inches, or standing height of 39 inches. Most libraries provide workstations of varying heights to accommodate the needs of all users. Tables or carrels with

adjustable-height worksurfaces have an advantage in offering flexibility to the library.

The size of worksurfaces to hold PCs for CD-ROM products and on-line catalogs is very important. A PC workstation with monitor and keyboard requires a worksurface that is a minimum of 30 inches deep from front to back. When selecting new furniture for purchase, libraries that are currently using dumb terminals for the on-line catalog should take into consideration the possibility that the smaller terminals may be replaced eventually with larger computer workstations connected to a local area network. Also, additional pieces of equipment not currently used, such as printers, will require space when they are added to a single workstation.

Workstations built in a starter-adder style with intermediate panels between worksurfaces. The workstation configuration was designed by the author and made by The Worden Company for Clayton Library, Houston Public Library. Steelcase® Sensor chairs are used here. *Photo: David J. Lund.*

FIGURE 54

In determining the depth of a workstation, provide enough space to allow some flexibility in the placement of the terminal and keyboard. Also, allow space at the back of the equipment to accommodate cords and cables and to allow access to power and data beneath the worksurface. As in a service desk, cords and cables can drop through a slot at the back of the worksurface or through grommets in the worksurface. A slot allows more flexibility in the placement of equipment, and the back panel on a piece of furniture serves to screen the back of the equipment. Overall, therefore, worksurfaces to hold a PC workstation should be a *minimum* of 30 inches deep, while depths of 36–42 inches may be preferred. (Microform reader/printers require very deep worksurfaces. In a

library where large reader/printers will be placed on furnishings, consider the maximum depth of worksurface needed.)

Likewise the width of a workstation must take into consideration the use that is made of the furniture item now, as well as possible uses in the future. Experience has shown that a space 30–36 inches wide may not be sufficient; a space 42–48 inches wide may be needed to accommodate a PC, a printer, and ample work area for the user.

Card Catalogs and Book Trucks

In spite of the increase in computerized catalogs over the last few years, librarians are still buying card catalog cases

Computer workstation custom-designed by the author for Helen Hall Library, League City, Texas. Double-faced, stand-up tables of the same design are also used in the library. Tables and 1100 series stools were manufactured by The Worden Company. *Photo: David J. Lund.*

FIGURE 55

and library furniture manufacturers continue to make them. Most catalog trays are now plastic rather than wood; the craftsmanship required to construct a wood catalog tray with full dovetail joints now makes the wood trays too expensive for most libraries to purchase.

Card catalogs are available with leg and full-panel or open-panel bases. The cases are made in vertical styles 60 inches or more high and "range" or "rancher" styles, 40–45 inches high. Card catalogs can be purchased as a unit or in modular sections. There is no standard size for catalog cases. If the library plans, therefore, to add cases

someday, it would be best to select initially a standard product from a manufacturer with a history in the business who is apt to be around in the future. Catalog cases made in special sizes or with special finishes can become a problem. Custom work may be affordable when purchasing the initial catalogs because of the quantity involved, but when a smaller number of pieces are needed later, the custom work involved may be very expensive.

Well-constructed card catalogs will last for years. All of the elements that determine quality in the wood construction of other library furnishings are applicable to cata-

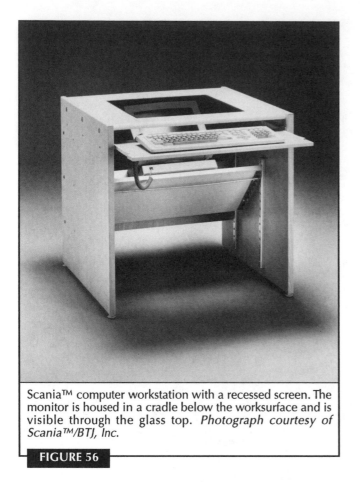

Scania™ computer workstation with a recessed screen. The monitor is housed in a cradle below the worksurface and is visible through the glass top. *Photograph courtesy of Scania™/BTJ, Inc.*

FIGURE 56

log cases: the materials used, the kinds and construction of joints, and the overall support system. In addition, a high-quality card catalog has the following attributes:

1. The trays move easily in and out of the box openings and are interchangeable with any other trays in that unit.

2. The side rails for the trays are constructed of solid wood, so they do not wear away with the friction of the moving tray.

3. The wood drawer fronts are attached to the plastic trays with a joint that imitates the dovetail or rabbet in all-wood cases.

4. The hardware on the drawer front is metal rather than plastic.

5. The case is adequately supported and does not sag in the middle. (Keels or intermediate panels are used to provide extra support for leg-base and open-panel-base cabinets.)

6. Sliding reference shelves are constructed of wood, rather than plastic, so they will not bend or break.

Wooden book trucks are usually purchased along with library furnishings. All of the major library manufacturers make them. Although they are subjected to very heavy use and abuse, a good wooden book truck should be serviceable for many years. A poorly constructed book truck is difficult to maneuver, becomes wobbly as the joints and wheels fail, and is more apt to tip over than a well-made truck. The book truck should be constructed of lumber core or solid edge-glued lumber. On high-quality trucks, the shelves and end panels are connected with mortise-and-tenon joints; the underside of each shelf is reinforced with a glue block. Rubber bumpers specified on the sides and the bottom shelf of the truck will help to prevent damage to walls, shelves, etc., when they are bumped by the truck. Most trucks have two swivel and two stationary wheels. For stability, the wheels should be five inches in diameter.

CHAPTER

Planning and Selecting Furnishings for Children's Areas

The selection of furniture for children involves many of the same considerations used in choosing furniture for adults; however, planning spaces for young people is done from a different perspective than that used in planning spaces for adults. Special spaces for children in public libraries have attracted a great deal of attention in the library profession in recent years. The opening of the Children's Center at the Dallas Public Library in 1989 and the planning of children's areas in other large libraries (Sacramento Public Library and Denver Public Library, for example) have encouraged creativity among library designers with regard to spaces for children.

Successful planning for children's areas, as with entire library buildings, is based on input from users and staff. Successful children's librarians are often special people in a public library who are admired by a following of dedicated young library users. Children's librarians who do their job well can provide valuable information during the library planning process. Based on their experience, librarians who work with children on a daily basis can tell a design team what elicits enthusiasm and interest from children in a library, what kinds of furnishings and equipment create problems, and what elements are needed in a children's area to support the work of the staff.

The planning process used by the Denver Public Library exemplifies one method for gathering input from the users themselves. Planning for the Children's Library of the Denver Central Library began by conducting a series of five focus groups discussions throughout the city. The groups included children of varying ages and ethnic backgrounds from various geographic locations around the city. As noted in an article about the project, "The objective of this research was to understand how children currently use the library and to explore their preferences for new technologies and innovative services." (Sandlian, p. 17)

The experience of Denver and other libraries provides planners with a list of qualities that young people and staff find desirable in spaces for children. Children express an interest in having public library spaces that:

- are accessible and welcoming;
- are safe and comfortable;
- are special, joyous, colorful, and fun;
- do not have a school-like atmosphere;
- allow for some noise and activity; and
- allow for both privacy and interacting with other people at different times.

Kin-der-Link™ stools double as seats and desks. The bent plywood stools are stackable and linkable for group seating. *Photograph courtesy of Skools, Inc. patent and trademark holder of Kin-der-Link™, New York, New York USA. Photo: D. Hamerman.*

FIGURE 57

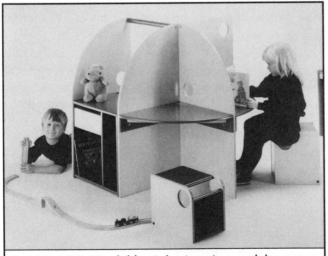

Scania's COPLA™ children's furniture is a modular system that includes tables, stools in two seat heights, and carrel configurations. *Photograph courtesy of Scania™/BTJ, Inc.*

FIGURE 58

Slatwall browser truck designed and manufactured by Library Display Design Systems. *Photograph courtesy of Library Display Design Systems. Photo: K. Ribnicky.*

FIGURE 59

The staff of children's areas would like to have spaces that:

- are separate from adult areas, but are visible and easily accessible;
- attract children to use the library;
- can be controlled by the staff to provide a safe environment for users;
- market library materials and services successfully;
- are designed to support the interactive nature of children's services (staff and users, children and parents, caregivers and children, a young person and other siblings or peers);
- provide maximum flexibility to allow for changing collections, equipment, displays, arrangement of furnishings, areas of emphasis, and services.

These desired qualities for children's libraries can be used as guidelines for planning widely varying spaces. Input from staff and users suggests that the following considerations should be included in the planning of any children's area:

1. The location and design of the entrance to the children's area is particularly important. The entrance should be readily visible from the other parts of the library building and should attract children by its design or by its color. The entrance to the children's area should provide the nonverbal message to a child that "I'm welcome." The scale of the furnishings and fixtures should make the area inviting to children.

2. The children's area should provide some visual stimulation to make the environment interesting. Colors should set the mood of the space.

3. The children's area should include a variety of spaces (if space is available). Spaces should be available for various age groups of young people and for various activities and interests. Some

Entrance to the children's area, Frankford Village Branch, Carrollton Public Library, Carrollton, Texas. Children's reference desk, custom-designed by the author with Worden Diametrix™ accents. Entrance design by HH Architects, Dallas, Texas. *Photograph courtesy of The Worden Company. Photo: Paul Colburn.*

FIGURE 60

spaces should allow a single person or a parent and child to read quietly in a semi-private environment; other spaces should allow for more activity and interaction, noise, and group activities.

4. The design of the children's area should reflect the interactive nature of library services for young people. The arrangement of the area and the furniture itself should enhance sharing and communicating. The furnishings should facilitate group activity.

5. Library services to young people begin at birth. The children's area should provide learning experiences for preschoolers that will enhance their prereading skills and provide services, collections, and activities appropriate for school-age children.

6. The design of the space and the selection of furnishings should be based on providing a safe and comfortable environment for young library users.

7. Just as in the rest of the library building, built-in flexibility should be a primary concern in designing the space.

Unfortunately, children's areas are sometimes designed without input from experienced librarians, and sometimes children don't respond to a feature in a library as adults expect. If library planning involves touring other buildings, do not assume that a particularly interesting feature in a children's area, such as a multilevel storytime pit, has been used successfully or is appropriate for every library. Ask the library staff who have used the space to discuss the advantages and disadvantages of elements of interest in the children's area.

Computer stations custom-designed by the author with Worden Diametron™ accents for the children's area of Frankford Village Branch, Carrollton Public Library, Carrollton, Texas. Diametron™ chairs are shown at the workstations. *Photograph courtesy of The Worden Company. Photo: Paul Colburn.*

FIGURE 61

Keep in mind that the design of a library space will affect how children behave in the library. Even the simplest platform or change in floor level in the children's area is apt to result in running and jumping. As one librarian wisely stated, "Don't lure a child into an activity and then reprimand her/him for the resulting behavior."

The design of a children's area often reflects the philosophy of the library manager in regard to services for young people. Some librarians continue to view a traditional library collection of books, audio-visual materials, and periodicals as appropriate for the children's area. Other librarians hold the opinion that the children's area should provide a greater variety of kinds of materials for young people to explore, including science centers with live animals, microscopes, and space to conduct experiments; educational manipulatives (toys!); arts and crafts centers; and computer centers.

Proponents of science centers note that activities that take place in such spaces appeal to children's natural curiosity and expose them to an investigatory process. Science centers also promote the idea of the "partnership" that should exist between local schools and the public library in educating young people; the public library is often open when schools are closed. The science center serves preschoolers and families who are involved in home schooling, as well as children who attend formal classes in local schools.

The value of parents and children reading together in the library and at home is well accepted. Toy collections, science activities, and computer centers in the library pro-

vide additional opportunities for parents and caregivers to interact with children.

Library planners hold varying views about how the children's area in a public library should be designed. Some people prefer to have the children's area designed as a reflection of the adult area, with furnishings that are smaller versions of the adult furniture and with one color scheme used throughout the library. Other people prefer the children's area to have an entirely different color scheme and children's furniture that does not imitate adult versions in other parts of the library. Final decisions about the children's area often reflect a compromise between these two extremes. Colors may be the same throughout the building, but furniture styles differ; or colors may differ in the children's and adult areas, but some details on the furnishings may remain the same in both areas. The design of the children's area may depend on the size of the building. In very small libraries, adult and juvenile areas are usually separated only by the furnishings; staff at one desk must be able to view both the adult and children's area. In this situation, design of the adult and children's areas are usually coordinated in some manner by carpet, by color, or by furnishings.

Many styles and brands of children's furniture appropriate for the library are now available. Children's furniture is manufactured by companies that serve libraries generally, by companies that market to schools and libraries, and by companies that serve the general contract furniture market. At one time, library chairs and tables for children were merely downsized versions of standard

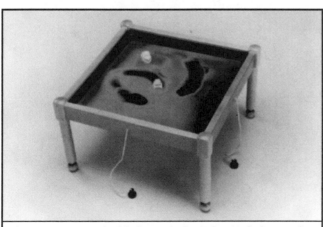

The magnetic sand table has wands underneath the top that are used to move vehicles through the sand to create imaginary highways and construction sites. Designed by Harry Loucks. *Photograph courtesy of The Children's Furniture Company. Photo: David Sharpe.*

FIGURE 62

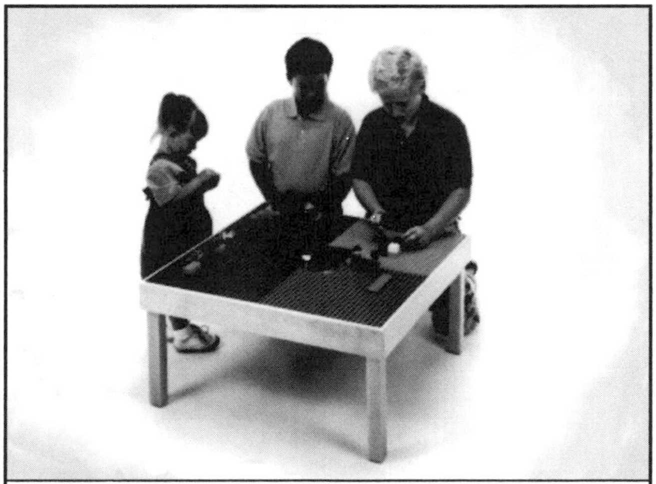

Table Toys®, available in several sizes and heights, can be used with Lego®, Duplo®, and other similarly sized blocks. *Photograph courtesy of Table Toys®, Inc.*

FIGURE 63

Bodyform™ table and chairs for children. *Photograph courtesy of Peter Danko and Associates.*

FIGURE 64

ICF's Aalto multi-section table and chairs for children. *Photograph courtesy of ICF.*

FIGURE 65

Modified Worden Academy-style chairs and tables in the children's area of Pitkin County Library, Aspen, Colorado. *Photograph courtesy of The Worden Company. Photo: Paul Colburn.*

FIGURE 66

Metro's Rubber children's furniture. Designed by Brian Kane. *Photograph courtesy of Metro Furniture. Photo: Steve Burns.*

FIGURE 67

Leaf chair and table. The chairs are available in five different back shapes. Designed by Christopher Murray. *Photograph courtesy of The Children's Furniture Company. Photo: David Sharpe.*

FIGURE 68

Shape-stacking chairs used with a Tip Toe table. The chairs are available with circle, square, or triangular backs. Designed by Christopher Murray. *Photograph courtesy of The Children's Furniture Company. Photo: David Sharpe.*

FIGURE 69

chairs and tables designed for adults. Little attention was paid to the need to proportion the members of chairs and tables as they were redesigned for young people. The major library and contract furniture manufacturers, however, have become more responsive in the last few years to the need for better, more attractive products for children. Many of the products now available are shown in the accompanying photographs.

Although no ADA guidelines presently relate specifically to children, the selection of worksurfaces for the children's area of a library should take into consideration barrier-free access for young people. Some guidelines for children's furnishings developed by The People's Center for Housing Change are provided on page 26.

Throughout this book the emphasis has been on selecting high-quality library furnishings that can withstand heavy use from "the public": local residents, high school and college students, or the staff of a company. The ultimate testers of quality in library furniture are, however, children. It is very important when selecting children's furniture to research use of the product. Obtain the service history of the product by talking to librarians who have used the items under similar conditions. Even heavy schoolroom use does not equal the amount of unintentional abuse to which children's chairs or tables in a pub-

lic library are subjected. For example, one library selected a very expensive European line of plastic children's furniture that was promoted as being able to withstand use in a busy preschool-age classroom. The tables and chairs looked indestructible; however, they all were destroyed by "normal" use in the public library within a couple of years' time.

Juvenile furniture is not used only by children. Most of the chairs selected for children should be capable of providing seating for adults as well. The arms of children's chairs get in the way of adults; most of the reading chairs in the area should, therefore, be armless. Adult-sized and child-sized rocking chairs are also popular items and are often used in children's areas. (Lombard is one company that makes a reasonably priced rocking chair in two sizes.)

It is imperative that children's reading chairs are well balanced and designed in such a manner that they do not tip over easily. The selection of children's chairs involves seeking a compromise between a chair that is heavy enough not to tip over and light enough for children to move. As with seating for adults, obtain sample chairs from vendors and have them "child-tested" at your library before making a final selection.

Too often, toddlers, the ones who seem most to enjoy climbing on a chair just their size, are neglected as librar-

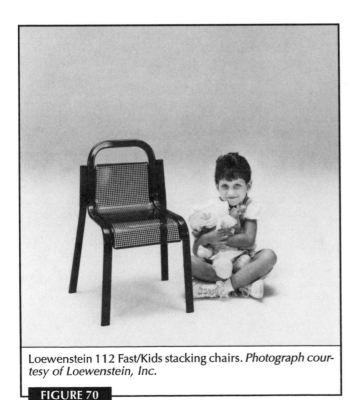

Loewenstein 112 Fast/Kids stacking chairs. *Photograph courtesy of Loewenstein, Inc.*

FIGURE 70

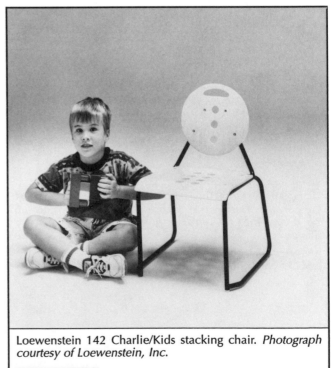

Loewenstein 142 Charlie/Kids stacking chair. *Photograph courtesy of Loewenstein, Inc.*

FIGURE 71

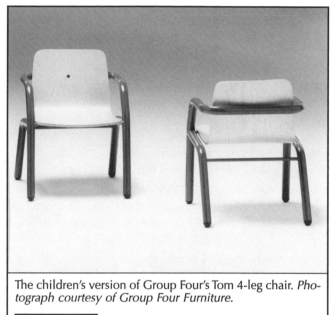

The children's version of Group Four's Tom 4-leg chair. *Photograph courtesy of Group Four Furniture.*

FIGURE 72

Kinetic®'s Scamps[RD] children's furniture. *Photograph courtesy of Haworth.*

FIGURE 74

Nemschoff children's table and chairs. *Photograph courtesy of Nemschoff Chairs, Inc.*

FIGURE 73

ians compromise by selecting larger furniture in order to maintain one consistent style. If funds are available, it may be preferable to have more than one size of furniture in the juvenile area: very small tables and chairs near the picture book shelving for toddlers and preschoolers up to age three or four, and larger furnishings for youngsters between the ages of five and eight or nine. In some cases, a third category of users—young adults—might be distinguished also.

The youngest library users should have tables approximately 20–22 inches high and chairs with a seat height of 12–14 inches. The older children will require tables about 24–26 inches high and chairs with a seat height of 15–16 inches. Some young adults areas are furnished with chairs of standard adult height used with a table 26 or 27 inches high, rather than the standard adult height table of 29 inches. (Other librarians advocate that furniture in the department should include just two sizes of furniture: preschool sizes with seat heights of 14 inches and adult sizes with seat heights of 18 inches. This point of view is based on the belief that by the time children are five or six years old, they are ready to use an adult-sized chair.) Just as with adult furniture, if reading chairs for children have arms, it is important to make sure that the arms will fit comfortably under the worksurface. Also, there should be ample leg room between the seat of the chair and the underside of the table. Tables and chairs for parents and caregivers should be provided adjacent to collections selected especially for adults, such as books on parenting and child care, and close to the toddler section for supervising young children.

Furniture for children should not have any sharp corners. Round or oval tables are safer than square or rectangular tables and enhance the tendency of children to interact with each other. A low table (approximately 15 inches high) provided without chairs can be used by children seated on the floor for reading and doing puzzles and by toddlers who pull up and stand by the table.

The strength of a chair or table for children depends on the same construction features that determine the strength of an adult chair or table. Chairs can be selected that have wood seats and backs, upholstered seats and backs, wood seats with upholstered backrests, or upholstered seats and wood backs. Most children's librarians prefer wood seats for maintenance reasons; however, fabric or vinyl upholstery is sometimes chosen over wood because the materials add color to the area.

Backless stools, rather than chairs, are sometimes preferred for use at on-line catalog and computer workstations. One library that provides numerous computers and educational software for children notes that computer use often involves more than one person, for example, an adult and one or two children, or two or more children. In order to accommodate the users comfortably, therefore, each computer station should include three stools, and, just as with computer stations for adults, each workstation should be 42–48 inches wide. An adult stool or chair with a seat height of 18 inches can be used with children's computer stations that have a worksurface 27–29 inches high.

To be approachable for children, the information desk in the children's area should be an appropriate height: a desk with a standard 29-inch-high worksurface and a 36-inch-high transaction top works satisfactorily. Children can see the person standing behind the desk, and the transaction top keeps the staff's paraphernalia out of sight and out of reach. The desk should be located, if possible, away from the adult area and in the part of children's area that is designed for activities of an interactive nature.

Color can be provided in children's areas by specifying plastic laminate tops on tables, counters, and desks; by selecting stained wood-framed furnishings or metal furnishings with epoxy-coated frames in bright colors; or by adding visually interesting accents, such as neon signs, cloth banners, or upholstered cushions. Every children's space should have plenty of display capabilities that add to the visual interest of the area. Tackable walls rather than framed bulletin boards should be specified. An empty bulletin board makes a negative statement; an empty tackable wall is just that, a wall.

In keeping with the concept that libraries serve people from birth, the discussion of "furniture" can be stretched to include provision of a place for diapering a baby conveniently and safely. However, ready-made, wall-mounted changing tables are a liability consideration for the library because of the weight and hygienic restrictions placed on the products by the manufacturers. A simple alternative is to build a large seat or bench in the rest room adjacent to a sink. The module addresses several needs and has several advantages over a changing table: The bench is

Texwood dictionary stand for children has a sloped top and two shelves for additional storage. *Photograph courtesy of Texwood Furniture Corporation.*

FIGURE 75

Texwood reading seat for children provides 14-inch-high bins for storage. *Photograph courtesy of Texwood Furniture Corporation.*

FIGURE 76

large and sturdy enough for changing toddlers, as well as babies; the adult doesn't have to leave the baby alone on the surface to walk to the sink (but can sit next to the child for changing, hold her/him on the bench, and still reach the nearby sink for water); the bench can be used by a mother breast-feeding a baby; and a child can sit on the bench to wait for an adult (rather than sitting on the floor).

Satisfying early experiences in a library contribute to lifelong library use. A young person should always feel welcome upon entering a children's library and should have a positive experience during each visit that encourages her/him to return again and again.

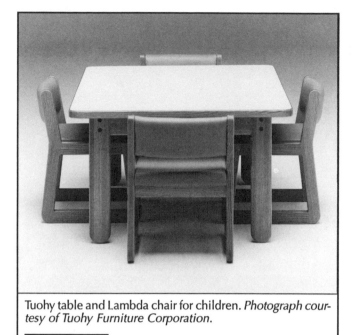

Tuohy table and Lambda chair for children. *Photograph courtesy of Tuohy Furniture Corporation.*

FIGURE 77

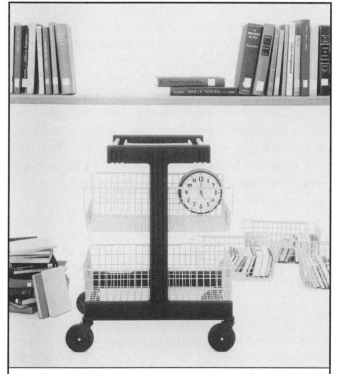

Worden's Media Transport Cart can be used to store and move materials for children's programs and activities. *Photograph courtesy of The Worden Company.*

FIGURE 78

Steelcase®'s Activity Carts are available in widths of 36 inches and 48 inches and are offered with optional footrails, tote bins, and power strips. *Photograph courtesy of Steelcase®, Inc.*

FIGURE 79

CHAPTER

Furniture for Work Areas

Anyone who visits a library is immediately aware of the highly visible library employees who check out books or answer questions at the reference desk. However, those librarians or members of the support staff who play a vital role *away* from public view are often forgotten or ignored. Unfortunately, some vendors and design professionals do not understand that a wide range of library functions have the same power distribution and wire management requirements of a general office. Although there is a difference between contract office furniture and many items manufactured for use in the *public* section of the library, furnishings used by staff in workrooms and technical services areas are the same as those used in any office.

Libraries are in various stages of transition from conventional to automated offices. Unfortunately, funds are often not available for completely refurbishing an office area to accommodate new equipment and procedures. Administrators recognize the necessity for allocating funds to purchase furnishings for public areas; afterall, expenditures for these items will be readily noticed by those receiving service or those responsible for funding. Staff members, therefore, often receive the short end of the proverbial stick and may be left with makeshift workstations, desks designed for typewriters no longer used, odds and ends of furniture, and jerry-built power distribution. In many libraries, technical services functions are allo-

cated inadequate space. Staff members are forced to share much of their work area and have little privacy and definition of their "territory;" many tasks are going on in one small area so noise and distraction are common problems.

Librarians with funds for renovating work areas or building new facilities have a unique opportunity to furnish space that will accommodate the automated office now and in the future. Furthermore, they have an obligation to their organization to take advantage of current knowledge of human factors in the workplace by designing areas that contribute to the productivity of the employees and that are safe, comfortable, and functional.

The details of building design—power distribution into and throughout the area, acoustics, lighting, heating/ ventilating/air conditioning (HVAC), and the structure itself—are crucial to the success of work areas. Indoor air quality, ADA concerns, and the importance of coordinating power and data in a building and its furnishings (issues discussed in chapter 2) are all considerations relevant to the design of staff, as well as public, spaces.

Mistakes made in designing work areas may cause costly problems later. Poorly designed work spaces (or makeshift accommodations) have one or more of the following: lighting that is inappropriate for computer use or other tasks; inadequate acoustical treatment of noisy areas; dangerous and unsightly power distribution involving extension cords, cables taped to the floor, dangling wires and power poles; and HVAC that does not provide a comfortable environment for the staff or correct conditions for proper maintenance of equipment.

ISSUES RELEVANT TO SELECTING FURNISHINGS FOR WORK AREAS

Although the subject of furnishings for the workplace is too extensive to cover comprehensively here, the discussion in this chapter does point out the importance of making thoughtful decisions when purchasing task furniture and does provide many suggestions about the questions and issues that should be raised with vendors about their products. Just as with furnishings for the public area of the library, life-cycle costing of products to be purchased for the workplace should be considered. A little more money spent on an initial investment of furnishings can save hundreds of dollars in replacement costs in the future. Task furniture—chairs, desks, files, etc.—should be serviceable for 10 to 20 years or more.

The same considerations of function, maintenance, and appearance that are used to select library furnishings for the public area of a library are used in choosing task furniture also. Aesthetics may be a secondary issue in selection, while function and maintenance are of primary importance. As in library planning generally, flexibility should be a major consideration in selecting furnishings for work areas.

Workplace issues that are of concern to general office employees are matters of concern to library staff members also. According to data collected in the *1991 Steelcase Worldwide Office Environment Index,* 85 percent of the workers in the United States report that they are using computers, and 33 percent are using their computers five or more hours a day. These figures have increased from five years ago, when 66 percent of the workers reported using computers and only 21 percent used them five hours or more a day. The increase in the use of computers has been accompanied by growing concern about work-related health issues, such as eyestrain, radiation, and cumulative trauma disorders (CTDs). Eighty-nine percent of U.S. workers reported in the Steelcase survey that it is very important for them to have the right tools and resources to do their jobs correctly. Adequate worksurface and storage/file space; comfortable, adjustable seating; proper lighting; privacy; and comfortable heating and air conditioning in the workspace continue to be matters of importance in the physical environment of staff. (Steelcase Inc., 1991)

In libraries, as in any office environment, computer users are subject to a wide range of repetitive strain injuries, including back pain; eye and muscle fatigue; and soreness in the lower arm, wrist, and hand. The Herman Miller company has identified five variables that may play a part in the high incidence of job-related health concerns: (1) job design (movements and repetition required by the job), (2) equipment design, (3) furniture design, (4) worker habits (how the person performs the job), and (5) overall worker health. (Herman Miller, Inc., 1991) All of these variables involve ergonomic issues. Ergonomics is the aspect of technology that is concerned with the application of biological and engineering data to problems relating to people and machines. In the workplace, ergonomic issues involve the relationships between people, their equipment, and the tasks they perform. In order to reduce the incidence of work-related injuries, responsible library employers must address ergonomic issues in the work environment by designing jobs properly and by providing appropriate furniture and equipment that will allow employees to work safely.

Unfortunately, many library work areas are improperly furnished because of a lack of funding to replace out-of-date items or because of a lack of understanding of the health issues related to unsuitable furniture. For example, desks and worksurfaces that were designed for typewriter use cannot be used safely and comfortably for most computer work. The desk top is the wrong height; the worksurface is not deep enough to hold a terminal and keyboard; and no accommodation is made in the furniture to manage power and data safely.

Just as libraries are encouraged to take a proactive approach to maintaining indoor air quality and achieving barrier-free design, organizations are encouraged to take a proactive approach in addressing workplace safety issues that will, in all likelihood, be mandated by law in the future. At the national level, the Occupational Safety and Health Administration (OSHA) is preparing proposed legislation that will mandate measures to prevent or control workplace hazards, including those related to the design of workstations and work methods. Existing and anticipated state and local regulations also affect the selection of furnishings and the design of work areas. A number of states already have OSHA-approved ergonomic and safety regulations in place. In San Francisco, an ordinance that was approved and later repealed set standards of acceptability with regard to chair adjustability and support, computer viewing area and quality, workstation height and support, lighting, glare and noise levels, document placement and screen image, job design, rest breaks, and ergonomic training. Although the San Francisco law was overturned, the ordinance has served to focus concern nationwide on the possibility of legislation that will mandate ergonomic standards in the workplace.

Industry standards, as well as laws, are applicable to office furnishings. Manufacturers of high-quality furnishings for work areas design and engineer their products to comply with all applicable industry standards. For example, customer-responsive manufacturers comply with ANSI/HFS 100-1988 (American National Standard for Human Factors Engineering of Visual Display Terminal Workstations) in regard to dimensional requirements for workstations and task seating. The standard is currently under review and will soon be updated and expanded. Two other recently revised standards are ANSI/BIFMA X5.1-1993, American National Standard for Office Furnishings–General Purpose Office Chairs–Tests, and ANSI/BIFMA X5.6-1993, American National Standard for Office Furnishings–Panel Systems–Tests. A committee of ANSI, known as Z-365, is currently writing a standard for the control of workplace cumulative trauma disorders. Although application of an ANSI standard is voluntary, the work of Z-365 could become the basis for future OSHA regulations. In addition to the national industry standards identified here, some companies are using ISO 9241, an international standard, as their guide in regard to ergonomic issues.

Decision makers in the furniture selection process do not need to know all of the details of laws and standards affecting task furnishings; however, it is important to be aware of ergonomic issues, to identify any state and local regulations that apply to a particular library, and to discuss compliance with regulations and guidelines with vendors. Both manufacturers and suppliers should be able to provide information about their products as they relate to laws and standards.

Barrier-free design of work areas includes considering the same factors that are used in space planning and selecting furnishings for public areas of the library. In workstations, 60 inches of clear floor space is required for turning a wheelchair. The use of an L-shaped, rather than a U-shaped, workstation is one way to eliminate the potential problem of adequate turnaround space in a workstation. Space under worksurfaces should be kept free of all obstacles. Components in a workstation should be planned to allow easy access to all items needed to com-

plete a job. ADA guidelines mandate the maximum high forward reach from a wheelchair of 48 inches and minimum low forward reach of 15 inches. The maximum high side reach from a wheelchair is 54 inches and low side reach is no less than nine inches above the floor. Knee spaces should be a minimum of 27 inches high, 30 inches wide, and 19 inches deep. The tops of worksurfaces should be 28–34 inches above the floor. Haworth, manufacturer of office furnishings and panel systems, makes the following recommendations in designing barrier-free workstations:

- Worksurface heights with a clearance of 30 inches to allow a wheelchair to slide underneath the worksurface and to access the full depth of a worksurface.
- Worksurface depths of 24 and 30 inches.
- Curved wraparound worksurfaces, adjustable keyboard pads, and sloped worksurfaces.
- Files a maximum of three drawers high.
- Overhead storage mounted no more than 62 inches from the floor.
- Smaller width overhead storage compartments that are easier to open from a wheelchair.
- No overhead storage above corner worksurfaces.
- Pedestals located away from main worksurface to allow for maximum wheelchair clearance.
- Worksurface-height access to power and data outlets and channels.
- Height-adjustable worksurfaces.

(From Haworth, not dated)

Steelcase suggests in its literature on ADA that the level of panels for workstations designed for hearing-impaired staff should be placed below a level that will allow the user to see co-workers from a seated position. Windows in the panels will serve the same purpose as lowering the panels. (*Americans With Disabilities Act*, Steelcase Inc., 1992)

DETERMINING WHAT IS NEEDED

Decisions made in designing work areas and selecting furnishings should be based on a clear understanding of: (1) personnel, space, work flow, and equipment needed for the tasks to be performed in the work area now; (2) possible growth and changes needed in the size of the staff, space, equipment, and tasks to be performed in the future; and (3) special needs of the staff now and in the

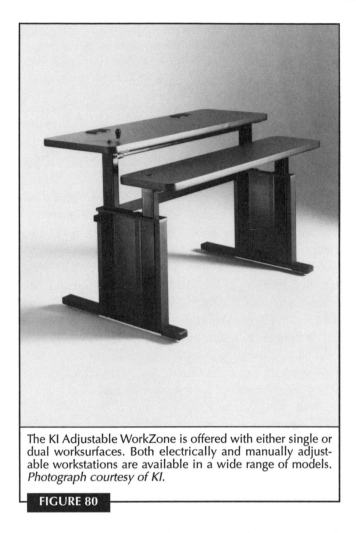

The KI Adjustable WorkZone is offered with either single or dual worksurfaces. Both electrically and manually adjustable workstations are available in a wide range of models. *Photograph courtesy of KI.*

FIGURE 80

future. A library that is planning or redesigning a work area should conduct a formal audit or informal assessment to gather information needed to make sound decisions about work areas. Information can be collected by having staff members complete a survey form or by conducting interviews or meetings with staff. For a major renovation or building project, the interior designer or consultant will conduct the audit with the assistance of the library staff. For a small project, the library staff may gather and use the audit themselves and provide relevant information to the architect. (Representatives of major contract office furniture manufacturers will provide direction and assistance in performing an audit and planning a work area if you express serious interest in their product.)

Some of the information to be gathered in an assessment of work areas generally includes the following:

- Number of private offices required.
- Maximum number of workstations to be assigned to individuals.

- Maximum number of workstations to provide shared space or space for equipment to be used by more than one person at different times.
- Special areas needed, for example, conference and training rooms.
- For a technical services area as a whole, a formal or informal flowchart that illustrates how materials move through from department to department, from receiving to the library shelves.
- For each department (for example, receiving, cataloging, book return), a formal or informal flowchart that illustrates workflow through the department.

The general information gathered regarding work flow will be used to determine the adjacencies of departments within the building and/or the layout of workstations within a department.

In addition to the general information collected in the workplace audit, the following kinds of information should be gathered for planning individual departments or workstations:

- Kinds of tasks performed at each workstation or each type of workstation (individual or shared), such as data entry only, computer use and manual work, discharging returned books, sorting mail, reading, conferencing with other employees, checking returned audio-visual materials, answering telephone reference questions, etc. (In some situations, it is also necessary to note how tasks are performed and how various tasks are carried out in a single workstation by an individual.)
- Kinds and maximum amount of materials to be stored at each workstation or each type of workstation, such as book collection, computer printouts, large computer manuals, paper in legal-sized files, plastic book covers, mailing supplies, etc. (Sometimes appropriate storage of materials may depend on how they are used with other items located in the workstations. Note how materials should be stored in relation to other items and how they are used in performing a task.)
- Kinds of equipment to be used at each workstation or each type of workstation, such as computers, scanners or light pens, printers, calculators, microform equipment, telephone, fax machine, typewriter, etc.
- Approximate dimensions and power and data requirements of equipment to be used at each work-

station or each type of workstation. (The same information needed for coordinating power and data with the building as discussed in chapter 2.)

- Special equipment or furnishings needed in or adjacent to particular workstations, such as loaded book trucks, drafting table, adjustable-height worksurface, guest chairs, conference table, display capabilities, etc.

The information gathered about specific work area needs can be used to determine the approximate size of each workstation or type of workstation and each office. Individuals who perform several different kinds of tasks that require different kinds of space usually require a larger workstation or office than those individuals who perform only one task repeatedly.

The workplace audit provides the information needed to ensure that workstations enhance the ability of staff to perform their work efficiently. A well-designed workstation should have the following characteristics:

- The overall size is adequate to allow for ease of movement from one task to another or from one part of the workstation to another.
- The overall arrangement of the workstation facilitates efficient work performance.
- The area under the worksurface is free of obstructions that might interfere with movement around the workstation.
- The workstation includes all of the elements necessary to perform the job, such as worksurfaces, special computer accessories, storage components, and conferencing area.
- The worksurface is adequate in size and dimensions to accommodate all needed equipment and to allow for safe and effective performance of all tasks to be completed in the workstation.
- Worksurface heights are appropriate for the tasks to be performed (standing, seated, computer use); tilted and height-adjustable worksurfaces are provided where appropriate; and worksurface heights allow adequate clearance from the floor and from the seat of a chair to the underside of the worksurface.
- The workstation provides the privacy needed to carry out all aspects of the job successfully.
- The workstation has appropriate storage components that facilitate ease of access.

- The workstation has built-in flexibility and adjustability to allow for changes in personnel, tasks, and equipment in the future.
- The work area has adequate lighting, acoustical treatment, and display capabilities.
- Power and data distribution and wire management are handled safely and conveniently.
- The workstation is attractive, comfortable, and easy to maintain.

Most libraries have open office areas for technical services and support functions; the individual workstations are not enclosed by panels or walls that run floor-to-ceiling. However, administrative and supervisory staff are usually assigned office space that is fully enclosed. Office system panels that are less than ceiling height don't offer enough privacy for most supervisors, and although high panels provide visual privacy, conversations taking place inside a panel enclosure can be heard by those nearby. A workplace created by a panel system in an open office environment is not satisfactory, for example, for a counseling session between a supervisor and an employee.

Work areas can be furnished with conventional freestanding furniture (desks, tables, lateral or vertical files, and credenzas), with furniture that is part of an office panel system, or with a combination of freestanding and system furniture. Freestanding furniture includes traditional wood case goods, as well as steel office furnishings. The concept of system furniture is one that is familiar to librarians who are used to working with shelving and other items constructed in 36-inch modules. Panel systems define individual work areas and make the most efficient use of space by utilizing modular components available in fixed sizes (worksurfaces, file and box drawer pedestals, and overhead storage compartments).

Numerous products representing a wide range of prices and a wide range of levels of quality are available. Many manufacturers offer more than one line of furniture with costs and level of quality varying from one product line to another. It is important to consider information about the manufacturer as well as the specific products selected for purchase. The parts of office systems, chairs, and freestanding furnishings are not standardized among manufacturers; replacements for lost or damaged parts must be obtained from the company that currently manufactures the furniture line. (Note: The ownership of particular office furnishing lines changes as businesses are bought and sold. An item purchased from one manufacturer originally may be available from a new owner later.)

Steelcase® Context® system used for computer workstations and offices. Shown with Steelcase® Sensor chairs. *Photograph courtesy of Steelcase®, Inc.*

FIGURE 81

It is important to know whether or not a manufacturer has been making office furnishings for a number of years and is likely to be around for several years to come. One key to this information is the warranty offered by the company. A company that offers a five- to ten-year warranty should be considered more reliable than one that offers only a one-year warranty. The reputation of the manufacturer is also important. The giants in the industry are well known, and the service histories of their products are readily available. Other indications of the reliability of the manufacturer include the following: (1) the company is involved in new product development that demonstrates customer responsiveness and a commitment to technology; (2) the manufacturer has a continuous program of quality control and product performance testing; (3) the company is concerned about indoor air quality and compliance with the letter and the spirit of the ADA; and (4) the products are readily available from reliable dealers who provide satisfactory installation, user training when necessary, and service after the sale.

Many libraries choose modular panel systems or a combination of panels with freestanding furniture in order to have the flexibility needed in the automated office. Furniture systems also accomplish the following: define personal work space, provide privacy, alleviate some of the problems of distractions and noise, aid in the organization of work, direct communication between particular staff members, and allow for time-sharing of equipment. Panel systems are designed to make the most of the vertical space in each workstation. Spaces can be reconfigured, enlarged, or reduced as tasks are reorganized.

The selection of an office system to specify for the library may involve talking to the representatives of several manufacturers and comparing their furnishings before deciding what to specify. For a large building project, the selection process may be much more complicated. The planning process for the work area of the San Francisco Main Library, for example, involved gathering the input of the staff and completing an extensive study of desirable workplace features and available products.

Early in the process at San Francisco, full-size mockups of typical workstations were constructed by the interior designers to allow the staff to observe and discuss desirable options in regard to worksurface heights, depths, and shapes; panel heights; overall size of the workstation; and types of overhead and pedestal storage. In order to study basic performance characteristics and features of systems furniture, the design team issued a preliminary questionnaire concerning products to 12 manufacturers of 24 office systems. The questionnaires were evaluated by the design team with regard to performance, aesthetics, indoor air quality, and manufacturer. From the initial information gathered, the design team selected nine systems made by nine manufacturers (narrowed to eight eventually) for further study. The design team and the library management team then completed showroom tours to study and observe the nine systems. The tours allowed the team to begin identifying the furniture system characteristics that were desirable for the library project. Following the tours, a detailed questionnaire was issued to the remaining eight system manufacturers. The questionnaire covered, for example, panel types, construction, and dimensions; worksurface construction, finishes, and shapes; storage components; accessories; electrical systems; and lighting. The questionnaires were used to give each of the eight systems a numerical rating. Four systems were eventually selected from the eight to provide the basic information to be used in preparing specifications for the project. The resulting specifications included the performance, aesthetic, and indoor air quality criteria that must be supplied by the furniture system purchased for the library.

Dozens of companies manufacture and sell office furniture systems. High-quality panel systems are constructed mainly of steel, with some wood members or wood

veneer surfaces. The structural panels that define workstations and support the components of the system are available in several widths and in a variety of heights, ranging from approximately 34 inches high to ceiling height. Acoustical and tackable panels are frequently used in open office situations to aid in noise reduction; however, glass, vinyl-clad, or veneer- or laminate-faced surfaces are also used on panels. Panels are available with chrome, wood, painted, and fabric-covered trim or caps. Panels support brackets used to mount components of a workstation and contain channels for handling wire management and power, data, and telecommunication distribution throughout a unit. Panels allow for configuring and clustering workstations in many, many ways.

If a manufacturer sells freestanding furnishings, as well as office systems, the freestanding units can be used along with modular components. This combination allows for moving the freestanding units to some other location, such as into a closed office, and reconfiguring or adding components to the original workstation.

Freestanding units and system components are available with either painted or wood veneer finishes on the vertical surfaces. A variety of sizes of worksurfaces (including corner units) are available. Worksurfaces are constructed of particleboard or steel-core faced with either veneer or high-pressure laminate. Worksurfaces can be placed at varying heights to accommodate several different tasks. Other components of office furniture systems include pedestals that carry box and file drawers and overhead storage compartments in several difference sizes. Task and ambient lighting are available as part of the systems. Many accessories and components that aid in the use of computers, such as articulating shelves for keyboards and paper-flow trays, are also part of the systems.

In addition to the full line of panel systems and conventional units offered by the manufacturers of steel office furniture, some companies sell items designed specifically to support computerized functions. These furnishings include straight and curved word processor workstations, mobile pedestals, individual computer tables with dual-height worksurfaces to accommodate the keyboard and the terminal, printer stands, and mobile terminal stands. Some of these specialized furnishings are designed to be flexible with such features as height-adjustable worksurfaces; extendable keyboard platforms that can be used to adjust the eye-to-screen distance for computer user; and keyboard and terminal platforms with adjustable tilt mechanisms and height-from-floor adjustment capabilities. Many accessories for use with comput-

A Herman Miller height-adjustable worksurface shown in an Ethospace® Interiors workstation. *Photograph courtesy of Herman Miller, Inc. Photo: Phil Schaafsma.*

FIGURE 82

3. Does the system allow for adjusting the height, position, or angle of the components of the workstation?

4. Does the system allow for expanding and contracting the size of the workstation? Can workstations be easily adapted in shape?

5. Does the system have the simplicity and flexibility of design to allow for ease in dismantling and relocating workstations?

6. Can additional components be added to the initial installation? Does the system allow for retrofitting pieces?

Panels

1. How are slotted uprights/channels attached to the end of a panel frame? Bolted? Screwed? Force fitted? How secure are these attachments?

2. Is the system designed in such a manner that panel-mounted components can be installed easily? Does the panel allow for attaching brackets (which support the components) into slots placed every 1"–1½" along a vertical channel? Do the brackets that attach to the panels lock securely in place?

3. Are panels both tackable and acoustical?

ers are also available, such as locking security cabinets for computer equipment, foot and palm rests, carousels for holding equipment shared by adjacent workstations, and document holders.

The following list of questions can be used in evaluating a line of furniture. (The word "system" in the questions below refers to any type of modular workstation, regardless of whether it contains freestanding units, components of a panel configuration, or a combination of both.)

Adjustability and Flexibility

1. Is a variety of module options and configurations available? Are both freestanding and systems components available from the same manufacturer?

2. Are the components from one module of the system interchangeable with other components of the same system?

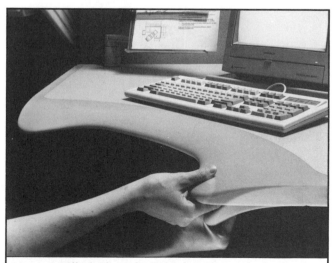

Herman Miller's Flex-Edge™ Work Surface was designed to reduce strain on wrists and hands while working on computers. *Photograph courtesy of Herman Miller, Inc. Photo: Cory Knoll, Labaak Studios.*

FIGURE 83

4. Can panels be repaired in place, or does the workstation have to be dismantled to repair panels?

Worksurfaces and Support

1. What kind of core material is used: particleboard, steel, or another material? (Generally, consider the fact that people sometimes sit on worksurfaces, whether they should or not, and that some worksurfaces may hold several pieces of equipment.)

2. How are worksurfaces cantilevered off of the panels? Do cantilevers extend the full depth of the worksurface?

3. How is the worksurface located in relation to the panel behind it? Is there a space between the worksurface and the panel? Is a space to drop cords desirable, or will a space be a nuisance because small desk items will drop through it to the floor?

4. What are the manufacturer's load restrictions on the worksurfaces?

Overhead Storage Bins

1. What material is used to construct the end brackets of overhead storage bins, particleboard or steel?

2. How are the bins attached to the panels?

3. Does the overhead storage have a backstop or solid steel back to prevent items like binders from damaging the panel to which the bin is mounted?

4. Does the door on the overhead bin open into the bin or does it open over the top of the bin, so nothing can be placed on top?

5. How easily can the doors on bins be opened and closed? Can the door be opened easily by someone seated in a chair? Does the door "hang up" or bind when opened at certain angles? Is there a possibility that the door might fall shut if it is accidentally opened only partway? How heavy is the door?

6. How does the bin lock? Can the lock on the bin be popped open with a letter opener or other tool?

Pedestals, Drawers, and Shelves

1. How much filing space is available? How deep are pedestal drawers? Are they the same depth as the worksurface?

2. Do drawers have double or single-wall construction? Does the drawer have a paper hood to keep papers from falling behind the drawer?

3. Do drawers and doors operate smoothly and conveniently? Are drawers designed with rubber bumpers or some other means of preventing metal-to-metal contact when a drawer is closed? What kind of drawer suspension is used?

4. What are the manufacturer's load restrictions on drawers?

Computer Accessories

1. What kind of specific keyboard tray/shelf options are available for a system? (Consider the following: amount of vertical height adjustment, degrees of shelf tilt, availability and size of built-in palm rests, degree of shelf swivel, ease of adjustment, storage height and knee clearance under tray, and degree of "bounce" to absorb the shock of excessive keying force.)

2. What other computer accessories are available to support the system, such as height-adjustable computer stands, printer stands, and foot and palm rests?

Power Distribution and Wire Management

1. What kind of electrical system does the system provide? How flexible is the electrical system? Can changes be made in power distribution as needs change?

2. Where are cable distribution channels located? Are they standard at the top and bottom of the panels and at worksurface height? Does the system have the capability for providing routing of cables from channel to channel? Can power and data be separated?

3. Where are outlets located? In the base? At worksurface height?

Steelcase® Activity tables are available in a variety of sizes and shapes. The tables can be used alone or configured in groups to create a larger worksurface. *Photograph courtesy of Steelcase®, Inc.*

FIGURE 84

A Steelcase® Activity post can be positioned next to an activity or other table to provide power and data access to multiple worksurfaces. The posts are available in a pre-wired version or can be wired in the field. *Photograph courtesy of Steelcase®, Inc.*

FIGURE 85

General Construction and Maintenance

1. Is the system designed for strength and stability? Can the manufacturer provide performance data or other evidence that worksurfaces and other components will not sag?

2. Are replacement parts readily available?

3. Is the system designed to allow easy access to areas or components that might require servicing?

4. Are the construction materials and finishes desired available? Can materials and finishes be easily maintained?

TASK AND OFFICE SEATING

Experts on ergonomics in the workplace agree that the selection of properly designed task chairs is vital to ensuring safe conditions in the office environment. Just as dozens of manufacturers sell desks, panel systems, and workstations, dozens of companies also sell chairs for offices. The leading companies in the office furniture industry will supply potential customers with a wide range of information about chairs, such as forms and criteria for determining the seating needs of the office; reports on seating research and design, seating safety standards, and the safe use of office seating; and forms for evaluating particular styles of seating.

The selection of seating involves considering the use of a chair within the context of the work environment. Because of the variety of tasks performed by someone seated in a chair in a library, the same chair is not appropriate for everyone. In fact, a single person may use a different chair for different tasks. The selection of a chair depends on many factors, such as the types of tasks to be performed by the person seated in the chair (reading, conferencing, intensive computer activity, a combination of tasks involving computers and paperwork, telephoning, reference work, circulation of materials, etc.), the kinds of equipment that will be used, the length of time that is spent on any one task, the length of time a person will remain seated in the chair, and whether or not the chair will be used primarily by a single individual or will be used in shared work space by several different people. Other factors that may be considered in chair selection include special requirements of particular staff members, personal preference, the hierarchy of positions in the or-

KI Vertebra® chair. *Photograph courtesy of KI.*

FIGURE 86

Herman Miller Equa® chair. *Photograph courtesy of Herman Miller, Inc. Photo: Bill Sharpe.*

FIGURE 89

Herman Miller Ergon 2™ chair. *Photograph courtesy of Herman Miller, Inc. Photo: Earl Woods.*

FIGURE 87

Haworth® Accolade chair. *Photograph courtesy of Haworth®.*

FIGURE 90

Vecta® 4 O'Clock chair. Designed by Jeff Cronk. *Photograph courtesy of Vecta®. Photo: Andy Post.*

FIGURE 88

Steelcase® Sensor chair with adjustable back. *Photograph courtesy of Steelcase®, Inc.*

FIGURE 91

ganization, and the kinds of workstations at which the chair will be used.

Task chairs are often classified into two types: those designated as having *active* ergonomic design and those designated as having *passive* ergonomic design. Chairs are also available that are designed with both active and passive features. Active ergonomic chairs have several levers and knobs that allow the user to make a wide range of chair adjustments. When a chair is used primarily by one individual, the person adjusts the chair to fit her/his needs and learns to change the chair when necessary. Studies have shown, however, that when a chair with active ergonomics is used at a shared workstation by several staff members, individuals often do not take the time to adjust the chair to fit her/his own needs. Adequate training in the use of a chair with active ergonomic design should, therefore, be provided by the vendor who supplies the chair. Chairs with passive ergonomic design are essentially self-adjusting. The chairs are designed to respond automatically when the user changes position or changes from one task to another.

Task chairs selected for the library should meet ANSI/HFS (American National Standards Institute/Human Factors Society) standard 100-1988, or revisions of the standard as they are made in the future. The standard applies to tasks involving text processing, data entry, and data inquiry; however, the standards may also be used as guidelines in selecting seating for other kinds of work. The standards are summarized as follows:

Seat height: 16–20.5 inches, minimum range of adjustment.

Seat depth: 15–17 inches maximum.

Seat width: 18.2 inches minimum.

Angle between seat back and seat pan: within the range of 0–105 degrees.

Seat pan angle: between 0 and 10 degrees.

Lumbar support: backrest required in the lumbar region; support to be placed between the L3 and L5 vertebrae.

Back width: 12 inches minimum in lumbar region.

Armrests (width between): 18.2 inches minimum.

Prior to selecting task chairs, staff members should be given an opportunity to try out several chairs. Vendors will supply chairs for evaluation. Staff should be encouraged to notice the overall comfort of the chair, as well as the comfort of the backrest, seat, and armrests; the ease

of adjustment of the chair; the range of adjustments and how appropriate the adjustments are for the work to be performed from the chair; the maneuverability of the chair; and the general appearance of the chair.

When selecting office chairs, it is essential to choose a manufacturer that has been in business a long time, is apt to remain in business, and has a reputation for being one of the leaders in the office furniture industry. It is interesting to note that a high-quality chair is not necessarily the most expensive one. It is possible to buy a chair that will last for 10 or 20 years and pay less for it than for a chair that is not as comfortable and will not last as long. The price is often based on the way a chair looks—its aesthetic appeal—rather than on functional considerations. It is also important to remember that even very inexpensive office chairs in a high-tech style may look good when they are new, but if the chairs soon fall apart or have broken parts that cannot be replaced, they are no bargain. With so many options available, however, it is important to try out several chairs, talk to more than one dealer, check references, and ask about performance testing.

In addition to meeting the ANSI/HFS standards, a high-quality office chair should have the following attributes:

1. The size and design of the backrest should allow for proper back support and distribution of the user's weight and correct curvature of the spine. The chair back should allow for differences needed in the height, angle, and tension of the backrest for different people. If upright posture is needed for computer-intensive activities, the chair should include the capability for locking the backrest into an upright or forward-tilt position. The chair should include back tension adjustment so that a range of support can be provided when a user leans back in the chair.

2. The chair should be designed and contoured properly in order to distribute the user's weight and support the body correctly. The chair should provide uniform support as the user leans back and forward.

3. The seat should be shaped and angled to position the spine properly and to distribute the user's weight correctly. The front of the chair should have a radius edge that will not cut into the leg of the user. The chair seat should have

enough foam to make it comfortable. The chair should be designed in such a manner that the user's feet don't rise off the floor when leaning back.

4. The arm should be designed in such a manner that it does not impede movement of the user from side to side. The arm should also allow for pulling the chair under the worksurface. A chair with adjustable-height armrests should be considered for maximum flexibility of use.

5. The chair should have a five-point steel base for stability. The base should be designed to minimize interference with the feet and legs of the user.

6. Chair adjustments should be easy and convenient to make. The chair should allow for height adjustment, either manually or with a pneumatic lift, so the user's feet can rest flat on the floor. Other chair adjustments to consider may include front and back tilt tension adjustment and lock, back height adjustment, and seat pan angle adjustment.

7. Preferably, a "family" of chairs will be selected that includes a variety of chairs appropriate for different tasks and different levels in the organization (manager's or executive's chairs, operator's or task chairs, secretarial posture chairs, high swivel stools, and side chairs). Consideration should be given to the size options available in the family of chairs selected.

8. Several different choices in the kind of casters for the chair should be available. The purchaser should specify the caster that is appropriate for the floor on which the chair will be used. The chair should maneuver easily, while still allowing the user to maintain control.

9. The chair should allow for ease of reupholstering and field replacement of some parts. Service and parts for broken chairs should be readily available.

FILE CABINETS

Office panel systems include steel files; however, lateral or vertical files are often purchased as freestanding items to be used singly or in groups in public areas, workrooms, or offices of the library. In addition to cabinets for paper storage, steel cases are also designed for other media—microfiche, microfilm, audiocassettes, videotapes, com-

puter printouts, and compact discs. Many poorly constructed files are on the market, but there is no reason to purchase files with drawers that do not operate smoothly, or with frames that bend easily when the cases are moved. High-quality files are available at reasonable prices from several reputable manufacturers.

A 1982 article, "Lateral Roll-out File Cabinets," in *Library Technology Reports* reviews tests performed on lateral files. Drawers, doors, cabinets, and finishes were tested in order to determine the following: stability of the files, quality of the hardware, ease of removing and replacing drawers and dividers, maximum extension of drawers, suspension, usable drawer space, thickness of the steel, and maintenance required. Although the particular files tested in 1982 may no longer be available, the information about the testing is still valid and can be used in selecting files today.

Fully loaded files are as dangerous as fully loaded bookstacks. Before files are purchased, the librarian should provide the vendor with information as to how the files will be arranged, where they will be located in the building, and the kind of material that will be stored in them. Some files were not designed, for example, to hold the weight of microfiche or microfilm. Also, how and where the files are placed determines how they will need to be anchored for stability. If they are placed in groups, several cases can be bolted together for strength. Single cases can be anchored to the floor or wall, or a counterweight can be added to them for stability.

Once the information regarding use of the files has been provided, it is the job of the vendor and installer to make sure they can be used safely. Sometimes, when changes

KI Perry high-density stacking chair with articulating backrest. *Photograph courtesy of KI.*

FIGURE 92

are made in a library, the original purpose of the files changes. As with steel bookstacks, it is a good idea to go back and check on the stability of files installed several years before. There should be no possibility that a case will fall over when a drawer is pulled out.

Lateral files are available in standard widths of 30, 36, and 42 inches. The height of the files varies from one manufacturer to another; however, most companies have files available in the height ranges of 28–30 inches, 40–42 inches, 51–53 inches, and 63–65 inches. Lateral file cases come with two, three, four, and five drawers. Drawer heights differ from brand to brand, but several companies have standard drawer heights of 3, 6, 9, 12, and 15 inches. Although the standard drawer depth for lateral files is 18 inches, some companies offer files in both 18- and 20-inch depths.

The same companies that make lateral files also make vertical files that are available with two, three, four, and five drawers. The files are 15 inches wide for letter-size and 18 inches wide for legal-size filing. The drawers are 25–30 inches deep. Vertical files come in heights of approximately 30, 42, 53, and 60 inches. Both lateral and vertical files can be purchased with a variety of inserts for the interior including dividers and trays for cards in sizes of 3" x 5", 4 x 6", and 5" x 8".

High-quality files have welded steel frames consisting of uprights and horizontal members under the outer steel cabinet. The better files have extra steel reinforcement at the stress points in the case. The case should be engi-

neered in such a manner that the frame (and therefore the cabinet) will not bend when the file is moved, pushed, or placed on an uneven floor. (The drawers will not operate properly in a cheaply made file with a bent case.) The vendor should be able to supply evidence that the file has been performance-tested. Ask about a warranty. Some companies offer ten-year warranties; some offer five-year warranties. Other necessary features of lateral or vertical files include: full-extension drawers riding on steel ball-bearing suspension, a safety interlock system to prevent the user from opening more than one drawer at a time, leveling glides, and counterweight packages.

Lateral and vertical files are also available in highly flexible, modular, stackable units. Additional modules can be added later, to be stacked on the initial installation. Also, with modular files, it is easy for a consumer to design a file that will allow for storing a variety of media. Modules usually are available in several heights, and half-height drawers are also available.

Although some lateral and vertical files allow for the storage of multimedia, cases specifically designed to hold microforms and audio-visual materials are also available. Steel storage cabinets purchased to hold these items should have the same heavy-duty construction as other high-quality files. Russ Bassett, Borroughs, and JB Engineering are some of the companies that make files to hold a variety of materials. These manufacturers and others offer full lines of high-quality modular files that are specifically designed for microfiche, microfilm, compact disc, video-tapes, and aperture cards.

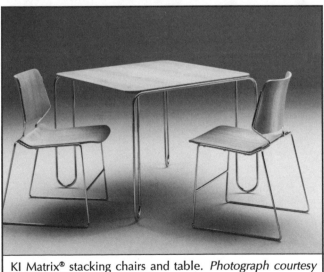

KI Matrix® stacking chairs and table. *Photograph courtesy of KI.*

FIGURE 93

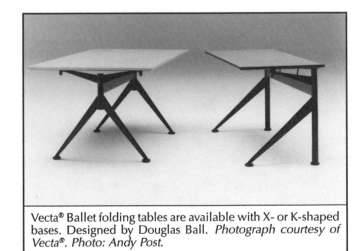

Vecta® Ballet folding tables are available with X- or K-shaped bases. Designed by Douglas Ball. *Photograph courtesy of Vecta®. Photo: Andy Post.*

FIGURE 94

STACKING CHAIRS AND FOLDING TABLES

Many of the contract furniture companies that sell office furnishings and tables and chairs for public places also sell products that can be used to furnish library staff lounges and meeting rooms. Lunch tables with metal legs or pedestal bases and high-pressure laminate tops are often purchased for staff lounge areas. Wood or metal-framed side chairs can be used with lunch tables. A library that selects a metal-framed stacking chair for the meeting room may decide to use the same chair in the staff lounge.

Many manufacturers produce stacking chairs for meeting rooms. Just as with task chairs, try out several chairs before selecting the one to purchase. Stacking chairs are available with wood or plastic seats and backs and with upholstered seats and backs. Many stacking chairs can be purchased with caddies on which they are placed for moving and storage. The design of a chair often determines how many can be stacked on top of each other on a caddy.

Many companies make folding tables, as well as stacking chairs. Folding tables are available in a variety of widths and lengths, with fixed and adjustable-height bases, and in four-legged and T-base styles. The tables vary in style from very institutional-looking training tables to very stylish tables that look like similar products with fixed bases. Caddies are usually available to hold the folding tables.

The type of folding table to be selected may depend on the funds available, what use will be made of the tables, how often they will be taken up and down, and the staff who will be responsible for setting up and arranging the tables. In selecting folding tables, consider whether the tables are light enough in weight to be handled by the staff who will need to be lifting them frequently. Folding tables constructed with tops with a "honeycomb" core are lighter than tables constructed with particleboard tops. Consider how easily the folding mechanism of the tables can be operated. If the tables will be handled by staff or users who are not familiar with how the folding mechanism works, the means of folding or unfolding the tables should be readily apparent and should be easy to operate. If the tables will be used by children, as well as adults, tables with adjustable-height mechanisms should be considered. Just as with chairs, try out several products before deciding which one to purchase.

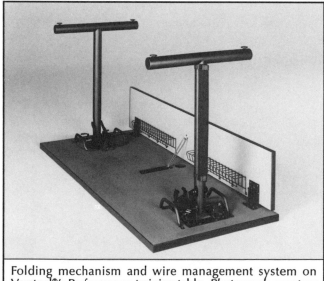

Folding mechanism and wire management system on Versteel®'s Performance training table. *Photograph courtesy of Versteel®.*

FIGURE 95

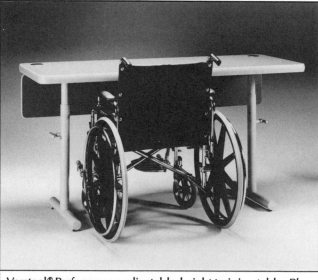

Versteel® Performance adjustable-height training table. *Photograph courtesy of Versteel®.*

FIGURE 96

CHAPTER
9

Sign Systems and Display

SIGN SYSTEMS

One of the most important, yet neglected, aspects of the library interior is the sign system. The emphasis here is on the word *system*. Even in a new building, the effect of good planning and design is destroyed when a library opens with signs in many shapes, colors, and styles. The lack of systematic signage also leads to a proliferation of hand-lettered or other makeshift signs. In the excellent book *Designing Places for People*, authors C. M. Deasy and Thomas E. Lasswell note:

> The principal concern in designing libraries is the special aspect of cue searching called *wayfinding*. This is because so much of library use takes the form of a search for specific information or material. The searcher must quickly learn how to use the system in order to improve the chances of finding what is sought. (p. 107).

Many aspects of a building's design affect signage: the placement and kinds of lighting; finishes and colors selected for the building interior; architectural features, such as soffits, concealed spline ceilings, stairways, halls, entrances, and exits; and the placement and styles of furniture. Planning of the sign system should take place along with the building design and the furniture selection.

Regulations in the Americans with Disabilities Act (ADA) apply to signage in the library. Signs that designate permanent rooms and spaces, directional signs, and informational signs must comply with ADA Accessibility Guidelines for Buildings and Facilities (ADAAG). Accessible elements of the building, such as entrance doors, rest rooms, water fountains, and parking spaces, must display the international symbol of accessibility. Temporary signage, such as building directories, does not have to comply with ADAAG. Both upper- and lower-case letters are permitted. ADAAG requires that all signs have a width-to-height ratio between 3:5 and 1:1 for letters and numbers. Letters and numbers on signs are required to have a stroke width-to-height ratio between 1:5 and 1:10. Signs placed overhead must be placed a minimum of 89 inches above the floor and must have letters and numbers at least three inches high. Permanent signs for rooms and spaces installed on the wall next to a door should be mounted on the latch side of the door 60 inches above the floor to the center line of the sign. Letters and numbers on permanent signs must be at least $^5/_8$-inch and no more than two inches in height, must be raised $^1/_{32}$ of an inch, and must be accompanied by Grade 2 Braille. Signs with pictograms must be six inches high. If pictograms are used for permanent signs, the verbal equivalent must be placed directly below it. The characters and backgrounds of permanent signs must be flat, matte, or nonglare. The characters must contrast in color with the background. Signs should have light-colored characters on a dark background or dark-colored characters on a light-colored background.

117

The new Main Library in San Francisco includes an extensive ADA-compliant, state-of-the-art system of signage to assist all users with wayfinding and provide barrier-free access to all collections and services. At the entrance to the library and at 150 other locations throughout the building, "talking signs" provide directions to visually impaired users. Infrared transmitters placed at numerous locations throughout the library provide spoken information that replicates adjacent visual signs to users who are carrying a receiver. Messages can be transmitted within a range of 75 feet. Because "talking signs" have been designated as San Francisco's standard technology for orientation and wayfinding for the blind, an increasing number of visually impaired individuals in San Francisco are purchasing their own receivers. In addition, receivers will be available for loan at the library entrance. Jerry Kuns, field consultant for HumanWare, assisted the SFPL with plans for signage and designed a "talking map" with touch tablet technology for the library. When a person touches a particular point on the relief map, a voice-output message identifies the location touched. The PC-based system allows each spoken "label" to have a maximum of 250 characters. LED announcement signs in the library's elevators will identify floors with both enunciated and scrolling script and will provide information about library programs and events.

Wayfinding in the library can be aided by architectural features as well as signs. Hearing-impaired library users can be assisted in the library by pathways or service areas differentiated by color; visually impaired users benefit from textural changes in floor coverings that separate pathways or service areas. Libraries are encouraged to work with consultants or design professionals with expert knowledge of the ADA and signage in purchasing signs for new libraries or upgrading signs for an existing building.

The three factors considered when choosing furnishings— function, maintenance, and appearance—are also relevant to the selection of a sign system. Because signs play a vital role in public relations, their appearance is especially important. Inadequate, makeshift signage makes a poor impression on a public that is surrounded daily by effective systems in department stores, shopping malls, hospitals, and professional office buildings. Attractive signage demonstrates that the library operates like a well-run company: The business is organized; planning has been done to ensure that the consumer finds needed goods and services easily; and the interior has been designed to show that the organization is customer-reponsive.

Just as the first step in a building project or the furniture selection process is the development of a program, the planning of a functional sign system begins with making decisions about what kinds of signs are needed and what they should accomplish. The system must include at least some of the following: (1) a directory or map near the entrance to identify locations for major departments or functions; (2) signs throughout the building to direct users to specific locations—up or down floors, around corners, and through halls or doors; (3) signs on doors or at the entrances to departments to identify the function or service within that room or area; (4) signs to provide information about regulations, warnings, procedures, instructions, and hours; (5) signs to highlight particular collections and services or to announce events taking place in the library; and (6) signs on the end panels of stacks to identify which books are shelved in that range.

A successful sign system is one that can be learned easily and is truly helpful to the library user. Here are some guidelines:

1. Consistency is essential to the development of an effective sign system. It allows the user to learn the system quickly and easily. Signs that serve the same function throughout the building, such as those giving instructions or those identifying specific departments, should have the same shape, size, layout, type size, and placement (height, location on the wall, etc.).

2. The sign system should be logical. Directions should be given in a progression from the general to the specific. Levels of information should be established so that some messages receive more emphasis than others.

3. Signs should use terminology consistently— only one term should be applied to any one area, service, etc. The words used should be as descriptive as possible and easily recognized by the public. Avoid using jargon that is familiar only to the staff.

4. Redundancy should be avoided. Too many signs, all providing the same message, can be as bad as having no signs at all.

5. Signs should be placed appropriately at decision points in the building—at the entrance to the

library, by elevators or stairs, at the end of a hall, etc.

6. The text of a sign should be clearly and accurately written in order to communicate the intended message effectively. The phrases used and the length of the lines of text should be short, so the sign can be easily read and understood. The tone should be appropriate for promoting good public relations.

7. Signs should complement the architecture of the library. The dimensions of signs should be in proportion to the scale of the building. The colors and materials should coordinate with the colors and finishes of the building. Place signs where they will not be obscured by parts of the building, fixtures, or furnishings.

8. Signs should be made in accordance with the principles of good design. These principles pertain to typeface, size and spacing of letters and lines, contrast, use of symbols, and color. (Information about the effective design of signs can be found in a number of books. Some of them are listed in the bibliography at the back of this book.)

9. As the situation in the library changes, signs should be changed promptly to reflect the new conditions.

10. Signage should comply with ADA guidelines.

Three important maintenance aspects must be considered when selecting a sign system for a library. First, the system should be one that can be easily installed and has the flexibility to allow for frequent changes. Second, the system should remain attractive and useful for a long period of time and should be constructed of materials that will not fade or wear out. Third, the system should be one that will be available in the future. If the signs are commercially produced, the manufacturer should be one who is likely to be in business for several years to come. If the signage is for a large building and involves a substantial investment, the service history of the product should be obtained and references for similar jobs should be checked. If the signs are to be produced in-house or by a small local supplier, the library should select materials that will be available for a number of years.

A workable sign system is dynamic, allowing a library to make changes frequently while still maintaining the integrity of the original design concept. Once a library

has planned a sign system, the resulting information should be documented in the form of a sign manual that will provide long-range guidance on signage for the organization. The manual should include guidelines and policies regarding the use of signs, placement and mounting, terminology, sizes, shapes, colors, design (typography, symbols, spacing and size of letters and lines), construction, maintenance, and the use of temporary signs. Libraries seeking a model sign manual should read *A Sign System for Libraries* by Mary S. Mallery and Ralph E. DeVore (1982), which documents a system developed for the Western Maryland Public Libraries.

Just as with furnishings, some vendors will be glad to discuss signage for the library, suggest possible systems, and provide specifications and pricing, even for small buildings. Because of the scope of the project and amount of detail involved, the development of a sign system for a large building should be done with the assistance of a sign consultant or a vendor with expertise in the area.

Signs that are considered permanent (identification of doors and major areas, directions to other floors, etc.) can be obtained from companies that supply a full range of

Directory board made by Modulex® for Transylvania University, Lexington, Kentucky. *Photograph courtesy of Modulex®/ ASI Sign Systems®.*

FIGURE 97

products constructed of metal, wood, and plastic with letters applied by a variety of processes. A wide variety of interior signs are also available from the major library suppliers, such as Brodart, Demco, and Gaylord. Signs that require changing frequently, such as identification on the end panels of bookstacks or announcements of upcoming events, can be replaced in-house or purchased from a local source that can supply new signs quickly and inexpensively.

A sign system may comprise several different kinds of signs. The Irving Public Library in Irving, Texas, for example, has a well-developed system of signs constructed from a variety of materials. Signage was not part of the architectural drawings, but was part of the work of the interior designer. The designer hired a consultant, who worked with the library director, Dr. Lamar Veatch, to plan the signs for the new central library that opened in 1986. The key element in the ongoing process of sign making for the Irving Public Library is a computerized sign making machine for producing die-cut vinyl letters. The machine is used to make call numbers and subject headings for custom-designed plastic sign-holders on the end panels of the bookstacks. For identification and directional signs throughout the building, the letters are applied to acrylic panels or glass walls and doors. The sign maker is also used to cut letters for instructional signs and posters.

Major areas in the Irving Public library are identified by hanging signs ingeniously made of polyvinyl chloride (PVC) pipe. The ends of the pipe were filled in with discs of plexiglass. The pipe and ends were then painted to coordinate with the building interior. Vinyl letters were cut by the machine and applied to the pipe to create a finished sign. (See Figure 98.)

Hanging signs made from PVC pipe at Irving Public Library, Irving, Texas. *Photo: David J. Lund.*

FIGURE 98

Although the computerized signmaker is an expensive item, it should be considered for purchase by large libraries. Perhaps the cost could be shared with another city department, department of a university, or with a network of libraries. Life-cycle costing could also be used to justify the expense. A public library with a main library and branches can use the machine to produce signs for all of its buildings. In Irving, large inexpensive sheets of plexiglass are purchased and cut into smaller pieces; the machine is then used to produce the lettering for signs to be used in the branches as well as the main library.

A variety of kinds of information can also be supplied on video monitors that are part of an electronic directory system, such as SelfInform™. A computer-based system has the capability for using a wide range of graphics for displaying an unlimited number of listings or directories that can be easily updated. The system can be integrated with other library networks and allows for user interaction by way of a touchscreen or keyboard.

Several available modular sign systems are especially useful for libraries because they allow for ease in changing signs. Modular, flexible systems are manufactured, for example, by Modulex/ASI Sign Systems and Changeable Sign Systems. Signs are available from both companies that work on the principle of the LEGO® building-block toy. The systems are an excellent solution to the problem of continually changing signs on the end panels of bookstacks. Aluminum frames are used to hold a plastic knob base. Letters, symbols, numbers, etc., are printed on LEGO-like pieces—one letter, symbol, or number on each piece. Users have an assortment of letters (pieces) that fit onto the knob base to create a line of text that is locked in place. Because the individual pieces fit together so well, seams between individual letters (pieces) do not show on the finished line, and the individual pieces provide correct alignment and spacing between letters. The changeable format can be used to create text on signs attached to walls, doors, or bookstacks, on hanging signs, and on many kinds of directory boards. The concept can also be used to make maps. Lines of the changeable type can be combined with modules of permanent silk-screened or vinyl die-cut text. Another attractive feature of the system is that panels with a baked enamel finish in bright colors are used with the lines of changeable type to allow for coordinating the system with the color scheme of the building. (See Figure 99.)

Many libraries purchase plastic or metal sign holders from library suppliers and generate signs, as needed, using

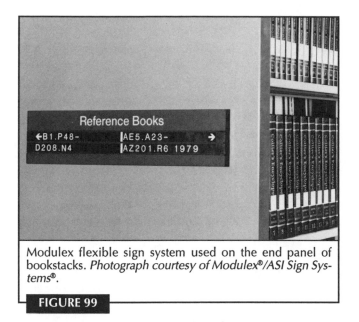

Modulex flexible sign system used on the end panel of bookstacks. *Photograph courtesy of Modulex®/ASI Sign Systems®.*

FIGURE 99

a PC and a laser printer. Another possibility for making small changeable signs, like those on the end panels of stacks, is a relatively inexpensive sign-making machine that produces prespaced and aligned vinyl letters that are attached to a self-adhesive strip. An example of this system is one made by Leteron. (This is actually a small, manual version of a sign maker like the one used at Irving.) The lines of text produced in-house can then be used on modular sign panels of a commercial system, on plexiglass panels, or on other materials.

These are only a few approaches that can be taken to signage in the library. It is interesting to note that an increasing number of companies are exhibiting signs at conferences. The library supply catalogs are also now selling a wider variety than they have in the past. Signage is an area of interior planning that can benefit from new ideas. With encouragement, perhaps staff members will discover other ingenious, attractive, and inexpensive ways of constructing signs for the buildings in which they work.

DISPLAY

Public librarians no longer sit quietly at their desks (if they ever did) as caretakers of a collection of the world's best books, waiting for someone to make a request for an item from orderly shelves. In recent years, librarians have had to react to new kinds of materials, competition from other multimedia sources, an increasing number of informal educational organizations, and an aware public with access to a variety of leisure-time activities. Once again, libraries have looked to profit-making businesses to learn

ways of taking a more aggressive approach to service. Librarians are seeking methods of drawing people into the library, where they are then offered a wide range of readily accessible materials and services. Librarians have begun merchandising materials to promote their use.

Merchandising of the library product involves continuous staff attention to the arrangement of the materials in the building and to the manner in which items are displayed. Patron use of some library materials depends to a great extent on how the materials are presented. Moreover, what works today to promote a product is not necessarily what will work tomorrow. Librarians who are skilled at promoting the use of their collections are aware of the value of change. Materials that are seldom used may be checked out more frequently if they are both moved to another location and displayed in another manner. Many libraries have taken a cue from bookstores where lighted signs and display shelving are used to promote products. As soon as the customer enters the store, books and other products are encountered in displays. In a mall, the display even spills out into the corridor. The titles currently being promoted are changed frequently, and displays are moved around or rearranged regularly. In grocery and department stores, the same kind of merchandising techniques are used. Displays are found at the ends of aisles and at the entrances to departments. This method of promoting products takes advantage of the user's tendency to browse and to pick up items that are within view and most readily accessible.

Display furnishings should be treated as the most dynamic element in the library. They should allow for rearrangement of the materials displayed, as well as possible movement of all or part of the fixture itself.

All of the standard steel and wood-and-steel bookstack lines discussed in chapter 3 include special accessories that can be used for the display of multimedia collections: sloped shelves with a back for paperbacks, compact discs, videotapes, and talking books; two-tier cassette and compact disc shelves; browsing boxes for paperbacks, cassettes, and compact discs; bars for hanging bags; zigzag paperback inserts; and in-stack media cabinets. The multimedia specialty shelves improve the flexibility of standard shelving greatly; any section of shelving in the library can become a "display" fixture simply by removing the standard shelves and inserting a specialized component. Face-out display of hardbacks can be accomplished using a standard fixed display shelf (designed originally for periodicals) or any sloped shelf with a back. Either standard

MJ Industries Circa 2000 shelving and display system photographed at Loudoun County Public Public Library, Leesburg, Virginia. *Photograph courtesy of M.J. Industries. Photo: Paul Colburn.*

FIGURE 100

Worden Diametron™ periodical display module custom-designed by the author for FrankfordVillage Branch, Carrollton Public Library, Carrollton, Texas. *Photograph courtesy of The Worden Company. Photo: Paul Colburn.*

FIGURE 101

Scania Tiltbox™ Periodical Storage Units have boxes that can be tilted to stay at an angle for easy removal of an item. *Photograph courtesy of Scania™/BTJ, Inc.*

FIGURE 102

Bretford®'s LEGACY Library System includes library furniture as well as shelving. A display unit for audio-visual and other materials is shown here. *Photograph courtesy of Bretford® Manufacturing, Inc.*

FIGURE 103

shelving units or steel display units with sloped shelves can be supplied with lighted canopy tops.

Several specialty shelving systems are also available to libraries. Although the systems are sometimes used throughout a building, many public libraries buy standard steel shelving for most of their book collections, limiting themselves to just a few sections of specialty shelving for an audio-visual or a new book/high-demand browsing area. The systems provide the capability for using one basic shelving framework that supports a wide variety of interchangeable display and standard shelf components.

BCI's System Arc and MJ's Circa 2000 are examples of two specialty shelving products. (See Figure 100.) The systems are of the starter/adder type with an open base. The systems meet the LTR recommended standards for steel shelving. The shelving end upright assemblies consist of vertical steel tubes welded to horizontal steel tubes. H-shaped and straight crossbars bolted to two adjacent frames provide stability to the shelving. Integral back shelves and a variety of multimedia shelves can be used on the frames. A number of options for changing the look of the shelving are available. The basic tubular frame can be used alone for shelving with an open look, or perforated steel plates can be inserted between the tubes of the end frame to give a more finished appearance. The tops of the upright tubes can be finished with arc-shaped inserts that loop from upright to upright on the end frames, or the tops can be finished with end caps. The shelving systems can be used either with or without lights. The light fixtures are supported by an arc insert placed in the top of the uprights on either side of a section of shelving. Sign holders are available with the systems.

Scania/BTJ's wood-and-steel shelving system has some interesting display capabilities. A special storage unit allows for housing back issues of magazines (or other library materials) in a plastic file box that can be tilted away from the shelf; a user can access the contents without removing the box from the shelf. (See Figure 102.) The Scania

line also includes HyLyter shelves. On the HyLyter system, fluorescent tubes are attached to the underside of each shelf to enhance the display of library materials on the shelf below. (BTJ is in the process of having the shelf and attached fixture tested for safety by Underwriters Laboratories.) Flat adjustable shelves, sloped periodical display shelves, and multimedia display shelves can be used in the HyLyter system. (See Figure 104.)

Another specialty starter/adder shelving is the Enem system (a subsidiary of Borgeaud Bibliotheques, France). The system is constructed of three components: ladders, connectors/crossbars, and shelves (or other display units). Ladders consist of steel tube uprights welded to double steel rods. Solid aluminum connector joints are used to connect steel tubing crossbars to two adjoining ladders. The system accommodates a wide variety of shelves and multimedia display units constructed of particleboard faced

On Scania™'s HyLyter™ wood and steel shelving system, each shelf is supplied with its own light. Flat adjustable, periodical, and display shelves are available as HyLyter™ shelves. *Photograph courtesy of Scania™/BTJ, Inc.*

FIGURE 104

with melamine. The system also includes a variety of worksurfaces. The modularity of Enem allows for configuring sections of the shelving in dozens of arrangements that can be used to divide various spaces in a library. (See Figure 105.)

Frameworks (available from Gaylord) is another display system that can be used to merchandise books, magazines, records, compact discs, and audio- and videocassettes. The modular system consists of wooden "slatwalls" and wire "gridwalls," from which can be hung a variety of units, including sloping shelves, display bins, wire racks, and individual angled holders. Rotating paperback, audio- and videocassette, and compact disc racks can be placed in wood frame units that are part of the system. Fabric-covered Velcro-tack board modules are also available. One of the advantages of a multimedia unit like

Frameworks is that it can be used to display community notices and giveaway items, as well as library materials.

Fixtures designed and sold to bookstores are another possibility for book or audiovisual display. Keep in mind, however, that many bookstore fixtures do not have the same level of quality as those designed for library bookstacks. Such fixtures are not designed or built to last for the life of a library. Many display systems now use slatwall to hold special racks or shelves for multimedia. The slatwall material can also be used on wooden end panels for steel shelving. (See Figure 107.)

Paperback book and multimedia display racks are available in a wide variety of styles with new models coming out all the time. Many of the multimedia display systems have racks for audio-visual materials, as well as books, on the same unit. All of the library supply companies have

Enem® Systems components, used here to display audio-visual materials, include a variety of shelving options, as well as workstations for children and adults. *Photograph courtesy of Enem® Systems, Inc.*

FIGURE 105

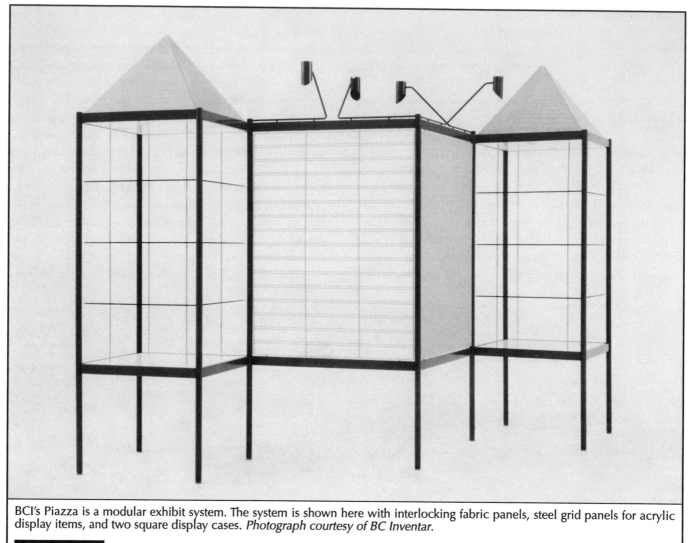

BCI's Piazza is a modular exhibit system. The system is shown here with interlocking fabric panels, steel grid panels for acrylic display items, and two square display cases. *Photograph courtesy of BC Inventar.*

FIGURE 106

racks available for displaying videocassettes, audiocassettes, records, and compact discs.

Because the companies selling these items, such as Brodart, Demco, Gaylord, and Highsmith, add new products frequently, don't assume that an item purchased five years ago is still the best one for your situation. Furthermore, it may not be possible to buy a unit to match one that was purchased several years ago. Check the catalogs for new products and, if possible, take a look at those you are considering for purchase at conference exhibits or at another library. Make sure you are getting a sturdy piece of equipment that will be stable when filled and will not fall apart when moved around the library. Some of the racks with rotating towers, for example, have no means for locking the towers in place. When the rack is moved,

the towers have to be completely removed. If the towers fall off, the plastic parts break easily. Also, many display units are just not very attractive. Spend a little more money, if necessary, to purchase a rack that matches the decor of the library and the level of quality of the other furnishings.

One of the details of library storage that is too frequently ignored involves the display of dozens of bibliographies, brochures, class and bus schedules, and tax forms that are free to library users. Because planning for the housing of giveaways is often neglected, public libraries can end up with stacks of messy papers on the tops of service desks, shelves, and tables. The problem is not that appropriate display racks are not available for these items, but rather that the question of what to do with these materials

Worden Diametron™ display kiosk shown here with slat wall and corkboard panels. *Photograph courtesy of The Worden Company.*

FIGURE 107

is not addressed along with other plans for the library interior.

In a project that involves a new building, the architect and/or interior planner should be involved in deciding what to do with giveaways. Custom display units for literature can be designed by the architect or interior designer, or ready-made, wall-mounted, or freestanding plastic literature holders can be purchased. The units come in a variety of sizes and styles and are available from local vendors and from library supply catalogs. The most important characteristics of literature holders are flexibility and visibility. The racks must handle a variety of sizes and shapes of literature in a neat, attractive manner, and items placed in the rack must be highly visible.

CHAPTER

10

The Bid Process

When public money is to be used for the purchase of library furnishings, a formal bid process is usually employed to award contracts for furnishings and shelving. A competitive bid situation allows the purchaser to analyze and judge comparable products for a particular project on the basis of quality and cost. Over a period of time, as a number of contracts are awarded, the bid process ensures the distribution of public funds among a number of suppliers. Unfortunately, the buying process involves many variables, and a number of problems inherent to the process sometimes make bidding difficult for both the purchaser and the vendor. This is especially true of a project that involves large sums of money and requires a full set of detailed specifications.

The preparation of a bid package requires expertise in the writing of specifications and knowledge of the elements of the bid document. Care must be taken to ensure that the package covers a wide range of contingencies. Even when the documents are well written, they are subject to misinterpretation by the bidders. Subjective judgment is often involved in qualifying bidders, approving alternates, and awarding the bid. As will be discussed further in chapter 11, the best that can be hoped for in a bid process is that all parties involved will act with integrity and understand their responsibilities in the process.

The written programming done at the beginning of the selection process (as outlined in chapter 1) becomes valu-able when making actual purchases. Furniture selections made on the basis of a particular level of quality can now be defended with authority, *provided all parties involved in awarding the bid have been educated throughout the process.* It is a critical error for a librarian to select particular furnishings and put them out for bid without involving all of the decision makers in the process. If a purchasing agent or any other person involved in the process does not truly understand the level of quality needed, poor-quality items may be purchased because a low bid is awarded as a matter of course. Architects, designers and consultants, purchasing agents, library boards, Friends of the Library, college or university administrators, school boards, members of the city council, the city administrator, etc.—any of these groups or individuals may play a vital role in awarding the bid. It is the responsibility of the librarian, designer, or consultant to see that key people understand why a particular level of quality is necessary, and what products can provide this level. One of the points to make in educating those involved is that high-quality furniture is apt to be higher in price than furniture of a lower quality, but the latter will not hold up with heavy library use. It is easier to justify furniture selections prior to the start of the purchasing process than to explain why a low bid is not acceptable when the decision makers have the bids in front of them and are able to compare dollars. Your best ally is a purchasing agent or representative who knows

128

the value of using sound judgment in awarding a bid and has the confidence to stand behind a decision based on factual evidence.

THE BID PACKAGE

A complete bid package consists of two parts: (1) documents detailing the requirements for bidding and successful completion of the contract, and (2) specifications for the particular items of furniture to be purchased. The document that provides the legal basis for the contract should be reviewed by an attorney or a purchasing agent.

The bid process may include a prebid conference to be held approximately one week after the package goes out for bid. Potential bidders are encouraged to attend the conference in order to ask for clarification of the bid process and document and to ask questions they may have about the specifications of the particular items included. Purchasing agents, design professionals, librarians, and other parties directly involved with awarding the bid may be in attendance to review the documents with the bidders, answer questions, and make note of items that may require an addendum to the original bid package.

A complete sample bid document can be found in *The Procurement of Library Furnishings, Specifications, Bid Documents, and Evaluation*. (Poole and Trezza 1969) The book contains the proceedings of a Library Equipment Institute conducted in 1966. Even though the book was published more than 25 years ago, the information is still relevant. Valuable information can also be obtained from chapter 16, "Specification Format and Content," in *Specifications for Commercial Interiors*. (Reznikoff 1989)

Bid documents customarily include the sections discussed in this chapter. However not all bid packages require every section; it is more important that essential items be covered somewhere in the document than that they are included in a specific section. The quotations from bid packages included in this chapter are designed to provide readers with examples of how the documents *might* be worded; there are many ways to state the stipulations of the bid and the specifications. In some cases, the examples do not apply to the usual bid situation, but are provided to illustrate how a number of contingencies can be covered in a bid document in an unusual situation.

Invitation to Bid

This section gives notice of what will be purchased and includes details of when and where bids will be accepted. Information may also be given regarding the withdrawal of bids and any bonds required for bidding. The invitation to bid is used to advertise the project in newspapers.

Instructions to Bidders

The legal aspects of the bidding procedure are covered in this section, including damages to be incurred by the contractor for failure to execute the contract on time, details on how bids are to be submitted, bid and performance bonds required, insurance requirements, and statements about the owner's right to request samples and to require performance testing. This section should have a paragraph noting the right of the owner to accept or reject any or all bids and to reject bids submitted with irregularities or qualifications. The instructions also include procedures for bidding and awarding particular sections of the package. For example:

> Bidders must bid on each and every item in any section for which a bid is submitted. Bids will be considered only by complete sections; partial section bids will be regarded as "no bids" on the particular section involved.

Or:

> Awards may be made by line item, by section, or on an "all or none" basis.

One of the most important statements in this section establishes the owner's right to gather evidence of the bidders' qualifications and to reject the bids of those who cannot prove their ability to complete the project successfully:

> The owner reserves the right to visit the factory of the manufacturer of the furniture offered in this bid in order to determine the capability of the company to produce furniture in the quantities required. The owner also reserves the right to make inquiries to determine the financial condition of bidders. The bidder must be in a financial position to obtain all materials, services, and labor to carry out the obligations of the contract. In no case will a purchase order be issued until the owner is completely satisfied with the bidder's professional craftsmanship, financial condition, and manufacturing capability.

It is essential that bidders be informed of the factors that will be considered in awarding the bid, and that they understand that the contract will be granted to the lowest *responsible bidder*.

> The owner will award the contract to the lowest and most responsible bidder who submits the most advantageous bid to the owner. In determining the most advantageous proposal, the following factors will be considered: conformity to specifications, delivery capabilities, purchase price,

life expectancy of items bid, cost of maintenance, product warranty, and past performance in similar projects.

Or:

The owner reserves the right to reject any or all bids and is not bound to accept the lowest bid submitted. If the lowest bid is not the best bid of value received for monies expended in the owner's opinion, the right is reserved to make awards in the best interests of the owner. In making awards, intangible factors, such as bidder's service, integrity, reputation, and past performance will be weighed, as well as tangible evidence of equipment quality and aesthetic appeal.

Many times, specific manufacturers are referenced in the detailed specifications; therefore, in the instructions to bidders, a statement should be made that brand names are given in order to establish a level of quality. This information can be combined with instructions for obtaining "approved equal" status where the detailed specifications use this terminology. The bid document should identify clearly who will have the responsibility for determining equal status. (Sometimes this information is given in the General Conditions section, rather than in Instructions to Bidders.)

It is not the intent of the specifications, drawings, or schedules to limit the materials or items to be procured by these documents to the product of any particular manufacturer, distributor, or supplier. Where any article, item, material, or thing is specified by a proprietary name, trade name, manufacturer, catalog number, or any other identification, it has been done so as to set a definite standard and/or style and to provide a reference for comparison as to quality, design, appearance, physical conformity, approximate dimensions, and other required characteristics, including equivalent value. It is not the intention to discriminate against or prevent any manufacturer, distributor, or supplier from furnishing an "approved equal" product, subject to the approval of the owner as to the equality thereof, which meets or exceeds all the characteristics of the item specified.

It is distinctly understood (1) that the library consultant (or interior designer) will use his or her judgment in determining whether or not any article or thing proposed to be substituted is the equal of any article specified; (2) that the decision of the consultant (or interior designer) on all such questions of equality shall be final; and (3) that in the event of any adverse decision by the consultant, no claim of any sort will be made or allowed against the consultant or the owner.

Actual samples of items bid as "approved equals" shall be submitted with catalog illustrations. Manufacturers' specifications, either written on their letterhead or printed in their literature, must accompany such items. Those items submitted for prior approval, which are then approved, will be listed in addenda to the specifications and

will be bound with the contract document. Submission of items for prior approval must be made no later than twenty-one (21) calendar days prior to date of bid opening.

The instructions to bidders may also include a statement about the owner's right to increase or decrease quantities slightly (usually no more than 10 percent) and procedures for bidding any add alternates (items that the library would like to purchase if funds are available) that are part of the package. These items are usually presented as a group in the bid package with the library retaining the right to purchase all or any of the items in the quantity noted or fewer. The actual schedule of items to be purchased and forms for submitting unit prices and total amounts may be in this section or may be included with the detailed specifications.

General Conditions

This section should cover information that relates more specifically to the job. This section includes statements covering the following: contractor's obligations to furnish materials and labor for installation, the owner's right to inspect items furnished, requirements for the contractor to replace rejected or damaged pieces, penalties paid by the contractor in the event of delays or failure to fulfill the contract, acceptance of work completed, guarantees, and a referral to floor plans attached to the document. The General Conditions section also outlines the contractor's obligation to make field measurements of the building:

It is the successful contractor's responsibility to obtain and verify all field measurements to ensure proper installation of all work. No additional costs shall be charged to the owner for modification of library custom wood furniture required to provide proper installation.

A project involving a new building or major renovation often presents problems in regard to delivery. The problem lies as much with the difficulty of predicting when a building will be completed as it does with the availability of the furniture. It is very difficult to time the purchasing of furnishings so precisely that the factory can schedule production and deliver the items as soon as the building is completed. Although bid documents include penalties for late delivery by a vendor, no provisions are made, unfortunately, for the charges incurred by a contractor who can supply items on time but is forced to accommodate delays in the completion of a building. Sometimes the scheduling of delivery can be complicated (as in the example given here); the details need to be included in the bid document in order to avoid misunderstandings:

Delivery and installation of furniture to be provided in this contract shall be performed in two (2) phases that will coincide with the completion of phases of the general construction contract. The two phases are as follows:

PHASE I—Completion of the first- and second-level additions to the library building; PHASE II—Completion of the interior renovation of the existing library building. Completion of the general construction contracts for each phase, for the purposes of this furniture contract, shall occur after all final inspections are approved and an occupancy permit is issued by the city.

All furniture included in Phase I (as represented by Drawings F-2 and F-3) must be delivered, installed in place, and clean within a period of ten (10) calendar days immediately following the general construction contract completion of Phase I. All furniture included in Phase II (as represented by Drawing F-1) must be delivered, installed in place, and clean within a period of ten (10) calendar days immediately following the general construction contract completion of Phase II.

Completion dates of the general construction work in each phase as projected at this date are as follows: Completion of Phase I—June 1, 1996; Completion of Phase II—August 15, 1996. The general construction completion dates will be revised as work progresses in the general construction. The contractor should, however, be prepared to furnish all items for Phase I any time between June 1, 1996 and September 1, 1996. In like manner, the contractor should be prepared to furnish all items for Phase II any time between August 15, 1996 and November 15, 1996. The architect reserves the right to adjust these "delivery windows" in the event of unusual, unforeseen events. In an effort to minimize problems with delivery of furniture and conflicts with this contract, the architect shall issue written updated completion schedules to the successful contractor(s) during the first week of each month.

The contractor shall be responsible for all coordination of the delivery of furniture to be provided as required, to coincide with the completion of each phase of the general construction contract.

No furniture shall be delivered and stored on the site prior to its installation. The Contractor shall be responsible for any and all storage of furniture prior to delivery and installation.

Requirements regarding where, when, and how deliveries are to be made are also covered in the General Conditions section, along with statements about protection of the building during installation, cleanup required, and final acceptance of the furnishings:

All delivery shall be made during regular business hours. Contractor or his representative shall be at the job site to accept all deliveries. No drop-shipping shall be allowed.

Under no circumstances will the owner be obligated to receive deliveries. The Contractor shall be required to provide protective runways (plastic or other suitable material) on all finished floors throughout the building in areas where furniture is being transported or installed. All furniture will be initially delivered at the loading dock on the north side of the building. Furniture delivered for Phase I shall enter the new addition through the Receiving Room, No. 120. (See Drawing F-2.) Furniture delivered for Phase II shall enter the existing building through the Theatre, No. 106. (See Drawing F-1.)

The bid document should also spell out terms of payment of the contract:

For the satisfactory fulfillment of the order for furniture, payment in full shall be due as stated below: First—85 percent of the value of the material and items on the premises, when substantially all of it has been delivered and installed or placed in storage awaiting installation. Second—the balance of the order sum within 30 days after acceptance of all installed items.

Either the General Conditions section or the detailed specifications must include a statement about the submission of shop drawings by the successful contractor and details concerning the approval of the drawings. Shop drawings should be required for any items that are custom designed or are modifications of a standard item. The dimensions and construction of items illustrated on the shop drawings should be examined by the architect, the designer or consultant, and the librarian.

Standard Forms and Agreements
The legal agreement for the contract between the owner and supplier is given here, along with other necessary forms.

Miscellaneous Items
This section will include such items as wage scales, taxes and other charges, patents and licenses, and required insurance.

Detailed Specifications by Bid Group
Furnishings are usually grouped in such a manner that vendors who supply certain kinds of items can bid all of one group and as many groups as they wish. Library bids may include the following groups: steel bookstacks, wood technical furniture and bookstacks, standard contract office furniture, meeting room furnishings, and upholstered items, including chairs and sofas. Sometimes, the chairs are included with the technical furniture.

The specifications may include details regarding the mandatory submission of samples. Because the provision of samples is expensive for the manufacturer, the practice of requiring them tends to discourage bidders who really are not qualified to handle the level of quality and magnitude of some projects. Sometimes samples are required prior to the bid process and are used as part of the process of prequalifying bidders.

Bidders can be prequalified either by submitting samples or by receiving "approved equal" status for their products as noted earlier. The results of the prequalification process are published as an addendum to the original bid documents. Prequalification lengthens the time needed to complete the bid process. The timing of the bid might be something like this: The package is put out for bid with an announcement of a prebid conference to be held a week later; the bidders are given three weeks following the conference to submit samples; the library requires two weeks prior to the day of the bid opening to review the samples and mail out addenda with the results of the prequalification. The process, therefore, requires at least six weeks.

Only the bids submitted by those companies approved as qualified prior to the bid opening should be considered legitimate bids. When samples are required, the procedure for accepting and evaluating samples should comply with the exact stipulations of the bid document. It is an abuse of the bid process, and is unfair to reliable manufacturers, when an owner waives the requirement for a sample or extends the submission deadline because some company that was expected to bid did not provide the sample in time. Failure to submit the sample according to the bid document should automatically disqualify that company as a bidder. Furthermore, samples should not be requested if they are not really needed, or if the decision makers are not absolutely sure of the level of quality and style desired. It is a waste of everyone's time and money if a sample for a particular item is requested, and the purchaser then decides that the library didn't really need that quality or want that style after all. Here is a sample statement for requiring samples prior to the bid opening:

> To ensure that the specified products are furnished and installed in accordance with the design intent and the level of quality desired, procedures have been established for advance submittal of sample for review and approval by the owner prior to receipt of bids. All samples shall be of the exact design, size, construction, material, detail, and finish of the products proposed to be furnished in this contract. The samples received shall be inspected and reviewed by the owner to determine each contractor's acceptability to bid on the contract. All determinations shall be based on the initial samples submitted; contractors shall not be permitted to resubmit samples if the initial samples are rejected. Decisions by the owner shall be final.
>
> The samples, when approved, shall be used as the basis of the minimum acceptable quality of all similar furniture to be supplied by the successful contractor. Any and all subsequent furniture delivered to the job site that does not meet the quality of the approved samples shall be rejected and removed by the contractor.
>
> Samples must be received in the office of the architect at least fourteen (14) days prior to the opening of bids. Contractor is responsible for any unpacking, setup, or installation of samples necessary for complete review in the office of the architect. Each contractor submitting samples shall be notified in writing by the owner of approval or rejection of the items submitted. Only those contractors who are approved shall be permitted to submit a bid for this contract.
>
> Submit one complete sample of all of the following items: 1) Item W-21, adult reading chair; 2) Item W-14, adult lounge chair; 3) Item W-8, catalog and computer table, including complete operable electrical system (Contractor must demonstrate, to the satisfaction of the owner, evidence of an understanding of and compliance with the electrical requirements of this project by providing literature or documented statements of the same information. Evidence of completed projects including this type of electrical requirement will suffice for meeting this criterion, also); 4) Item S-5, one (1) double-faced section of steel shelving, 66" high x 24" deep with one 24"-deep closed-base shelf, and eight adjustable 10"-deep shelves with one end panel and a canopy top.
>
> Samples shall remain the property of the submitting contractor. All arrangements and charges associated with the shipping and handling of submitted samples shall be the responsibility of each contractor. All samples shall be removed from the architect's office within seven (7) days after receipt of written notice to do so. Samples submitted by the successful contractor shall be retained to be incorporated into the project at the appropriate time.

Samples are sometimes requested from the successful bidder following the awarding of the contract in order to ensure that the furnishings will be built according to exact specifications and with the level of quality desired. Here again, the owner retains the sample to use as a model against which the quality of the rest of the shipment can be measured.

The specific qualifications of bidders are also set out in this part of the bid document. For example, manufacturers must have produced items of the type specified for at least five years and be able to provide the names of at least three installations of equal or larger size that they have done in the last five years. The bidder can also be required to provide evidence that the furniture in the referenced projects was actually made in the company's manufacturing plant or in a factory where the company had responsibility for controlling the quality of the products. If there is any question about the qualifications of a bidder or the ability of the manufacturer to supply the item as specified (especially in a large project), the librarian and/or others involved in the project should tour the factory and visit some of the referenced projects.

The introduction to the detailed specifications for each group of furnishings may include background information about the project, requirements for style or design, workmanship, testing, samples of finishes, cleanup, and guarantees. General paragraphs should cover the requirements for wood and other materials, standard construction methods, electrical requirements, and finishing processes.

Detailed specifications can be written in several ways, depending on the kinds of furnishings specified. Specifications for steel bookstacks usually include a list of the individual components needed by size, as well as a general section describing the construction, material, and finish of the shelving. Standard contract office furniture is often specified simply by stating the relevant ordering information. Guarantees and performance specifications can also be included if the purchaser wants to ensure a particular level of quality:

High-density articulating stack chairs, armless, sled base. 19 ¾" wide x 21 ½" deep x 32 ½" high, seat height 18". Seat and back shall be constructed of injection-molded polypropylene. Seat shall consist of one piece screwed to frame. Backrest shall be two sections that form a snap fit and are then screwed together. Chair frame shall be constructed of $7/16$" o. d. steel rod welded into a one-piece unit. Seats shall have two die-formed, 11 gauge straps welded to side frames. Back articulation will be achieved with a single piece frame that flexes as the back pivots around its upper and lower crossbars. The seat will be hung from the lower back so that the user's weight counterbalances the tilting pressure of the upper back. Stacking bumpers shall be an integral part of the frame and shall be welded to the lower front frame radius. Twenty-five (25) chairs shall stack on a dolly. Chairs shall have leg/frame finished in IF1179 Red; polypropylene seat and backrest shall be finished in warm gray (KI Perry chair, PRY-P/RD/WG or equal).

Performance specifications are sometimes used. Unfortunately, many products have not been performance-tested, so it is difficult to describe what is needed in these terms. Also, performance specifications do not allow for meeting the needs of the library in terms of design. As discussed in earlier chapters, performance tests are available for steel bookstacks, wood finishes, and some tables and chairs.

Most specifications are detailed descriptions of the materials and construction to be used in manufacturing an item. Performance specifications can be included with the description. An individual specification will include the kind of item; dimensions; finishes and upholstery; electrical requirements; type of wood construction (three-ply particleboard, five-ply lumber core, etc.); joinery to be used; hardware; special features or modifications required in construction; and the name of a vendor to establish the level of quality. If the furniture of more than one manufacturer is acceptable from the standpoint of style and construction, include the names and model numbers for several products. This is likely to be the case where furniture to be purchased will be a standard library chair to be used with a manufacturer's standard leg-base table and technical furniture. It is possible to list only one product for some items and reference several brands for another item. Do not include special features of an item unless they are necessary. If you will accept a product that does not have the feature, do not mention it in the specifications. An example of a detailed specification for a table with custom features and a lounge chair with required performance testing would read thus:

Catalog and computer table. 68" wide x 74⁷/₈" long x 42" high. Double-faced with electrical system and four- compartment call slip units. (Stand-up reference table)

Tabletop will be constructed of five-ply lumber core, 1¼" thick with a .050" high-pressure laminate face. The two sides will be edged with a 2" x 2" band of solid oak, shaped to a $1^3/8$" radius, splined and glued to the lumber core and flush with the laminate. Panel ends will be constructed of $1^7/16$" five-ply lumber core with select oak veneer on the face and back. The panel will be edged with a 4" wide band of solid oak, splined flush to all four sides of the core. The band will be shaped to a 1½" radius on the top two corners and a ½" radius on the bottom two corners. All four corners will be mitered and double-doweled. The edges of the oak band will have a continuous bullnose shape. The panels will have a double-rout detail. The first rout will be 2½" from the edge of the panel and will be ¼" x ¼". The second rout will be ½" from the interior edge of the first rout and will be $3/16$" x $3/16$". Both routs will be curved to match the radiused edges on all four corners of the panel. Each panel end will be equipped with a pair of adjustable leveling glides. The table will have a longitudinal stabilizing keel 1" thick x 8" wide, five-ply lumber core construction with select oak face and back. Bottom edge shall be banded with $1/8''$ solid oak and machined to receive a steel bracket. The keel shall be attached to the underside of the top by means of ¾" square screw cleats and at the bottom by means of a $5/16$"

x ¾" black oxidized truss head machine screw passing through a bracket into threaded inserts embedded in the end panel. Each side of the table will be equipped with a three-compartment call slip unit. The assembled unit will have all edges rounded, then finished to match the table. The finished unit will be positioned at the center of each table edge and screwed to the underside of the tabletop. The interior dimensions of each compartment will be 3½" high x 3½" wide x 5" deep. The table will be equipped with an electrical raceway mounted flush with the writing surface and located in the center of the table along the full length of the top. See specifications above for Electrical System. Laminate: Formica, Storm, #912 (Worden X-2800 series modified or equal).

Single lounge chair. 29½" high x 27½" deep x 29" wide; seat height 17"; arm height 25½". Chairs to be upholstered in Designtex Autumn, 1006-401 Baltic (Worden Regis 3521-25-0 or equal).

The lounge chair shall be of suspended frame design with the frame rising above the floor approximately 6" and supported by oak structure legs. The chair shall have an upholstered seat, back, and side panels. The back of the chair shall have an eased arch detail. The front, top, and back of the upholstered side panels shall be banded with solid oak and shall have a solid oak dowel stretcher running between the front and back legs. The front profile of the side panels shall be arched both out at the legs and eased up to the armrest at the top of the chair. The upholstery shall be tightly stretched and tailored around side panel frames with no welts.

All interior frames shall be soft maple, a minimum of 1¹⁄₆" thick. Exposed parts (arms and legs) shall be constructed of select solid red oak. All joints shall be double-doweled and double-glued.

The inside back of the upholstery shall be webbed with elasticized fabric and shall be covered with 2½" fire retardant, polyurethane foam. The foam shall be of 2.8 lb. density and 30 lb. IFD (30 lb. IFD at 25 percent deflection). The outside of the back shall be webbed with elasticized fabric and covered with a ¾" thick fire retardant polyurethane foam with 1.2 lb. density and 32 lb. IFD.

The seat shall be constructed with a spring unit at each seating position that shall consist of six (6) 9-gauge sinuous springs. The seat shall be covered with 2" thick, fire-retardant polyurethane foam of 2.8 lb. density and 45 lb. IFD; the bottom shall be covered with black fabric.

The arms shall be webbed with elasticized fabric and covered with ¾" thick, fire-retardant polyurethane foam with 1.2 lb. density and 32 lb. IFD. The seat, back, and arms shall be of tight upholstering design with all seams backed and double-stitched.

The legs and arms shall be of red oak. Each leg shall be furnished with a ¾" nylon button glide.

The lounge seating must be tested by an independent testing laboratory and shall be certified as being tested as prescribed in GSA Specification FNAE-80-214. BIFMA standards or other "Pass or Fail" standards will not meet the criteria for this specification.

The following test levels must be satisfied for each seating position. (For sofas, the total load values shall be tripled.)

1. Seat Load Foundation Test: 225/112.5 lbs. and 250,000 cycles successfully completed.
2. Backrest Foundation Test: 150 lbs. and 225,000 cycles successfully completed.
3. Backrest Frame Test: 150 lbs. and 100,000 cycles successfully completed.
4. Back Leg Test: 300 lbs. and 100,000 cycles successfully completed.
5. Side Thrust Load Test on Arms Outward: 200 lbs. and 175,000 cycles successfully completed.
6. Side Thrust Load Test on Legs: 350 lbs. and 100,000 successfully completed.

Specification writing requires specialized knowledge and expertise. Most vendors and manufacturers will provide detailed specifications for their products. Designers and library consultants who are hired to plan the interior of the library will write the specifications as part of their job. Specifications are also written by members of architectural firms, purchasing agents, or facilities managers.

Awarding bids for furniture is seldom a simple matter of accepting the lowest bids. Usually, a number of factors have to be studied in making purchasing decisions. Although every item of furniture in the library does not have to be made by one manufacturer, it is wise to remember that splitting a package among several manufacturers on a small project may mean the library will not obtain the best price from any one of the suppliers. The more specific and clearly written the bid requirements are, the easier it is to decide which suppliers will receive the contracts. If the low bid deviates from the bid documents or does not meet the specifications in regard to style or level of quality, or if the bidder cannot meet the delivery date or has not supplied required samples, the bid should not be considered "responsible." If information regarding the qualifications of the manufacturer cannot be obtained, the bid should be rejected. Likewise, the burden of demonstrating that an alternate item is an equal lies with the bidder, not with the purchaser. The bid process works only if all parties act responsibly. These responsibilities are discussed in detail in chapter 11.

CHAPTER

11

The Library Furniture Market

The bid process discussed in chapter 10 should benefit both the purchaser and the supplier, the two parties involved in the market transaction. The market transaction can be mutually advantageous if both parties accept and carry out their responsibilities in the selection and purchase process.

In making purchases, buyers do their part by selecting furniture according to the process discussed in chapters 1 through 9. To summarize the process, librarians, designers, or consultants begin by developing a furniture program that outlines what is desired in terms of function, maintenance, and appearance. Then they, in conjunction with the others involved in the purchase, research the available products. The librarian talks to vendors in the area and visits relevant booths at conferences. (It won't take long for word to get around to suppliers that there is a library in the market for furniture.) Vendors who may want to bid or submit a quotation for prices are given an opportunity to discuss the project and explain why their products will be best for the library. The librarian and designers ask lots of questions, evaluate how well the particular furnishings of each manufacturer will fill the needs of the library, and take the time to educate and inform other parties who will play a key role in awarding the bid. The others may also read this book, talk to manufacturers and dealers, or visit a factory. The investigation of products continues until the decision makers feel certain that

they will be able to stand behind their choices when the bids or quotations come in and to objectively justify the purchases.

Librarians can benefit from knowing how furniture is sold. Different manufacturers of library and contract furniture sell their products in different ways. Some manufacturers submit bids directly from the factory. Some products are "open lines" and can be sold by any dealer. (Dealers are companies that handle the products of many different manufacturers.) Some items are sold by a limited number of dealers "authorized" by the factory to sell in a given area. Other manufacturers have "exclusive" dealers who are the only ones allowed to sell the product within a particular geographical area. Some large companies have representatives, showrooms, or regional managers who coordinate the market in a particular area and provide information and pricing to authorized dealers, but do not themselves generate orders or submit bids.

Most library manufacturers have representatives ("reps") who handle the market in a specific geographical area. The rep acts as a liaison between customers and the factory, or between dealers and the factory, by answering questions and providing information about the product, providing pricing to dealers, placing orders, and sometimes, providing additional services to customers, such as space planning or the writing of specifications. In a bid situation, the rep may bid the furniture or may supply pricing to dealers who bid.

Salespeople in the library business often have the knowledge and expertise to assist with space planning, preparation of a bid document, and the writing of specifications. Some of them will say that they are doing this for you for free; however, it is important to remember that these companies *are* in the business of selling furniture and shelving. It is reasonable to expect that somewhere along the line, someone is going to pay for the work. It may be built into the prices of the items bid on the project, or your neighboring library may pay in its project, or you may pay the next time you go to the same supplier for something else. It's all right to take advantage of this service, but understand that *someone* is paying for the work. Also, keep in mind that vendors are going to write specifications only for products they sell.

In a bid situation, the final version of the bid document and specifications should be reviewed or written by an individual who does not sell furniture or shelving and who is, therefore, in a position to provide the library with an independent opinion regarding the documents. Bid documents can be prepared, for example, by a library consultant who specializes in doing interiors. The consultant should have the library experience needed to understand what functional considerations are important in selecting furniture and the knowledge of furniture necessary to select the best product for a situation. If interior designers are also involved in the project, the library consultant acts as a liaison between the staff and the designer or architect. While the designer will know about furniture generally, the consultant will be better informed about how libraries operate and about products designed specifically for the library. Consultants should be familiar with the manufacturers and vendors of library furniture, should have visited the major factories, and should know what's happening in the industry. They should know the capability of the manufacturers, the kinds of materials typically used, and standard construction techniques.

Consultants are aware that there are many different ways to furnish a library and many different products available; some are appropriate in one situation, some in another. An independent consultant is not bound, like a salesperson, to specify only the products of particular manufacturers. A library that works with a consultant should receive information about a wide range of products and have an opportunity to purchase the best quality available for the money. The funds spent for a consultant

are not hidden. Because of the specialized knowledge provided, however, the library hiring a consultant will very likely receive more quality for its money and will be assured of furnishing the building at or below budget. Because of the time and expertise needed, a consultant can be as helpful on a small project as on a large one.

The best interests of both librarians and those in the library furniture business are served if all parties act honestly and responsibly in the purchase process. Actions that are unfair to either the buyer or the seller are a detriment to the industry, resulting in higher prices and possibly lower overall quality. It is very frustrating for everyone who understands the role of the parties in the market—both librarians and those in the industry—when individuals and organizations do not act responsibly.

SUPPLIER RESPONSIBILITIES

The responsibilities of the supplier include the following:

1. The vendor should be knowledgeable about the product lines represented and be able to provide information about standard products, basic construction and materials, the capability of the manufacturer to do custom work, the limitations of the factory, special features of the products, and where and how the items can best be used. The salesperson should be able to discuss the positive aspects of the product without making unfounded negative comments about the work of competitors.

2. Once the decision has been made as to what products best fit the needs of the library, the vendor should supply budget pricing and specifications upon request. In some cases, the vendor may also assist with space planning.

3. Vendors should understand the purchase process and be reliable in following the procedures exactly as they are stipulated in the bid document. They should attend the prebid conference, if one is announced. Having accepted the terms of the bid and asked all relevant questions in regard to approved items, equivalents, etc., prior to submitting a bid, the vendor should accept the decision of the purchaser, if all of the terms of the bid document have been carried out in the selection process.

4. A vendor who has been awarded a contract should provide the purchaser with regular updates in regard to the delivery date, supply ac-

curate shop drawings in a timely manner, discuss any problems or questions that arise in the production of the items, and work cooperatively with the purchaser to accommodate changes in schedule on the part of either party. The vendor is obligated to supply the items as specified and bid, unless a change has been agreed upon by both parties.

5. It is the responsibility of vendors to see that the items are correctly and expeditiously installed, whether the work is done by the primary contractor or a subcontractor. If the vendor subcontracts the job, the scope and details of the work should be carefully reviewed with the subcontractor prior to the installation. Likewise, the installer should have all relevant shop drawings and specifications as well as the knowledge and expertise to interpret the documents. The supplier should provide any special instructions needed for the use or maintenance of the products. If parts are missing, or items are not received or are incorrectly supplied, the installer should notify the vendor, who should then take action immediately to work out a solution to the problem and correct the mistake.

6. The vendor should follow up on all questions that appear at the time of the installation and correct any problems that are the result of faulty workmanship, materials, etc. The most reliable suppliers will work cooperatively to correct problems even after the warranty period, if it is obvious that the manufacturer was at fault.

7. Manufacturers have an obligation to be customer-responsive. They should know how libraries function, attempt to develop new products or improve old ones to meet the needs of the library, and maintain quality control of their products.

PURCHASER RESPONSIBILITIES

The purchaser also has a set of responsibilities. In order to keep prices reasonable and keep the market competitive, it is as important for the librarian to act responsibly in the selection and purchase process as it is for the supplier. This side of the transaction is, unfortunately for our profession, sometimes ignored:

1. It is the responsibility of the librarian or other purchasing agent to gather information and make selection decisions based on knowledge and understanding of the products available. Only after the decision has been made as to the particular product or level of quality desired should a librarian ask a vendor to supply space planning services and/or provide furniture specifications for a project. A librarian not genuinely interested in a product should not waste a salesperson's time. A purchaser is not doing a vendor a favor by "letting" the vendor assist on a project in order to make all parties involved think the work is being spread around. A vendor cannot be expected to be up-front and frank with the purchaser if the librarian is playing games.

2. Decision makers have a responsibility to their funding bodies to purchase the highest level of quality that their money will buy. All parties in the purchase process should agree on the level of quality expected and be prepared to defend the level specified when the bids come in. Whenever possible, evidence of level of quality should be obtained by requiring proof of field or performance testing during the purchase process. Laboratory testing of products is done voluntarily by manufacturers. The level of quality for furnishings should not be lowered in writing specifications or in awarding a bid because some manufacturers have decided not to make the commitment of time and funds needed to performance test their products. It is the responsibility of the purchaser to ensure that all of the stipulations of the bid documents are valid and maintained in awarding the bids. In other words, decision makers should not specify top-of-the-line, performance-tested items if they are going to accept lower quality furnishings that have not been performance tested when the bids come in.

3. It is the responsibility of the librarian and design professionals to educate and inform all parties who will eventually be involved in awarding a contract. The education process should go on throughout the decision-making process. If a library or Friends board, purchasing agent, or administrator will ultimately have some say in regard to the purchase, it is important to make sure that that person or group agrees with the librarian concerning what product(s) will be acceptable *before* the project is bid.

4. The librarian should ask for a reasonable amount of information regarding delivery dates without harassing the supplier.

5. If furniture arrives that has not been made according to specifications in regard to construction, materials, design, or quality, the librarian is obligated to reject it and demand that the job be done correctly. It is unfair to reputable manufacturers and vendors for a library to accept items that do not fulfill the contract. The practice of accepting inferior goods allows dishonest companies to stay in business and lowers the standards of the industry for everyone.

6. Once a project is installed, the librarian has a responsibility to go over all items carefully to make sure that any problems are called to the attention of the supplier immediately. It is better to ask a question or point out a problem and attempt to work out a solution than to let it go and then gripe about the mistake later. In many cases, the problem may be easily corrected. No project is perfect; be prepared to compromise in working out solutions.

7. A vendor cannot be expected to correct a problem that has nothing to do with the manufacture of the product, but rather, is a problem with the situation or environment in which the item is being installed. For example, if wall shelving cannot be properly installed because the wall is crooked, it is not the responsibility of the installer to straighten the wall. Once again, you get what you pay for. If a bookshelf made of particleboard, rather than lumber core, is specified and purchased, the vendor cannot be expected to replace a sagging shelf with one of solid wood.

SUMMARY

It would be wonderful if all librarians and all manufacturers and vendors could be depended upon to act responsibly and with integrity in all situations. Unfortunately this is not the case. There are members of every profession who do not act ethically or in the best interests of others with the same job.

The librarian who has made a decision based on a thorough investigation of what is available has a right to choose which furniture is best for the project. Unfortunately, not all salespeople want to accept this; sometimes a vendor will low-bid an alternate product that meets only part of the specifications, on the chance that the buyer will not stand behind the document and will make an award for an item that does not meet specifications. In cases where alternates that comply only partially with specifications are purchased, vendors who bid exactly to specifications have been treated unfairly.

Different librarians like different products, and there are enough projects for vendors who sell good products to get their share of the market without resorting to unethical behavior. The library that does not stand behind its bid, and gives in to intimidation or threats, does a disservice to other libraries as well as to the salespeople of integrity in the business.

In summary, the selection of functional, attractive, and easy-to-maintain library furnishings begins by determining the needs of the library and collecting information about what products are available. Once products equal to the level of quality desired are chosen, both the vendor and the librarian have responsibilities regarding the bid and purchase process. Sound decisions and responsible actions on both sides of the process will ensure that the library is getting the highest level of quality possible for the funds available.

APPENDIX

Goals, Objectives, and the Furniture Selection Process

Below is a mission statement and the goals and objectives developed for the Carrollton Public Library, Carrollton, Texas. The goals and objectives were developed to outline the long-range services and collections for a much larger building than that currently occupied by the library. In order to emphasize the relationship between the stated goals and objectives and the furniture selection and acquisition process, the impact of some objectives on interior planning and furniture selection is noted in italics. Although not all of the goals and objectives have an impact on furniture selection, the entire document as originally written is included here.

THE LIBRARY'S MISSION

Carrollton Public Library provides dynamic, state-of- the-art service to the diverse population of the community. The library is dedicated to improving the quality of life of its users by supporting lifelong learning and recreational library use. The library serves as a source of community pride and as an asset to the city that helps to attract new individuals, families, and businesses.

GOALS AND OBJECTIVES OF CARROLLTON PUBLIC LIBRARY, 1992-1997

I. Goal: Carrollton Public Library is located in a state- of-the-art facility that meets or exceeds com-

munity, state, and national standards for library buildings and that allows the staff to provide high quality service to the residents of the city.

Objective:

1. To construct library space that will provide a minimum of .7 square foot of space per capita (65,000–75,000 square feet) and adequate parking space on the present municipal complex site, or on a site in the general area of the municipal complex, that will include all of the improvements recommended in the library's long-range master plan.

II. Goal: As the city's major information center, the library serves to enhance the quality of life of Carrollton's diverse population by providing a well-balanced collection of books in English and other languages for people of all ages.

Objectives:

1. To develop a collection development plan that includes guidelines for the number of copies of titles to be purchased, that identifies "black-hole" subject areas that need continuous large quantity purchasing, that identifies areas targeted for expansion and new kinds of materials to be purchased, and that determines a general plan for

purchasing the opening-day collection(s). for the expanded building(s).

2. To expand the library's collections to provide a minimum of 2.5 books per capita (250,000–300,000).

[Bookstacks to house the 250,000–300,000 books will be needed.]

3. To improve the adult collection of nonfiction by purchasing multiple copies of high-demand titles in popular subject areas identified in the collection development plan.

4. To work to eliminate the need for a limit on the number of titles that can be checked out in some high-demand subject areas.

5. To expand the paperback collection based on demand and expanded space available.

[An increase in the number of paperback racks or stacks will be needed to house the collection.]

6. To purchase more language-learning materials and to develop collections of books in languages other than English (for both children and adults) that will serve the growing populations of residents seeking books in Spanish, Asian, and other languages.

7. To cooperate with organizations in the community who are interested in contributing to the library's book collections in languages other than English and in specialized areas such as genealogy and technical subjects.

8. To designate an area of the expanded library for the continuing development of a basic collection in genealogy and local history.

[The special collections noted in objectives 6, 7, and 8 may be designated in the building by particular furnishings or by a particular arrangement of the furnishings.]

9. To improve the children's collection by purchasing multiple copies of popular books as identified generally in the collection development plan.

10. To designate an area of the expanded building for young adults and to expand the young adult collection.

III. Goal: In order to fill a wide range of recreational and informational needs, Carrollton Public Library provides a comprehensive collection that includes books, periodicals, audio-visual materials, micro-

forms, and computerized resources that are easily accessible and prominently displayed.

Objectives:

1. To improve the access, arrangement, and display of audio-visual materials by designating a highly visible area of the expanded building to house all of these items in one convenient self-serve location.

2. To expand the collections of videotapes, books-on-tape, and audio-cassettes as determined in the collection development plan and to work toward eliminating the need to limit the number of videotapes that can be checked out at one time.

3. To develop a collection of compact discs and a collection of recreational and educational computer software for in-house use and possible check out.

[Expansion of the A-V collections and improvement in access indicate a need for appropriate furnishings to house these growing collections.]

4. To develop a listening and viewing area for the public with carrels for listening to cassettes and compact discs or looking at videotapes.

[Furniture selection will include carrels for listening and viewing.]

5. To maintain the collection of current issues of magazines for patron browsing and to increase the number of subscriptions in the expanded building by a quantity determined in the collection development plan.

6. To improve access to back issues of periodicals by adding the Journal Citation Module to the automated system.

7. To consider phasing out the purchase of back issues of magazines in microform and phasing in full-text access to back issues in computerized formats, either on-line or on CD-ROM, and to provide appropriate equipment in adequate numbers to provide convenient access to back issues in these new formats.

[Plans for furnishings should include more shelving for current issues and a number of workstations for periodicals in computerized formats.]

IV. Goal: The library introduces preschoolers and school-age children and their parents to books and reading and provides stimulating activities that enhance childhood learning.

Objectives:

1. To provide a large children's area in the expanded building that is separated from the other areas of the building by glass or furnishings.

2. To provide a storytime/activity room (with a stage) adjacent to the children's area for regular weekly programs, and to provide a prop storage and staging area for the preparation of programs next to the storytime room.

3. To provide a small parents "waiting area" close to the storytime room for 15 to 20 parents.

[Special furnishings may be needed for the storytime room and related space. Appropriate seating will have to be provided for the waiting area.]

4. To provide an office for the librarian, a work area for the staff, and appropriate storage for the children's program.

[Workstations or office furnishings will be needed to support the staff in the children's area.]

5. To provide restrooms specifically designed for children and located adjacent to the children's area.

6. To add a parenting collection, a basic reference collection, and a home schooling collection to the children's area.

7. To expand the kinds and number of children's activities to include, for example, a storytime in Spanish, a Great Books program for children, family reading programs, contests, and multi-cultural activities.

8. To eliminate the need to limit registration for regular, weekly children's programs.

9. To eliminate the need to run two one-month programs during the summer.

10. To move the children's audio-visual items from the adult area and to display them in the children's area, and to provide listening and viewing equipment for in-house use of the A-V materials.

[Additional A-V display furnishings will be needed in the children's area. Carrels or counters for listening and viewing should be included.]

11. To provide a large tackable wall and display case for the children's area.

V. Goal: An experienced and knowledgeable staff of librarians provide high quality information and reader's advisory service using an up-to-date collection of reference sources in books, microform, and computer formats.

Objectives:

1. To expand and improve the adult reference collection of books according to guidelines in the collection development plan.

2. To expand the reference collection to include computer- based sources in online or CD-ROM formats.

[More computer workstations for the public will be needed.]

3. To provide an improved and expanded reference desk/center with a place designated for holding private/confidential reference consultations with a patron.

[Plans for the reference desk must include a section or area for private consultations.]

4. To plan an area away from the public for providing ready-reference service by phone.

5. To provide a service desk near the entrance to the library, possibly staffed by volunteers, where users can stop to ask directional questions about locations within the library building.

[A desk to be placed near the entrance to the library will need to be purchased.]

6. To develop an improved procedure for answering all library telephones from one centralized switching location.

VI. Goal: Library circulation functions are performed by an experienced and knowledgeable staff dedicated to providing efficient, responsive, and friendly service to all patrons.

Objectives:

1. To provide an expanded, ergonomically-designed circulation desk that will hold all necessary equipment, supplies, and materials arranged in a convenient manner.

2. To study ways of handling circulation functions more efficiently in an improved work area.

3. To add more positions to the circulation staff so that every staff member can have some scheduled work time away from the public desk every day.

[A larger, more efficient circulation desk to handle automated functions will need to be designed.]

4. To provide adequate work space for every member of the circulation staff in a circulation workroom.

PLANNING LIBRARY INTERIORS: THE SELECTION OF FURNISHINGS FOR THE 21ST CENTURY

5. To provide an improved area for handling the discharge and sorting of returned library materials.

[Plans for furnishings will include a number of workstations or desks for the circulation staff.]

6. To reduce the number of activities performed at the circulation desk by arranging the library materials in such a manner that self-service is encouraged.

VII. Goal: An experienced and knowledgeable technical services staff efficiently handle the acquisition, processing, and cataloging of library materials in a timely manner.

Objectives:

1. To provide an improved and expanded work area that reflects the flow of materials from the delivery area to the shelves.

2. To provide a receiving area with space for checking in new materials and for the temporary storage of boxes and equipment.

3. To provide adequate storage for the temporary shelving of materials in process and the storage of supplies.

4. To provide an area designated for checking and repairing audio-visual materials.

5. To provide work space designed specifically for the processing of new books and audio-visual materials.

[Furnishings for technical services will include a number of workstations designed to accommodate a variety of specific tasks.]

VIII. Goal: The library provides specialized public services and a variety of kinds of seating for reading and study in a comfortable building designed to minimize noise levels.

Objectives:

1. To provide readers seats at tables and study carrels for approximately 330 people in the adult area, 20 people in the young adult area, and 100 people in the children's area.

2. To provide an ample number of lounge seats in both the children's and adult areas.

3. To provide a spacious and comfortable area for patrons reading current issues of newspapers and magazines.

4. To provide small rooms that will accommodate no more than four people for quiet or group study or proctoring exams.

[Furniture selections will include seating in the quantities and kinds indicated by the objectives.]

5. To provide key card or coin-operated computers and typewriters for public use in a designated room or rooms.

6. To provide an adequate number of photocopiers, computer terminals, microform reader/printers, and other equipment in an area designated and designed specifically for these items.

[More equipment workstations will be needed.]

IX. Goal: A specially designed area of the library is designated for the use of young adults and includes seating, display, and a collection of materials of special interest to users of this age group.

Objectives:

1. To provide seating for 20 people and shelving for a maximum of 10,000 books in a designated area that can be seen from a reference desk.

2. To provide display capabilities that will attract young patrons to the area.

3. To increase the kinds and number of library activities offered specifically to young adults.

[Furniture selections will include specific items for the young adult section including 20 seats, shelving for 10,000 books, and, possibly display racks.]

X. Goal: Carrollton Public Library contributes to the economic development of the city by providing a specialized collection of information in paper, microform, and electronic formats to fill the needs of businesses and industries located in the community.

Objectives:

1. To expand the library's collection of information about large and small local businesses, business and industrial directories, investment services, and other reference sources according to guidelines developed in the collection development plan.

2. To add computerized business resources on CD-ROM to support the book collection.

[More computer workstations will be needed!]

3. To purchase an online database service and to develop procedures and policies for patron and staff use of the services.

4. To expand the collection of audio-visual media on subjects of interest to the business community.

5. To develop a circulating collection of computer software that will include programs for interactive training.

XI. Goal: The library provides resources and space to support both formal and informal courses of study involving students of all ages.

Objectives:

1. To provide a designated area in the larger building for an expanded collection of literacy, adult basic education, GED, and ESL materials.

2. To provide small rooms for literacy tutoring and conference/meeting room space for adult education classes.

3. To provide flexible office space that can be used by individuals coordinating the literacy and other adult education programs.

4. To develop an adult literacy tutoring program that involves cooperating with other literacy organizations in the community.

5. To develop an expanded program of GED and ESL classes in cooperation with other organizations.

6. To develop a family literacy program that involves parents and children learning to read together.

[Special furnishings and shelving will be needed to support the library's expanded education program.]

XII. Goal: As a vital element in Carrollton, the library maintains a complete program of community outreach that involves delivering service outside the library building and cooperating with other service-providers to improve the quality of life of local residents.

Objectives:

1. To develop a community outreach plan that can be implemented in the expanded building.

2. To purchase the vehicles necessary for delivering library services outside the library building.

3. To provide regular library service to institutions in the city, including nursing and retirement homes, senior recreation sites, and day-care centers serving disadvantaged families.

4. To develop a program that provides books to the homebound, possibly a volunteer program co-

ordinated by the library staff, or a books-by-mail program.

5. To instigate an organization of service-providers in the community that includes the library and that meets in the library on a regular basis to discuss cooperative programs and resource-sharing.

6. To expand reference services to make the library the primary source for local information and a key information and referral agency in the community.

7. To develop a newcomers' program that dispenses information about the library on a regular basis to families and individuals moving into the city.

8. To develop a program for placing small deposit collections of paperback books in day care centers, apartment complexes, and other appropriate places.

9. To expand the collection of large print books to support the expansion of outreach services.

10. To develop a computerized file for providing information and referral service using the Dynix community resource module.

[Furnishings will be selected to provide an effective staging area for a variety of outreach programs that involve taking materials into the community. Expanded information and referral services may impact the design of the reference desk.]

XIII. Goal: The library serves as a community center by providing meeting space for non-profit organizations and by sponsoring a variety of informational and recreational programs for adults.

Objectives:

1. To provide a large, flexible meeting space (auditorium) with seating for 200–300 people, as well as smaller meeting spaces in the expanded building.

[Plans will include auditorium and meeting room seating for 200–300 people.]

2. To offer additional library-sponsored programs for adults on practical topics, such as job-related programs and programs for adults with special needs.

XIV. Goal: The library cooperates with area school districts and private schools to ensure that the library needs of students are adequately met and that local resources are used effectively.

Objectives:

1. To instigate a "library liaison board" that includes representatives from the Lewisville and Carrollton- Farmers Branch Independent School Districts and Carrollton Public Library and that meets on a regular basis to discuss cooperative programs and resource sharing.

2. To network with local school librarians and to host at least one annual meeting/social event with local school librarians.

XV. Goal: Carrollton Public Library provides a functional, efficiently-designed work environment that allows the staff to work productively and comfortably.

Objectives:

1. To provide two expanded workrooms (one for the circulation staff and functions and one for the technical services staff and functions) that are designed to expedite work flow.

2. To provide private offices for the library director, the assistant library director, the librarian in charge of adult reference, the head of children's services, the head of circulation, and the head of technical services; as well as offices for future staff members who will manage a young adult program, public information, grant application and library development, outreach, coordination of volunteers, training and staff development, and library business and personnel.

3. To provide a workstation or desk away from the public for every full-time staff member.

4. To provide adequate shared work space for every part-time staff member.

5. To provide a locker and coat storage for every library staff member and for volunteers.

6. To provide staff restrooms that are not in the staff lounge and that meet ADA guidelines.

7. To provide a larger staff lounge.

8. To provide ergonomically designed circulation and reference desks for public service functions.

9. To provide every staff member with an ergonomically designed work space and task chair.

10. To provide adequate storage areas for extra copies of books, supplies, equipment, and other materials.

11. To provide an improved book drop with convenient access for both users and staff.

12. To provide a production area for preparing programming materials, items for public relations, signage, and displays.
[Most of these objectives are directly related to the purchase of furnishings.]

XVI. Goal: The library has a well-trained and knowledgeable staff that is friendly, responsive, and helpful to the public and to co-workers; the number of employees is large enough to allow the staff to fulfill the library's mission and to fulfill the city's stated mission to provide effective and efficient service delivery to the residents of the community.

Objectives:

1. To provide enough staff members to adequately provide service when people are ill, during vacations, and when staff members attend training programs or conferences outside the building.

2. To provide enough employees to have both the children's and adult reference desks adequately staffed at all times.

3. To have enough Spanish-speaking staff that at least one Spanish-speaking staff member is in the building at all times when the library is open to the public.

4. To provide staff members who speak additional languages as indicated by the composition of the community.

5. To add positions to the library roster as needed to adequately staff an improved building and to implement the additional services indicated by these goals and objectives.

6. To study and implement re-structuring of the staff in order to provide an improved career ladder for some positions.

7. To develop a formalized training and development program for all employees that includes closing the library to the public for two to four days a year so that staff can attend in-service planning and training programs.

8. To develop a coordinated program for the use of volunteers to supplement and assist the staff in the library.

XVII. Goal: The library building is attractive, safe, and comfortable for all users and conforms to the guidelines of the Americans with Disabilities Act of 1990 (P.L. 101-336).

Objectives:

1. To improve and expand the public restrooms.

2. To provide a library that is barrier-free.

3. To provide an integrated and attractive sign system throughout the library that makes the building accessible to everyone.

4. To provide a telecommunication device for the deaf (TDD) in the library.

[ADA guidelines should be considered in all furniture selections.]

XVIII. Goal: Carrollton Public Library seeks to make its resources known to the community by implementing a well-planned public relations program.

Objectives:

1. To develop a complete program of public relations that is coordinated and implemented by one person and that includes contacts with the media, regular library calendars, special library publications, and the organization of library displays.

2. To improve library exhibit capabilities with large tackable walls for the display of community information, announcements, and posters and with freestanding display cases.

[An expanded public relations program may involve purchasing freestanding directories or display racks as part of the furnishings package.]

XIX. Goal: Carrollton Public Library seeks mutually advantageous ways of cooperating with other public libraries in the area.

Objectives:

1. To explore ways of cooperating with other Dynix users for the purpose of sharing bibliographic information and resources.

2. To expand the library's service area by placing Carrollton Public Library's computerized catalog in other libraries.

3. To participate in the ShareNETLs program.

XX. Goal: The library continues to enhance and upgrade its automated system in order to improve public and technical services.

Objectives:

1. To add the acquisitions module to the automated system.

2. To add the journal citation module to the system.

3. To add the serials module to the system.

4. To add the community resource file module to the system.

5. To add the capability for users to have dial-in access to the online computerized catalog.

[Journal citation module and community resource file module may impact the number of public computer workstations needed.]

XXI. Goal: Carrollton Public Library fulfills the requirements for membership in the Northeast Texas Library System and takes advantage of the support provided by the System.

XXII. Goal: Carrollton Public Library is supported by a Friends of the Library organization that serves as an advocate for the library in the community, that assists with library functions, and that carries out fundraising efforts on behalf of the library.

Objective:

1. To organize a Friends of the Library association to begin advocating for the library immediately.

XXIII. Goal: As part of an ongoing process of evaluation and improvement, Carrollton Public Library updates and revises its goals and objectives annually, and reviews and updates its long-range plans every five years.

BIBLIOGRAPHY

Amdursky, Saul J. 1993. Re-creating the Children's Room, A Renovation Project at Kalamazoo Public Library. *School Library Journal* 39, no. 2 (February): 25–28.

Architectural Woodwork Institute. 1993. *Architectural Woodwork Quality Standards*. 6th ed. Version 1.0 Centreville, Virginia: Architectural Woodwork Institute.

Arndt, Robert. 1991. *Ergonomics and Office Design*. Developed for the National Office Products Association, Office and Contract Furnishings Division. Alexandria, Virginia: National Office Products Association. Reprinted by Haworth, Inc.

Bernheim, Anthony. 1993. San Francisco Main Library: A Healthy Building. Fifty-ninth IFLA Council and Conference, Barcelona, Spain, August 22–28. Published as Booklet 6 by IFLA, Division of Management and Technology.

Boardman, Robert. 1981. Particle Board vs. Lumber Core, Panel Materials Used in Furniture and Cabinet Construction. Holland, Michigan: The Worden Company. Photocopy.

Bright, Franklyn F. 1991. Planning for a Movable Compact Shelving System. *LAMA Occasional Papers*, no. 1. Chicago: American Library Association.

Buyers Laboratory, Inc. 1982. Lateral Roll-out File Cabinets. *Library Technology Reports* 18, no. 4 (July–August): 423–473.

California State Department of Consumer Affairs. 1992. *California Technical Bulletin 133, A Fire Test for Seating, Furniture in Public Buildings, Questions and Answers*. Sacramento: California State Department of Consumer Affairs, Bureau of Home Furnishings and Thermal Insulation.

Camp, John. F. and Carl A. Eckelman. 1990. Library Bookstacks: An Overview with Test Reports on Bracket Shelving. *Library Technology Reports* 26, no. 6 (November–December): 755–894.

Chekon, Terry and Margaret Miles. 1993. The Kids' Sacramento, a Patchwork of Expertise, Hope, Conflict, and Compromise. *School Library Journal* 39, no. 2 (February): 20–24.

Computers in Libraries. 1992. Special Section: Library Equipment and Furniture. 12, no. 10 (November).

Cornell, Paul. 1989. *The Biomechanics of Sitting*. 2d ed. Grand Rapids, Michigan: Steelcase.

————. 1989. *Dynamics and Task Seating, Suiting the Chair to the Person, the Machine, the Task, and the Office Environment*. Grand Rapids, Michigan: Steelcase.

Crispen, Joanne L. ed. 1993. *The Americans with Disabilities Act: Its Impact on Libraries: The Library's Response in "Doable" Steps*. Chicago: American Library Association.

Deasy, C. M., and Thomas E. Lasswell. 1985. *Designing Places for People: a Handbook on Human Behavior for Architects, Designers, and Facility Managers*. New York: Whitney Library of Design, Watson-Guptill Publications.

DuPont. *FireLine: A Legislative Update for Contract Furnishings*. (Includes updates of legislation based on Cal 133.) Published by DuPont G52079, P.O. Box 80010, Wilmington, Delaware 19885-1010, 800-453-8527.

————. 1992. Furniture Flammability Laws: State Status Report. (Reprinted from DuPont newsletter *FireLine: A Legislative Update for Contract Furnishings*, September, 1992.) *Interiors and Sources* 6, no. 23 (September–October): 26.

———. 1993. Understanding Your Fire Liability, Guidelines to Minimize Exposure. (Reprinted from DuPont newsletter *FireLine: A Legislative Update for Contract Furnishings*, Spring, 1993.) *Interiors and Sources* 6, no. 27 (May–June): 24–27.

———. 1993. Why does Cal 133 Legislation Take So Long? (Reprinted from Du Pont newsletter *FireLine: a Legislative Update for Contract Furnishings*, Summer) *Interiors and Sources* 6, no. 30 (November–December): 20.

Dyer, Hilary, and Anne Morris. 1990. *Human Aspects of Library Automation*. Brookfield, Vermont: Gower Publishing Company.

Eckelman, Carl A. 1982. The Use of Performance Tests and Quality-Assurance Programs in the Selection of Library Chairs. *Library Technology Reports* 18, no. 5 (September–October): 483–571.

———. 1977. Evaluating the Strength of Library Chairs and Tables. *Library Technology Reports* 13, no. 4 (July): 341–433.

Fernberg, Patricia M. 1992. Laying Down the Law on Ergonomics. *Modern Office Technology* 37, no. 10 (October): 74–78.

———. 1992. Supporting Computer Support Furniture. *Modern Office Technology* 37, no. 9 (September): 39–42.

———. 1992. Tailoring the Workstation to the Worker. *Modern Office Technology* 37, no. 6 (June): 26–30.

Foos, Donald D. and Nancy C. Pack, eds. 1992. *How Libraries Must Comply with the Americans with Disabilities Act (ADA)*. Phoenix, Arizona: The Oryx Press.

Gale Research Inc. 1994. *Encyclopedia of Associations: National Organizations of the U.S.* 28th ed. Detroit: Gale Research Inc.

Gale Research Inc. 1994. *Encyclopedia of Associations: International Organizations*. 28th ed. Detroit: Gale Research Inc.

Gouin, Michelle D., and Thomas B. Cross. 1986. *Intelligent Buildings, Strategies for Technology and Architecture*. Homewood, Illinois: Dow Jones-Irwin.

Grandjean, Etienne. 1987. *Ergonomics in Computerized Offices*. Bristol, Pennsylvania: Taylor and Francis.

Gunde, Michael G. 1991. Working with the Americans with Disabilities Act, Part I. *Library Journal* 116, no. 21 (December): 99–100.

———. 1992. Working with the Americans with Disabilities Act, Part II. *Library Journal* 117, no. 8 (May 1): 41–42.

———. 1992. Working with the Americans with Disabilities Act, Part III. *Library Journal* 117, no. 21 (December): 90–91.

Hanna, Herbert L., and Nancy H. Knight. 1987. Movable Compact Shelving: a Survey of U. S. Suppliers and Library Users. *Library Technology Reports* 17, no. 1 (January–February): 7–105.

Harvey, David A. 1991. Health and Safety First. *Byte* 16, no. 10 (October): 119–128.

Haworth, Inc. Not dated. *ADA Handbook*. Holland, Michigan: Haworth, Inc.

———. 1993. *Facility Planning and Management*. Holland, Michigan: Haworth, Inc.

———. 1993. *How to Maximize Your Office Furniture Investment*. Holland, Michigan: Haworth, Inc.

———. 1989. *Individual Work Station Plan Survey*. Holland, Michigan: Haworth, Inc.

Healthy Buildings International. 1989. *Proactive Monitoring: Controlling Indoor Air Quality*. Data Sheet HBI-11/89. Fairfax, Virginia: Healthy Buildings International.

Helm, Randall S., and James R. Strobridge. 1991. *Indoor Air Quality in the Healthy Office*. Corporate case study by Daniel B. O'Malley. Grand Rapids, Michigan: Steelcase.

Herman Miller, Inc. 1991. *Cumulative Trauma Disorders, Rising Incidence, Rising Awareness*. (May) Zeeland, Michigan: Herman Miller, Inc.

———. 1991. *Equal Opportunity Facilities, Designing for Accessibility*. (October). Zeeland, Michigan: Herman Miller, Inc.

———. 1993. *Everybody Deserves a Good Chair*. (March). Zeeland, Michigan: Herman Miller, Inc.

———. 1992. *It's Here Somewhere, the Effect of Storage Methods on Job Performance*. (December). Zeeland, Michigan: Herman Miller, Inc.

———. 1991. *Office Workers and the Computer: Reconciling the Demands of Technology and the Needs of People*. Zeeland, Michigan: Herman Miller, Inc.

———. 1992. Special Issue: Focus on the Environment. *Salesmarts!* (March 13). Zeeland, Michigan: Herman Miller, Inc: 3–4.

Humphries, Anne Wood. 1993. Designing a Functional Reference Desk: Planning to Completion. *RQ* 33, no. 1 (Fall): 35–40.

Jackman, Dianne R., and Mary K. Dixon. 1983. *The Guide to Textiles for Interior Designers*. Winnepeg, Canada: Peguis Publishers Limited.

Kroemer, K. H. E. 1993. Fitting the Workplace to the Human and Not Vice Versa. *Industrial Engineering* 25, no. 3 (March): 56–61.

Levin, Hal. 1981. Building Ecology. *Progressive Architecture* 62, no. 4 (April): 173–175.

———. 1993. The Myths of Indoor Air Pollution. *Progressive Architecture* 74, no. 3 (March): 33–37.

Lewis, Christopher. 1992. The Americans with Disabilities Act and Its Effect on Public Libraries. *Public Libraries* 31, no. 1 (January–February): 23–28.

Macdonald, Hugh. 1986. Designing a Reference Desk. *Texas Library Journal* 62, no. 3 (Fall): 175–178.

McClure, Charles R., Amy Owen, Douglas L. Zweizig, Mary Jo Lynch, and Nancy A. Van House. 1987. *Planning and*

Role Setting For Public Libraries, A Manual of Options and Procedures. Prepared for Public Library Development Project. Chicago: American Library Association.

Mallery, Mary S., and Ralph E. Devore. 1982. *A Sign System For Libraries.* Chicago: American Library Association.

Metcalf, Keyes. 1986. *Planning Academic and Research Library Buildings.* 2d ed. by Philip D. Leighton and David C. Weber. Chicago: American Library Association.

Muth, Jim. 1993. *Achieving ADA Compliance with Mobile Storage.* Fort Atkinson, Wisconsin: Spacesaver Corporation.

National Fire Protection Association. 1993. *National Electrical Code Handbook, Based on the 1993 Edition of the National Electrical Code.* 6th ed. Quincy, Massachusetts: National Fire Protection Association.

O'Brien, Patrick M. 1989. Dazzling Center Opens in Dallas. *American Libraries* 114, no. 10 (June): 591–594.

Pata, Richard J. 1993. System Approach to Furniture Design. Unpublished memo. Oshkosh, Wisconsin: Busckstaff.

Peoples Center for Housing Change. 1985. *Accessibility Design Guidelines for Public Facilities Serving Children.* Topanga, California: Peoples Center for Housing Change.

Pollet, Dorothy, and Peter C. Haskell, eds. 1979. *Sign Systems For Libraries: Solving the Wayfinding Problem.* New York: R. R. Bowker.

Poole, Frazer G., and Alphonse F. Trezza, eds. 1969. *The Procurement of Library Furnishings, Specifications, Bid Documents, and Evaluation.* Proceedings of the Library Equipment Institute, New York, New York, July 7–9, 1966, sponsored by the Library Administration Division. Chicago: American Library Association.

Pulgram, William, and Richard E. Stonis. 1984. *Designing the Automated Office, a Guide for Architects, Interior Designers, Space Planners, and Facility Managers.* New York: Whitney Library of Design, Watson-Guptill Publications.

Reynolds, Linda, and Stephen Barrett. 1981. *Signs and Guiding for Libraries.* London: Clive Bingley Limited.

Reznikoff, S.C. 1989. *Specifications for Commercial Interiors: Professional Liabilities, Regulations, and Performance Criteria.* 2d ed. New York: Whitney Library of Design, Watson-Guptill Publications.

Sandlian, Pam. 1993. Designing a Children's Library: A Review. *Public Library Quarterly* 13, no. 1: 17–26.

Sannwald, William W., ed. 1990. *Checklist of Library Building Design Considerations.* 2d ed. Chicago: American Library Association.

Shelton, John A. 1990. *California State Library Manual of Recommended Practice, Seismic Safety Standards for Library Shelving.* Sacramento: California State Library Foundation.

Silberman, Richard M. 1993. A Mandate for Change in the Library Environment. *Library Administration and Management* 7, no. 3 (Summer): 145–152.

Smith, Charles R. 1987. Compact-shelving Specifications. *Library Administration and Management* 1, no. 3 (June): 94–95.

Smutko, Liz. 1993. Ergonomic Plans Protect Workforce While Preparing for Coming OSHA Rule. *Industrial Maintenance and Plant Operation* 54, no. 4 (April): 38–40.

Steelcase, Inc. 1992. *Adjusting to Your Needs in the Computerized Workplace.* Grand Rapids, Michigan: Steelcase, Inc.

———. 1992. *Americans with Disabilities Act.* Grand Rapids, Michigan: Steelcase, Inc.

———. 1991. *ANSI Standards and the Healthy Office, Toward a More Complete Understanding.* Grand Rapids, Michigan: Steelcase, Inc.

———. 1993. *Choosing and Using Office Chairs: Four Tips for Healthier Sitting.* Grand Rapids, Michigan: Steelcase, Inc.

———. 1992. *Ergonomics in the Healthy Office.* Grand Rapids, Michigan: Steelcase, Inc.

———. 1993. *Seating for People at Work, a Personal Guide to Evaluating and Selecting Seating.* Grand Rapids, Michigan: Steelcase, Inc.

———. 1994. Trouble in the Air. *Workwell, A Magazine for Steelcase.* Edition no. 1: 21–25.

———. 1991. *The Worldwide Office Environment Index, 1991 Summary Series.* Conducted by Louis Harris and Associates. Grand Rapids, Michigan: Steelcase, Inc.

Underwriters Laboratories, Inc. 1992. *Testing for Public Safety.* Northbrook, Illinois: Underwriters Laboratories.

———. 1988. *UL 1286 Standard for Safety, Office Furnishings.* 2d ed. Northbrook, Illinois: Underwriters Laboratories.

United States Department of Agriculture, Forest Service. 1987. *Wood Handbook. 72.* 2d ed. Washington, D.C.: United States Government Printing Office.

USGPO. 1991. *ADA Accessibility Guidelines for Buildings and Facilities.* Federal Register 56, no. 144 (Friday, July 26): 35605–35691.

VDT News. 1993. ANSI CTD Committee Favors Good Practices, Not Specific Limits. *VDT News* 10, no. 4 (July–August): 1, 9–10.

Weber, David C. 1990. *Library Buildings and the Loma Prieta Earthquake Experience of October 1989.* Sacramento: California State Library Foundation.

Zelinsky, Marilyn. 1993. ISO's Implications. *Interiors* 152, no. 5 (May): 52, 56, and 164.

———. 1993. A Symbol of the Times—ACT Makes a Specifier's Job Easier by Boiling Down Voluminous Textile Testing Information to a Program of Clear-Cut Icons. *Interiors* 152, no. 8 (August): 54–57.

———. 1993. Update: California Technical Bulletin 133. *Interiors* 151, no. 9 (September): 33–34, 118.

LIST OF MANUFACTURERS

Acme Design Technology
Magic Aisle
1000 Allview Drive
Crozet, Virginia 22932
(800) 368-2077

Adden Furniture, Inc.
26 Jackson Street
Lowell, Massachusetts 01852
(800) 625-3876

Advance Manufacturing
A Gaylord Company
P. O. Box 60689
Los Angeles, California 90060
(800) 638-8636

Automated Storage & Retrieval Systems of America
(ASRA)
Elecompack®
225 West 34th Street, Suite 1020
New York, New York 10122
(212) 760-1607

BC Inventar, Inc.
1404 North Belt, #160
Houston, Texas 77032
(713) 442-4334

Berco Industries
1120 Montrose Avenue
St. Louis, Missouri 63104
(314) 772-4700

Biblomodel
Ocampo Y Ayuntamiento 83-85
Col. Las Encinas
Apartado Postal No. 19
Escobedo, N.L. C.P.66050 Mexico
011-5283-8412-76

Blanton & Moore
P.O. Box 70
Barium Springs, North Carolina 28010
(704) 528-4506

Borroughs Corporation
Wilsonstak®
3002 North Burdick Street
Kalamazoo, Michigan 49004
(800) 748-0227

Bretford® Manufacturing, Inc.
9715 Soreng Avenue
Schiller Park, Illinois 60176
(708) 678-2545

Brodart Company
1609 Memorial Avenue
Williamsport, Pennsylvania 17705
(800) 233-8467

Buckstaff®
1127 South Main Street
Oshkosh, Wisconsin 54901
(800) 755-5890

CAN-AM Merchandising Systems
900 Hertel Avenue
Buffalo, New York 14216
(800) 387-9790

Changeable Sign Systems
999 North 1200 West
Orem, Utah 84057
(801) 222-0960

The Children's Furniture Company
P.O. Box 27157
1234 Leadenhal Street, #300
Baltimore, Maryland 21230
(410) 625-7908

Peter Danko & Associates
7492-F Old Alex Ferry Road
Clinton, Maryland 20735
(301) 868-5550

Demco Inc.
P.O. Box 7488
Madison, Wisconsin 53707
(800) 356-1200

Enem® Systems, Inc.
900 Bethel Circle
P.O. Box 456
Waunakee, Wisconsin 53597
(608) 849-6800

Estey Company
Division of Tennsco Corporation
P.O. Box 1888
Dickson, Tennessee 37056
(800) 251-8184

Fixtures Furniture®
1642 Crystal
Kansas City, Missouri 64126
(800) 821-3500

Franklin Fixtures
59 Commerce Park Road
Brewster, Massachusetts 02631
(508) 896-3713

Gaylord
P.O. Box 4901
Syracuse, New York 13221
(800) 634-6307

Group Four Furniture
25-5 Connell Court
Toronto, Ontario M8Z 1E8
Canada
(416) 251-1128

Hannecke Display Systems, Inc.
300G Route 17 South
Mahwah, New Jersey 07430
(800) 345-8631

Hausmann Manufacturing
925 West Russell
San Antonio, Texas 78212
(210) 734-9090

Haworth®, Inc.
Kinetics®
One Haworth Center
Holland, Michigan 49423
(616) 393-3000

Healthy Buildings International, Inc.
10378 Democracy Lane
Fairfax, Virginia 22030
(703) 352-0102

Highsmith Company, Inc.
W5527 Highway 106
P. O. Box 800
Fort Atkinson, Wisconsin 53538
(800) 558-3899

Howe Furniture Corporation
12 Cambridge Drive
P. O. Box 0386
Trumbull, Connecticut 06611
(203) 374-7833

HumanWare, Inc.
6245 King Road
Loomis, California 95650
(916) 652-7253

International Contract Furnishings (ICF)
10 Maple Street
Norwood, New Jersey 07648
(800) 237-1625

International Library Furniture
2140 South Main
Fort Worth, Texas 76110
(817) 926-8682

JB Engineering
1714 California Avenue
Monrovia, California 91016
(818) 303-2626

Jasper Chair Company
P. O. Box 311
Jasper, Indiana 47547
(812) 482-5239

Jasper Seating
932 Mill Street
P. O. Box 231
Jasper, Indiana 47547
(800) 622-5661

Johnson Industries
1424 Davis Road
Elgin, Illinois 60123
(800) 346-5555

KI
P.O. Box 8100
Green Bay, Wisconsin 54308
(414) 468-2701

Kardex
P. O. Box 171
Marietta, Ohio 45750
(800) 848-9761

The Knoll Group
P.O. Box 157
East Greenville, Pennsylvania 18041
(215) 679-7991

Library Bureau
801 Park Avenue
Herkimer, New York 13350
(315) 866-1330

Library Display Design Systems
P.O. Box 8143
Berlin, Connecticut 06037
(203) 828-6089

Loewenstein
1801 North Andrews Extension
P.O. Box 10369
Pompano Beach, Florida 33061-6369
(305) 960-1100

F.W. Lombard Company
34 South Pleasant
Ashburnham, Massachusetts 01430
(508) 827-5333

Lundia
600 Capitol Way
Jacksonville, Illinois 62650
(800) 726-9663

MJ Industries
P. O. Box 259

Georgetown, Massachusetts 01833
(508) 352-6190

McDole Library Furniture, Inc.
323 Brooke Road
Winchester, Virginia 22603
(703) 667-7983

Metropolitan Furniture Corporation
1635 Rollins Road
Burlingame, California 94010
(415) 697-7900

Herman Miller, Inc.
855 East Main Avenue
Zeeland, Michigan 49464
(800) 851-1196

Modulex®/ASI Sign Systems®
3890 West Northwest Highway, Suite 102
Dallas, Texas 75220
(800) 274-7732

Montel
4 Starter Drive
Frackville, Pennsylvania 17931
(717) 874-4800

Thos. Moser Cabinetmakers
72 Wright's Landing
P.O. Box 1237
Auburn, Maine 04211
(207) 784-3332

Nemschoff Chairs
2218 Julson Court
Sheboygan, Wisconsin 53081
(414) 457-7726

Nova® Office Furniture, Inc.
421 West Industrial Avenue
Effingham, Illinois 62401
(217) 342-7070

Nucraft Furniture Co.
5151 West River Drive
Comstock Park, Michigan 49321
(800) 453-0100

Protocol Contract Furniture
5121 Kaltenbrun Road
Fort Worth, Texas 76119
(817) 572-2266

Richards-Wilcox
600 South Lake
Aurora, Illinois 60506
(708) 897-6951

Rudd Industries
21641 Beaumeade Circle
Ashburn, Virginia 22011
(703) 729-5800

Russ Bassett
8189 Byron Road
Whittier, California 90606
(800) 350-2445

Scania™/BTJ, Inc.
150 North Michigan Avenue, #1200
Chicago, Illinois 60601
(800) 372-2642

SelfInform™
11910-G Parklawn Drive
Rockville, Maryland 20852
(800) 355-1464

Skools, Inc.
Kin-der-Link™
40 Fifth Avenue, Suite 15A
New York, New York 10011
(212) 674-1150

Smith System
P.O. Box 64515
St. Paul, Minnesota 55164
(800) 328-1061

Spacemaster Systems
155 West Central Avenue
Zeeland, Michigan 49464
(616) 772-2406

Spacesaver Corporation
1450 Janesville Avenue
Ft. Atkinson, Wisconsin 53538
(414) 563-6362

Steelcase®, Inc.
901 44th Street Southeast
Grand Rapids, Michigan 49501
(800) 227-2960

Suspa®, Inc.
Movatec® Lift System
3970 Roger B. Chaffee Drive Southeast
Grand Rapids, Michigan 49548
(616) 241-4200

TAB Products Company
1400 Page Mill Road
Palo Alto, California 94304
(800) 672-3109

Table Toys®, Inc.
2500 Central Parkway, Suite P
Houston, Texas 77092
(800) 999-8990

Talking Signs®, Inc.
812 North Boulevard
Baton Rouge, Louisiana 70802
(504) 344-2812

Texwood Furniture Corporation
P. O. Box 6280
3508 East 1st Street
Austin, Texas 78762
(512) 385-3323

Tuohy Furniture Corporation
42 St. Albans Place
Chatfield, Minnesota 55923
(800) 533-1696

Vecta®
P.O. Box 534013
Grand Prairie, Texas 75053
(214) 641-2860

Versteel®
P.O. Box 850
Jasper, Indiana 47547
(800) 876-2120

White Office Systems
50 Boright Avenue
Kenilworth, New Jersey 07033
(908) 272-8888

The Worden Company
199 East 17th Street
Holland, Michigan 49422
(800) 748-0561

LIST OF ASSOCIATIONS

American Association of Textile Chemists and Colorists (AATCC)
P.O. Box 12215
Research Triangle Park, North Carolina 27709
(919) 549-8141

American National Standards Institute (ANSI)
11 West 42nd Street, 13th Floor
New York, New York 10036
(212) 642-4900

American Society for Testing and Materials (ASTM)
1916 Race Street
Philadelphia, Pennsylvania 19103
(215) 299-5400

Architectural Woodwork Institute (AWI)
P.O. Box 1550
13924 Braddock Road, #100
Centreville, Virginia 22020
(703) 222-1100

Association for Contract Textiles
P.O. Box 8293
FDR Station
New York, New York 10150-1918

Business and Institutional Furniture Manufacturers Association (BIFMA)
2680 Horizon Drive Southeast
Grand Rapids, Michigan 49546
(616) 285-3963

General Services Administration (GSA)
General Services Building

18th and F Streets Northwest
Washington, D.C. 20405
(202) 708-5082

International Organization for Standardization (ISO)
1, Rue de Varembe
Case Postale 56
CH-1121 Geneva 20, Switzerland
011-22-749-0111

National Fire Protection Association (NFPA)
1 Batterymarch Park
P.O. Box 9101
Quincy, Massachusetts 02269
(617) 770-3000

Occupational Safety and Health Administration (OSHA)
Labor Department
Safety Standards Programs
200 Constitution Avenue Northwest
Washington, D.C. 20210
(202) 219-8151

People's Center for Housing Change
P.O. Box 1151
1424 Old Topanga Canyon Road
Topanga, California 90290
(213) 455-1340

Underwriters Laboratory (UL)
333 Pfingsten Road
Northbrook, Illinois 60062
(708) 272-8800

INDEX